BLANK VERSE

Also by Robert B. Shaw:

Poetry:
Comforting the Wilderness
The Wonder of Seeing Double
The Post Office Murals Restored
Below the Surface
Solving for X

Criticism:
The Call of God: The Theme of Vocation in the Poetry of Donne and Herbert

As Editor:
American Poetry since 1960: Some Critical Perspectives
Henry Vaughan: Selected Poems

BLANK VERSE

A Guide to Its History and Use

Robert B. Shaw

OHIO UNIVERSITY PRESS   Athens

Ohio University Press, Athens, Ohio 45701
www.ohio.edu/oupress
© 2007 by Ohio University Press

Printed in the United States of America
All rights reserved

Ohio University Press books are printed on acid-free paper ∞ ™

15 14 13 12 11 10 09 08 07   5 4 3 2 1

Library of Congress Cataloging-in-Publication Data
Shaw, Robert Burns, 1947–
    Blank verse : a guide to its history and use / Robert B. Shaw.
        p. cm.
    Includes bibliographical references and index.
    ISBN-13: 978-0-8214-1757-7 (alk. paper)
    ISBN-10: 0-8214-1757-6 (alk. paper)
    ISBN-13: 978-0-8214-1758-4 (pbk. : alk. paper)
    ISBN-10: 0-8214-1758-4 (pbk. : alk. paper)
 1. Blank verse, English—History and criticism. I. Title.
    PR509.B53S53 2007
    821'.009—dc22
                        2006033521

To the memory of William Alfred,

poet and friend of poets

CONTENTS

PREFACE

As ITS subtitle indicates, this book undertakes two tasks: to study the characteristics of the poetic form we call blank verse, and to study the achievements of poets who have used it from its first emergence up to our own day. These two strands of interest are intertwined throughout. While the first and last chapters concentrate on practical considerations for writers and readers of blank verse, the middle chapters, which are arranged as a historical survey, in fact carry on the discussion of technique by analyzing numerous examples written by masters of the form, as well as some by poets whose struggles with the meter fell short of mastery. The twentieth century and later receives more expansive treatment than earlier periods because this part of the story has been overlooked by scholarship. While one may feel some satisfaction simply in having filled a conspicuous gap, there is an even greater pleasure in demonstrating the continuing vitality of this form for poets writing today. There is plenty of poetic vitality to be found in earlier periods as well. Styles may change, but as Edwin Arlington Robinson reminds us in his fine blank-verse poem "Rembrandt to Rembrandt," "in Apollo's house there are no clocks" (313). For the young poet wishing to explore blank verse, lively models—both venerable and contemporary—abound. In examining these models, this discussion proceeds more like a poetry workshop than like a museum tour.

In the preface to his collection of essays on versification, *Vision and Resonance,* John Hollander candidly remarks, "English prosody has tended to be a subject for cranks."[1] No system of scansion or of prosodic symbols is without disadvantages; some become forbiddingly complicated in an effort to define the more delicate rhythmic nuances. I have opted for a simplified, uncranky notation, marking the feet of a line according to their patterns of syllables that are unstressed (x) or stressed (/). I have allowed myself an additional symbol (\) to indicate an intermediate level of stress. Some prosodists may see this as admitting too much flexibility, others as admitting not enough. While I hope the scansions offered here will be persuasive, their purpose is not to score points against competing systems. It is, rather, to be a stimulative device, reminding the reader to listen even more carefully than usual, so that the rhythmic effect of each line will register fully. A look at a contour map will alert a hiker to changes in terrain, but not with the same immediacy as the feel of an upward or a downward slope underfoot. While symbols and terminology, preferably applied with some consistency, are needed to discuss a verse passage efficiently and intelligibly, the ultimate key to its movement will be found by reading it aloud, weighing in one's own ear the levels of accent which any system of notation can only approximately chart. Readers of this book will be on the right track if they find themselves vocalizing, annoying librarians and alarming passengers in neighboring seats on the subway. This is one of the more virtuous ways I can think of to get in trouble.

My own trouble in writing this book would have been much greater without the help I have received from friends and associates. Several, in conversation or correspondence, have moved me to clarify points or have introduced me to poets and poems I might otherwise have missed. For thus sharing their experience and expertise, I am grateful to Daniel Hall, Eugene Hill, Heidi Holder, J. Wainwright Love, Joshua Mehigan, and Mary Jo Salter. Welcome encouragement came early on from Leslie Brisman and John Hollander. John M. Walsh offered valuable corrective remarks on initial drafts. My student, Sarah Giragosian, made many useful suggestions regarding the first and final chapters. David Sanders, my supportive editor at Ohio University Press, was of great help in determining the final structure of the book as well as augmenting, through his suggestions, the coverage of contemporary poets. I am uniquely indebted to Timothy Steele, who read the entire manuscript in installments and offered detailed commentary on it. Every part of the work has benefited from his vigilance, which prompted me to make many clarifications, additions, and corrections. As always, I am grateful to my wife, who put up with much strategizing and helped me through recurrent keyboard crises.

I am grateful also to Nancy Basmajian, whose thoughtful and meticulous copyediting has made the work more readable.

Two very different poets, both of them my teachers, influenced me in enduring ways when I was first beginning to write. I cannot write poetry, or write about it, without before long remembering Robert Fitzgerald and Robert Lowell with renewed gratitude. And I feel the same in remembering their friend and colleague, also my teacher, to whom this book is dedicated.

A NOTE ON REFERENCES AND SYMBOLS

Verse quotations are followed by author and title, if not already mentioned, and line numbers in parentheses. A list of sources for these quotations (as well as for any poems mentioned by title) appears at the end of the book. Prose quotations are cited in the notes.

In quoted verse passages, bracketed ellipses appear when a quotation breaks off in the midst of a sentence, except in the case of single lines or other very brief passages exhibited as specimens without terminal punctuation. Ellipses without brackets are the poet's.

The following prosodic symbols are used in scanning verse passages:

x	denotes an unstressed syllable.
/	denotes a stressed syllable.

The most common metrical feet are thus represented as follows:

x /	iamb
/ x	trochee
x x /	anapest
/ x x	dactyl
/ /	spondee
x x	pyrrhic

\   is used when needed to mark an intermediate degree of stress on a syllable.

| marks a pause or caesura.

A detailed discussion of these symbols and their use appears in the third section of chapter 1.

BLANK VERSE

THE SOUNDS OF BLANK VERSE

I

BLANK VERSE—unrhymed iambic pentameter—is not hard to find, and some-times it turns up in unexpected places. Julian Symons uses the form in a short poem, "The Guilty Party," which serves as preface to his historical study of the detective story.[1] The theme sardonically developed in the piece is that the writer of stories of murder and mayhem is in an unsettling way responsible for the violence staining his pages:

> It is the author who creates the crime
> And picks the victims, this blond dark girl sprawled
> Across a bed, stabbed, strangled, poisoned, bashed
> With a blunt instrument.
>
> (1–4)

Later, Symons pictures the author sitting in "his butter-bright smiling room / Where crimes are kept in filing cabinets / Well out of sight and mind" (21–23), haunted by visions of the victims and villains he has created:

> One paddling fingers in her own bright blood
> And staining his face with it, another
> Revealing the great wound gaping in his side,

> The sliced-up tart carrying a juicy breast,
> Inviting him to kiss it: and the villains all
> Crowding him with their horrid instruments,
> The rope that playfully tightens round his neck,
> The blue revolver used to mutilate,
> The dagger points to pierce out jelly eyes,
> The saw and hammer at their nasty work [. . .]
>
> (26–35)

There are mysteries surrounding—or we might better say emanating from—blank verse, and unlike questions in detective stories they do not allow for incontrovertible solutions. Some of the questions are historical. This poem, from the 1970s, uses a form that came into English in the mid-sixteenth century. What accounts for the longevity of this poetic form? Other questions, of the kind that tend to interest poets more, are practical and technical. How can the formal demands of blank verse be mastered (for that matter, what *are* its formal demands), and when one has learned to write it, what is it good for? To follow these questions where they lead us, even if that does not uncover proofs to persuade a jury, may still offer some enlightenment. And poetry being the innocent subject that it is, we may manage to get through this discussion without too much blood on the floor.

Craft is mastered only through imitation. To learn to write blank verse there is no substitute for steeping oneself in what has been written to date in the form, and the examples in this and the following chapters should supply numerous models to ponder and emulate and (why not?) surpass. Such direct confrontation with poetry of the past and the present is essential to any poet's stylistic development; commentaries can have at most an ancillary value. This book cannot pretend to teach anyone how to write blank verse apart from deeply attentive reading of the masters. It may justify itself, however, if it serves to highlight the expressive opportunities offered by the form, as these have been discovered and exploited by poets over more than four centuries. The issues treated here are useful ones to bear in mind in reading or in writing blank verse in the twenty-first century.

Let us set aside for the moment the technical aspects of prosody, with its plethora of Greco-Roman terms and its supralinear symbols. These will claim our attention in due course. Initially, though, let us consider the current and potential uses of blank verse and, as we do so, draw some broad distinctions between it and other forms.

The lazy way to think about blank verse is to view it as a compromise between rhyming metrical verse on the one hand and free verse on the other. A poet who devotes serious attention to these three forms will quickly realize that blank verse is something more than a halfway house between rhyme and open form. It has characteristics that give it a unique set of capabilities, setting it distinctly apart from either of these alternatives. It is not a "lite" version of formalist poetry; nor is it free verse in a coat and tie. Anyone who has ever tried to write a poem first in one form, then in another, knows that even if the basic content is reproduced, the overall effect will change, especially in relation to tone. Symons would certainly have been capable of rhyming his list of murder weapons in some fashion such as this:

> The rope that tightens round his neck in play,
> The blue-nosed gun that blasts his nose away,
> The dagger with an eyeball on its point,
> Hammer and saw to rend him joint from joint.

But this would make it a jokier sort of macabre catalogue. The actual poem is not without humor, but it is tinged with a bit of hysteria, as these lines, with their brittler wit, are not. Free verse would give the material another slant:

> One
> who paddles fingers in
> her own
> bright
> blood,
> who stains
> his face with
> it

This seems to concentrate attention on the lurid image with a sort of sloweddown voyeurism that has its own interest but is different from the disquieting glide of Symons's lines, which proceed like a sort of funhouse ride through a chamber of horrors.

It is in fact this commanding momentum, this sense of ongoingness, that is one of the leading characteristics (and advantages) of blank verse. This affects sound regardless of what we have been calling the tone of the passage (by which we meant its implied as well as its stated range of emotions). If we momentarily abstract the sound of the lines from the meaning of the words composing them—and it is difficult to do this more than momentarily—we glimpse, as the passage proceeds, a special quality of blank verse. Freedom and fixity are both at play in the form. Unchecked and unsegmented by patterns of rhyme, it can accommodate prodigious flows of utterance; in that sense it is freer. At the same time, unlike free verse, it has a set length of line and recurring number of beats, and while poets in practice may allow themselves flexible rhythms and even occasional metrical substitutions, these attain expressive power precisely because the standard iambic pentameter is there as a basis, a point to vary *from*. (Like many twentieth-century poets, Symons allows himself considerable deviation from the strict metrical pattern in several of his lines, but the standard sound of blank verse, which comes through starkly in

```
        x   / x / x  /   x  / x /
```
   The blue revolver used to mutilate,

is what he is consciously tugging against.) Developing these notable features of blank verse that set it apart from other forms into a strong and versatile array of tactics has been the communal effort of many generations of poets.

One obvious index of the form's versatility is the heterogeneity of subject matter to which it has been applied, which seems only to increase with the passage of time. If one does not care to be accosted by Symons's murder victims, the blank-verse canon offers more appealing images in sumptuous quantity. Many of these are mentioned in the following pages; but here, as a foretaste, are the beautiful closing lines of Wallace Stevens's "Sunday Morning":

> Deer walk upon our mountains, and the quail
> Whistle about us their spontaneous cries;
> Sweet berries ripen in the wilderness;
> And, in the isolation of the sky,
> At evening, casual flocks of pigeons make

> Ambiguous undulations as they sink,
> Downward to darkness, on extended wings.
>
> (VIII, 9–15)

Especially since the burgeoning of short descriptive or lyric poems in blank verse, it has become clear that it would be foolish to assume any topic ruled out. Classical notions of decorum, which deemed certain poetic forms proper for treating certain subjects, have never had much staying power among poets of the English-speaking world. Just as this form diversified in terms of mode—moving successively from drama through epic to other narrative, meditative, descriptive, and lyric types—so it has proven able to deal with subjects decorous or rough, exalted or mundane. The poet wishing to give blank verse a try has, in this respect, an apparently limitless field to explore, and it would be otiose to suggest any particular sorts of topic as more promising than others.

Some suggestions can be offered, though, in regard to modes. While the history of the form has demonstrated that virtually all modes are available to it, some have been less widely used than others, and some have been exercised within what may be an unwarrantably restricted scope. Narratives, for instance, have gravitated to shorter lengths; the book-length poems in blank verse that so frequently occupied E. A. Robinson and others have been in recent decades hard to come by. Truly enormous works like James Merrill's *The Changing Light at Sandover* are not blank verse in their entirety; Anthony Hecht's "The Venetian Vespers," at twenty-six pages, is what now seems to pass for a "long" poem in the form, though free-verse poems of the modern and contemporary eras run hundreds of pages without exciting surprise. The novel-in-verse is so neglected a notion that it might be possible to make something fresh of it, and in such a case blank verse would seem a more suitable medium than many others. If the thought of something this sizable is daunting (as it no doubt should be), there are other neglected areas. For instance, the epistolary poem is a much underused form in our time. Letters in verse, which may have seemed a stilted concept for much of the twentieth century, are now more intriguing to contemplate in a time when e-mail has made letters of the older sort exotic. The concept is so old that it might seem new. And if writing a letter which requires a stamp has become something of a ceremonial act, this would seem in many respects compatible with the assumptions and processes of formalist poetry.

Some of the most exciting possibilities are in the dramatic sphere. The monologue continues to attract poets who persist in mining the rich veins previously worked by Browning, Robinson, Frost, and others. The dialogue poem, or narrative largely in dialogue, is much less common. The interest in this (and the technical challenge) is in effectively differentiating the voices. This can be more difficult than creating a single speaking character; in a monologue there is ample room for gradual disclosure of character, whereas in dialogue the voices must define themselves more compactly and through contrast in the course of verbal interchange. Frost is talented at this. The married couples in "Home Burial," "The Fear," and others; the mother and son in "The Witch of Coös"—these offer pairs of easily distinguished voices. (Interestingly, the contrasts in temperament portrayed by Frost often parallel differences of gender.) Not many poets have followed Frost's lead; solo performances greatly outnumber duets. This is a pity, for blank verse remains a supple form in which to set one voice against another. We get a rare contemporary glimpse of how this is done in some of the dialogue-laden poems of Philip Stephens. Here are two derelicts escaping winter weather by camping out in the public library, conversing as they play a clandestine chess game:

> "Virge,
> You know how you said you'd like just one chance?"
>
> "Uh huh."
>
> "Well, I know how. Near Union Mission
> At this house called Men's Place, you get a room,
> Three squares, a job. They even let you stay
> Long as you like, but it don't cost you nothing.
> Just all you got to do is get the word
> Of God."
>
> "What do you mean I got to get it?"
>
> "You know, you got to beg for God's forgiveness."
>
> "What's God got to forgive me for? He needs
> To beg for my forgiveness, is what he needs
> To beg."
>
> ("March," 14–25)

Why is blank verse such a promising medium for dialogue? Probably it is because the form conveys a slight heightening to the material through its recurrent sound-patterns, holding our attention without distracting us by its artifice. Our attention thus engaged, we are reminded of the collaboratively creative nature of conversation, which is human drama in itself. Other animals communicate. Only we converse, and in doing so one never knows exactly what the person one is talking to will say in reply and how that in turn will affect one's own next utterance. Hearing two people converse in a language unknown to us can awaken us to a sense of strangeness, of specialness, in this exchange of sounds which we take to be meaningful even without knowing their meaning. Blank verse has something of the same framing or spotlighting effect, although it often is quite subtle. Even if the language is colloquial, the meter formalizes it and, in the way of many esthetic devices, entices us even as it distances us from the dialogue we are overhearing. We are carried by the rhythms as the speakers are. Because each speaker sustains similar rhythms, we feel the intensity of their connection to each other: they are in some sense on the same wavelength, even if what they are exchanging is mottled with misunderstandings. Their speech is the way they reveal themselves, and blank verse, in its unobtrusive though stylized way, draws our attention to disclosures of character. When one speaker stops talking in the middle of a blank-verse line and the other responds, completing the pentameter, we feel our expectation met, and in this way we may feel increasingly involved in the progress of what is being said. We *follow* it, and the iambic pentameter line offers an inviting path by which to do so.

As we shall have reason later to note, verse drama over the last hundred years has compiled a lackluster record at best. If a poet were emboldened to take blank verse back to its dramatic roots, the field could hardly be more open. The theater itself may, for economic reasons, be inaccessible in these times. But dramatic writing is not limited to the stage. Poems entirely or principally in dialogue are not dependent on a producer's largesse or enthusiasm, and such poems, particularly now, are waiting to be written.

Are there any kinds of poems for which blank verse would *not* be suited? Certainly, there are a few: poems whose forms and structures are so specialized and tailored for a specific effect that they could not lose these without losing their raison d'être. Any kind of free verse that depends on visual effects is, of course, one of these untransposable forms. This would include not only the freewheeling typewriter art of E. E. Cummings but many short-lined poems by William Carlos Williams and others, in which line groupings, enjamb-ments, and deliberate fragmentation contribute importantly to the ultimate meaning. While blank verse may be a reasonable (and possibly superior) stand-in for some kinds of free verse, it simply is not equipped to do what Cummings and Williams do when they split words into smaller components or poise them in collage-like assemblages on a page.

Again, blank verse can, arguably, substitute for traditional rhyming verse in many cases, but this is not to say it would necessarily be a superior or desirable choice. Good blank-verse sonnets exist, but one would not prefer having "Not marble, nor the gilded monuments" stripped of its rhymes. Rhymes are less dis-pensable, of course, when they contribute something beyond mere ornament. Some poems would founder completely without them. Consider these two epi-grams, the first by John Donne and the second by J. V. Cunningham:

> *A Lame Begger*
> I am unable, yonder begger cries,
> To stand or move; if he say true, hee *lies.*
>
> ~
>
> This Humanist whom no beliefs constrained
> Grew so broad-minded he was scatter-brained.
>
> ("Epigrams: A Journal" [30])

If, as an experiment, we substitute for the first rhyme-word in each couplet a close but unrhyming synonym (and also modernize the spelling in the case of Donne), we get:

> I am unable, yonder beggar calls,
> To stand or move; if he say true, he *lies.*

and:

> This Humanist whom no beliefs controlled
> Grew so broad-minded he was scatter-brained.

Notice, in each case, the change affects only the rhyme; the witty wordplay in each second line is preserved. Yet, in both cases, it falls decidedly flat in our revisions. These are punch lines that need to be led up to deliberately, and without the tight framing of the couplet rhyme and the additional force of closure afforded by the rhyme-sound to the final word, these are not effective as jokes, let alone as poems. Rather than being poems, the revisions, despite being in iambic pentameter, are little more than remarks. And as Gertrude Stein remarked to Ernest Hemingway, remarks are not literature.

Many students working with iambic pentameter have found it an instructive exercise to write two versions of a single poem, one with rhyme and one without. Although exceptions are always possible, it seems likely that blank verse, which can succeed brilliantly in poems of sonnet length or slightly shorter, may find it harder to do so in *extremely* short pieces (say, under five lines). Without room to display many of the devices that, for it, supply distinctive auditory and structural functions, the few lines may seem fragmentary or tentative jottings rather than finished works of art. To illustrate this general rule by an exception, here is a rhymeless epigram by Howard Nemerov, "What Kind of Guy Was He?":

> Just so you shouldn't have to ask again,
> He was the kind of guy that if he said
> Something and you were the kind of guy that said
> You can say that again, he'd say it again.

This piece does not fall flat in the way our rhymeless versions of Donne and Cunningham do. But that is because it uses parallel phrasing and repetition of words in place of rhyme to tie the little verbal knot together. And this formal device would probably not lend much weight to the piece if it were not thematically appropriate—the poem is *about* repetitiousness, and its own repetitious construction underscores the fact. This is not a momentous poem, but it is, in its tenuous way, an entertaining one. It suggests that so unusually compact a blank-verse poem may call for structural devices that are basically surrogates of rhyme if it is to have a hope of avoiding the feel of being a fragment. A poem this size or smaller that is centered on imagery rather than wit—a blank-verse haiku, we might say—is technically feasible, but even more of a challenge. Of course, these cautions need not discourage poets from trying the experiment. Sometimes remarkable things result from defying the odds.

II

Having taken some pains to differentiate blank verse from rhyming verse and free verse, we should do the same in regard to blank verse and prose. Prose is one of the places where blank verse unexpectedly turns up. Consider these sentences, each of which is the beginning of a well-known work of fiction: "And after all the weather was ideal" (Katherine Mansfield, "The Garden-Party"). "It goes a long way back, some twenty years" (Ralph Ellison, "Battle Royal"). "We didn't always live on Mango Street" (Sandra Cisneros, "The House on Mango Street"). All of these can be scanned as conventional iambic pentameter lines. And while something like the first sentence of William Faulkner's "The Bear"—"There was a man and a dog too this time"—bends further from the metrical pattern than the other three, it would not appear especially unusual were we to come upon it or its like in a twentieth-century blank-verse poem. (Adherents of a stricter prosody will find this regrettable, but it is the case nonetheless.) People reading these stories rarely notice anything verselike about such lines. They blend easily with the paragraphs they initiate. The affinity between blank verse and prose is something critics both hostile and friendly toward the meter have remarked on. Samuel Johnson, writing in the late eighteenth century, often disparaged blank verse and made use of this point to do so. Here is one of Johnson's more succinct statements for the prosecution: "If blank verse be not tumid and gorgeous, it is crippled prose; and familiar images in labored language have nothing to recommend them but absurd novelty which, wanting the attractions of Nature, cannot please long."[2] On the other side, a century after Johnson lodged this indictment, we find J. A. Symonds declaring, "Blank verse is indeed a kind of divinised prose."[3] If the blank verse of his own time was rarely "tumid and gorgeous" enough to distinguish it from prose in Johnson's view, that of our own day, so often keyed to conversational levels of diction, would please him even less. (And of course, it should be noted that the latter clause of his sentence suggests that tumidity and gorgeousness, even when achieved, were not likely to please him, either.) What is striking about these opposing statements by Johnson and Symonds is the certainty with which they present the affinity of blank verse to prose as one so close as to be near identity. They disagree only on whether the "prose" produced by writers of blank verse is "crippled" or "divinised." Readers may wonder whether the links between the forms are so self-evident that they may be taken for granted, as these critics seem to do.

In our own period the notion of blank verse as a blood-relative of prose is supported by the popularity of the conversational style. Blank verse is viewed as more natural than other verse forms because it can so easily occur as unpremeditated utterance. An acquaintance of this writer was attempting to reassure a student who was stymied by an assignment in a poetry-writing class. It was slow going; iambic pentameter seemed an impossible cliff to scale. Finally, when the student said,

> x / x / x / x / x /
> "I can't believe that I can write blank verse,"

the teacher was able to respond, with some satisfaction, "You just did." Surmounting fear of the demands of meter is to be applauded. Yet the assumption behind this pedagogically useful anecdote may raise questions. In minimizing the difficulties of writing in the form, are we in danger of presenting it as something all too easy? Blank verse may dovetail smoothly with prose and may at times be mistaken for it. But such misprisions are of short duration, as we can tell by playing tricks with margins. It isn't difficult to plant a line or two of blank verse in a paragraph, especially if the line-ends are disguised not only by a lack of lineation but also by enjambment. Is this prose? The longer it goes on, the less proselike it sounds to ears attuned to these two forms.

Those who emphasize the similarities between blank verse and prose—either to make the meter less threatening on the one hand or to condescend to it on the other—are not fantasizing a connection. Blank verse may well have taken root in the Elizabethan theater in part because the line mirrored the iambic rhythm dominant in English speech, and was capacious and flexible enough to accommodate numerous patterns of phrasing, as well as numerous levels of diction. Still, verse is not what most of us speak or write on ordinary occasions. It should be remembered that in William Shakespeare's plays there is a repeated deliberate *contrast* between prose and verse, sometimes in adjacent scenes, sometimes within a scene. Once the student has discovered that writing in meter depends not on some genetic predisposition but on skills that can be learned, it may be of greater value to stress the differences—sometimes subtle but nonetheless always crucial—rather than the likenesses observable between blank verse and prose.

Taking some well-known passage in prose and attempting to versify it can be an unnerving experience. The first sentence of Abraham Lincoln's Gettysburg Address reads, "Fourscore and seven years ago our fathers brought forth on this continent, a new nation, conceived in Liberty, and dedicated to the proposition that all men are created equal." If we versify this, trying to maintain Lincoln's meaning within the bounds of conventional meter, we might come out with this:

> Our fathers eighty-seven years ago
> Produced upon this continent a state,
> New, and conceived in Liberty, and sworn
> To faith in all mankind's equality.

This is dismal throughout, and the first line is particularly so. We feel the unflattering contrast between this line and the phrase it travesties for more than one reason. Most obviously, Lincoln's sonorously biblical "Fourscore and seven years ago" seizes attention, while the timidly archival "eighty-seven years ago" flutters by in a blur. But what is noticeable as well is the rhythmic contrast. While "Our fathers eighty-seven years ago" is a blandly paradigmatic pentameter line, Lincoln's opening words can be heard as a much more interesting pentameter line with a feminine ending:

$$\backslash \quad / \quad x \ / \ x \quad / \quad x \ / \ x \quad / \ (x)$$
"Fourscore and seven years ago our fathers."

"Fourscore" is either a spondee or a heavy iamb (for those who are wondering, we shall discuss this and other matters of prosodic terminology in the following section); but in any case it provides a salutary opening emphasis. Lincoln continues with something akin to verse rhythm in segments like "brought forth on this continent a new," which can be read as a clipped pentameter, and "and dedicated to the proposition," which scans as another pentameter with a feminine ending. Put these segments back into the sentence from which they have been lifted, however, and their verselike quality becomes less salient. They subordinate themselves to the stately prose rhythm of Lincoln's sentence. And in the remainder of the speech, which is dramatic and various in its rhythms, such buried pentameters are not conspicuous. One would have to depart even further from Lincoln's wording to versify the later passages. If blank verse and prose are forms as near akin as some have argued, it is puzzling to observe the awkwardness on exhibit in this exercise. It is not that one would expect the verse rendering to be "as good as" the original. (Or as interesting. The oddly perverse birthing metaphor—fathers "bringing forth" a nation with no mothers involved—is largely obscured in the verse revision.) What is striking above all is the cumulative difference of movement imposed on the language in the original and in the paraphrase. Someone who did not know the original, reading the blank-verse version, would more than likely think it uninspired verse, but it is altogether unlikely that such a reader would intuit a superior prose prototype from any clues lurking about the lines. The meter is an effective disguise in this case, although in esthetic terms it is a decidedly shabby one.

Some verse adaptations of prose passages are more successful than the hapless example above, and some have outshone their originals. The famous speech of Enobarbus in *Antony and Cleopatra* (2.2.193–219), which describes Cleopatra's journey down the Nile in her royal barge to meet and seduce Antony, draws sometimes word for word from an impressive passage in Thomas North's translation of Plutarch. The word "derivative" does not come to mind, however, in reading Shakespeare's rendering. It is possible that such transpositions came more easily to poets in earlier times, whether in drawing on others' writings or on their own. Ben Jonson is said to have drafted his poems in prose before recasting them in verse. For later poets this has not been a frequent procedure. Although W. B. Yeats is sometimes cited as writing in this fashion, most of his prose "drafts" are more like notebook entries or outlines than full-fledged versions of eventual poetic texts. The fact that most poems thematically dependent on prose sources borrow only sparingly from their actual wording suggests that blank verse is harder than one might have thought to reconcile with what John Milton called "the cool element of prose."[4] (Milton is here assuming a contrast between the rationalistic properties of prose and the fiery energy of the poetic imagination. With reference to the present discussion, we may note that when something hot is mixed with something cool, what results is something tepid.)

There is a fine and touching poem by Anthony Hecht, "Coming Home," which is subtitled "From the journals of John Clare." It draws on Clare's account of his escape, in July 1841, from the asylum where he had been committed for insanity, and his long, grueling attempt to return home on foot. Comparison of the poem with Clare's prose shows that Hecht, while following the journal's outline and narrating several of the same incidents, is cautious about borrowing Clare's phrasing. Direct quotations are scattered through the poem, but in their original setting these usually have little in them to suggest iambic pentameter. In recasting the episode in blank verse, Hecht has brought a remarkable delicacy to matching his highly selective borrowings with compatible turns of phrase. One brief example demonstrates the unusual blend of deference and originality involved in this adaptation. Here are a few lines from Clare, followed by Hecht's verse rendering:

> I scaled some old rotten paleings into the yard and then had higher pailings to clamber over to get into the shed or hovel which I did with difficulty being rather weak and to my good luck I found some trusses of clover piled up about 6 or more feet square which I gladly mounted and slept on[5]

> ~
>
> I made good progress, and by the dark of night
> Skirted a marsh or pond and found a hovel
> Floored with thick bales of clover and laid me down
> As on the harvest of a summer field,
> Companion to imaginary bees.
>
> (23–27)

The last two of Hecht's lines expand Clare's bare mention of clover in a way that has no parallel in the original but would be comfortably at home in Clare's own pastoral verse: Clare didn't say it, but he *could* have said it. This is a feat of dramatic plausibility, very different from slavish, line-by-line versifying. Paradoxically, the only way a poem like this could continue to be imaginatively faithful to its prose source was to situate itself at a carefully gauged distance from it.

Students who wish to experiment may try writing passages in prose and then versifying them or may take poems they have written in blank verse and rewrite them as prose. This can be a useful exercise for refining one's sense of how a set of blank-verse lines will sound when observant of meter and sensitive in rhythmic variation. It will not sound like prose. If this recasting turns out to be easy to do, without major alterations of tone or substance coming into play, the experimenter should be suspicious. In such a case the original, whether verse or prose, is probably not realizing the full potential of its form. Blank verse and prose can be regarded, if one likes, as neighbors, but a close look reveals a well-maintained spite fence between them. To put it another way, the dog and the rug it lies on may both be shaggy, and both may need washing, but that does not mean they came from the same litter.

III

Some of the terms and apparatus of versification have already crept into the discussion in the preceding section. Clearly it is time to deal with these matters head-on. How is the iambic pentameter line constructed? And how can we use symbols to graph its movement, whether in more or less regular versions?

Students in school most often learn about blank verse—if they learn about it at all—in connection with Shakespeare. The teacher may indulge in a certain amount of vocalizing to get the metrical pattern of the blank-verse line—iambic pentameter, or five iambic feet—drummed into impressionable heads: da-DUM, da-DUM, da-DUM, da-DUM, da-DUM. As a visual aid, the line may be charted on the blackboard, thus:

ᴜ / ᴜ / ᴜ / ᴜ / ᴜ /

Or, in the style used in this book, representing each unaccented syllable with x and each accented one with /:

x / x / x / x / x /

None of this is wrong. One can find numerous lines in Shakespeare's plays that hew very closely to this metrical paradigm, even as they exhibit a wide variety of content and tone. A few examples:

If music be the food of love, play on

(*Twelfth Night*, 1.1.1)

A little more than kin, and less than kind!

(*Hamlet*, 1.2.65)

A horse! A horse! my kingdom for a horse!

(*Richard III*, 5.4.7)

There's language in her eye, her cheek, her lip

(*Troilus and Cressida*, 4.5.55)

The caterpillars of the commonwealth

(*Richard II*, 2.3.166)

Your wit's too hot, it speeds too fast, 'twill tire

(*Love's Labour's Lost*, 2.1.119)

Yond Cassius has a lean and hungry look

(*Julius Caesar*, 1.2.193)

I wasted time, and now doth Time waste me

(*Richard II*, 5.5.49)

He jests at scars that never felt a wound

(*Romeo and Juliet*, 2.2.1)

Sans teeth, sans eyes, sans taste, sans everything

(*As You Like It*, 2.7.139)

Trouble develops when the schematic simplicity of the paradigm runs into variations, which in any good blank verse are plentiful. Inconvenient though the fact may be, not all iambs are created equal. To qualify as iambic, a foot need only have a second syllable that is stressed more than the first; but the relative *degree* of stress may vary noticeably from one foot to another. Therefore, it would be fairly rare for a line of actual poetry to conform exactly to the pattern that well-meaning teachers work so hard to drum into the heads of their students. A number of such lines in sequence would create an effect of stilted artificiality. Rather than adhering in lockstep fashion to the paradigm, well-written lines of iambic pentameter will correspond to it in more relative ways, generally following the fluctuations between weaker and stronger syllables, but doing so with ever-shifting modulations. The difference between weak and strong syllables will be at some points emphatic, while at other points it will be less pronounced.

We are recognizing here a distinction between rhythm and meter, one important to bear in mind throughout the discussion that follows.[6] When people describe verse as "singsong," they are responding to a lack of dynamic tension between the rhythm of the language and the metrical pattern in which it is arranged. The poet in such a case is meeting the requirements of meter robotically, by regulating his rhythms metronomically. A failure to grasp the distinction between rhythm and meter (as well as what might be thought of as the symbiotic relationship between them) can result in good poetry being read badly. We hear this when a student who has learned the iambic pentameter pattern all too well attempts to read a number of lines from one of Shakespeare's plays aloud. It is torture to listen to. Too strict a metrical reading damages both the sound and the sense of blank verse in extended passages and even in the single line, for it takes no account of the way the poet exploits the elasticity of the meter in its unrhymed form. If one reads the first line of a famous speech from *The Merchant of Venice* (4.1.183) by sticking slavishly to the iambic pattern, it scans this way:

> x   / x / x   / x / x   /
> The quality of mercy is not strained

Mercy may not be strained, but the meter is, if too rigidly imposed on this set of words. The degree of stress on accented syllables is not uniform, and a more sensitive reading of the line would recognize this. Using \ to represent a relatively weaker accent, we may scan the first part of the line more naturally:

> x   / x \ x   / x
> The quality of mercy

Most readers can easily hear the artificiality of

> / x /
> quality

as opposed to

> / x \
> quality,

so the understanding that not every da-DUM has an equally forceful DUM is not too hard to convey. Further problems await us, however, in the rest of the line. The three monosyllabic words "is not strained" do not rest easily within the iambic pattern, for the sense would seem to call for some stress on "not," possibly a stronger stress than on "is," perhaps as strong as the one on "strained." For that matter, it is hard to hear "is" as carrying much more stress than the last syllable of "mercy" which precedes it. Shakespeare has substituted other metrical feet for the last two iambs in his line, a pyrrhic (x x) and a spondee (/ /). A persuasive scansion of the line, then, would be:

> x   / x \ x   / x x   /   /
> The quality of mercy is not strained

If natural fluctuations in rhythm account for many variations from the strict iambic norm, so, too, do metrical substitutions. In the discussions that follow, we shall be saying a great deal more about these features, which some poets manipulate with more calculation than others do. Here at the outset we may insist, at the risk of emphasizing the obvious, that not all lines of blank verse sound alike. The metrical pattern is sometimes spoken of as the "skeleton" of a poem. It is a useful analogy up to a point—the meter provides structure— but it is misleading if it suggests rigidity. Iambic pentameter, as used by the masters of blank verse, is not skeleton alone but muscle and tendon, capable of bending and stretching to give adequate mobility to language and to the thoughts language embodies.

This bending and stretching takes many forms. The alert reader will have sensed it in operation in one of the "regular" Shakespearean lines quoted earlier: "The caterpillars of the commonwealth." If we scanned the line according to ordinary speech rhythms in a conversational context, we might well get something like this:

> x / x / x   x x   /   x   /
> The caterpillars of the commonwealth

And yet, especially when we come upon the line as part of a series in which the iambic pentameter pattern is often if not always audible, we are likely to find ourselves reading the line more "poetically":

> x / x / x   / x   /   x   /
> The caterpillars of the commonwealth

Prosodists describing what we have done here to "of" will speak of the word as having been "promoted" by the meter. "Promotion" is a misleading term if it suggests that the meter has imposed an artificial emphasis upon a syllable. What is happening here is that the meter is proving hospitable to the kind of shift in stress that often occurs in speech. It is in fact a natural tendency in speech to place more stress on such a word positioned between two unaccented syllables—at least when we are enunciating clearly—and a scansion that registers this does not do violence to ordinary intonation the way an accent on the last syllable of "quality" undoubtedly would. Exactly how much we are inclined toward or away from the paradigm in our reading will depend on the construction of the individual line and, even more, perhaps, on the construction of the passage of which it is a part. Certain combinations enhance or limit flexibility. For instance, if Shakespeare's line were paraphrased as "The worms of state," there would in that case be no possibility of an accent on "of."

The examples so far raise points that are applicable to any quotations cited in this book. First, any system of notation is an approximation, at best a stylized representation of the actual sound of a line. Second, while scansion is not a matter of whim, it is not, either, the exact science some might wish it to be. Experienced readers do not always "hear" a line of verse—especially a problematic one—in the same way. To return to our caterpillars, a reader not wishing to accept the full metrical promotion of the word "of" could reasonably argue for a secondary stress on the word:

> x / x / x \ x / x /
> The caterpillars of the commonwealth

In assessing relative levels of stress in a line, readers may scan according to differing assumptions, thus obtaining differing results. For instance, some readers would find our scansion of the earlier example,

> x / x \ x / x x / /
> The quality of mercy is not strained

unsatisfactory because they doubt whether pyrrhics and spondees truly exist in English verse.[7] Their preference would be to regard the fourth foot of this line as a "light iamb" (i.e., one whose second syllable is less heavily accented than usual) and the fifth foot as a "heavy iamb" (i.e., one whose first syllable is more heavily accented than usual). The lighter or heavier stressing of a syllable, in this view, is not sufficient to prevent these feet from being iambic as long as *some* difference, however slight, can be discerned between the more accented second syllable and the less accented one preceding it. The system of notation in use in this book could present such a reading by making more use of the intermediate stress mark:

```
    x    / x \ x    / x \ \      /
The quality of mercy is not strained
```

But this seems awkward, and a reader asked to recite the line according to both scansions in succession is likely to find little to distinguish one from the other. The nuances of relative stress are likely to challenge any system of scansion that attempts to be more precise than it is the nature of such schematic representations to be. And our awareness of the presence of a rhythmic shift in the line is more important than the particular symbols or prosodic terminology that we use to describe it.

Unreconciled to such uncertainties, some prosodists have proposed more finely calibrated systems of notation. Numbers and musical notes have been used to differentiate levels of stress; the study of linguistics has generated a widely accepted numerical system designating four levels of stress ranging from weak (1) to strong (4).[8] Helpful as this may be in some instances, it still cannot adequately address every nuance of stress variation in a line; and it may prove to be counterproductive if it lulls us into faith in a precision that turns out to be illusory. The older method of scansion by feet that we are using (and that most poets themselves use in writing accentual-syllabic verse) seems preferable for our purpose, as long as readers are aware that it is (and must be, and should be) open to question. The scansions offered in the following discussions are carefully considered but necessarily limited attempts to track the behavior of language within lines of verse. Readers should feel entitled to argue with them (as some undoubtedly will). One would hope, however, that their proposed alternatives will take heed of the accents inherent in words properly pronounced and of the additional emphases provided by thematic contexts and patterns of syntax. In disputed cases, those who are unpersuaded can agree to disagree.

It soon becomes apparent that studying isolated lines of blank verse cannot take us very far in understanding the quality, strained or unstrained as it may be, of the meter. Blank verse is called "blank," authorities inform us, through a translation of the French term *vers blancs* ("white verses"), referring to unrhymed verse. Both in French and in English the idea of the verse as colorless suggested a lack of ornament—the missing rhyme meant the verse was missing one of the "colors" of style. (The concept seems amusing in hindsight, since the last four centuries have offered so many examples of blank verse that are not only colorful but downright gaudy.) Absence of rhyme, at first regarded as a detriment, came to be appreciated as a strength once poets learned to make use of the liberty it afforded. Verse that is not confined to units by being cast in couplets or in larger stanzas can develop complex patterns of sound and of thought over extended passages, engaging the reader's attention in tantalizing, often surprising ways. Without the recurrence of end-rhyme or the visible patterns of stanzas, both poet and reader find themselves thinking, as the cant phrase goes, "outside the box."

It is often said that iambic pentameter comes closer than any other meter to the patterns of speech in the English language. In one well-known textbook, *Western Wind,* John Frederick Nims and David Mason offer a number of specimen lines, including "Deposit fifty cents for overtime," "I'd like to introduce a friend of mine," and "Suppose you take your damn feet off the chair."[9] Such demonstrations are useful reminders of the link between life and art in this case, but they cannot go very far to illustrate the actual use of the meter by poets. Why? Again, because a single line cannot give us the same impression of the meter's range that a longer passage can. Also, just as important, the deliberately conversational style of these examples represents only one of a spectrum of styles in which the meter has been successfully employed.

Once again, let us leave scansion aside for the moment and sample some of this stylistic range in passages of varying lengths from several periods. (As the reader will note, some of the later poets allow themselves much greater metrical liberty than their predecessors, but we shall discuss that in later chapters.) Certainly, with a nod to Nims and Mason, we can find any number of examples of the conversational style. Here is Robert Frost's country parson, recalling a Civil War casualty:

> He fell at Gettysburg or Fredericksburg,
> I ought to know—it makes a difference which:
> Fredericksburg wasn't Gettysburg, of course.
>
> ("The Black Cottage," 31–33)

And here are the first lines of Howard Nemerov's "She," in which the conversational manner and deliberately contemporary viewpoint jar amusingly with an exalted subject (in fact, "exalted" is the most exalted word in the piece):

So Dante exalted his Beatrice, a girl
"Of great beauty and utterly without charm"
Of whom his wife once wrote Ann Landers, Ann
My husband is a decent kindly man
Though on the road a lot, but has this thing
About a dame's been dead for half his life
He's writing this enormous poem about
And I want to know should I bring the matter up?
The wise woman answered Better leave it lay,
And added Gemma baby you need help.

(1–10)

There is plenty of conversational speech in Shakespeare. Juliet's nurse rambles on in recalling how old Juliet is:

Even or odd, of all days in the year,
Come Lammas Eve at night shall she be fourteen.
Susan and she (God rest all Christian souls!)
Were of an age. Well, Susan is with God;
She was too good for me.

(*Romeo and Juliet*, 1.3.16–20)

These passages in the conversational style illustrate just a few of the possibilities for dramatic uses of blank verse. Frost and Shakespeare each delineate a single character by means of a voice. In the Nemerov passage the narrator's offhand, satirically edged tone alternates easily with the voices of his characters. A particularly intriguing aspect of blank verse is its chameleonlike way of accommodating various levels of tone. Looking at the following passage by John Keats, we cannot see anything especially ornate in the language, and yet "conversational" would not likely be the first word to come to mind to describe it:

Hyperion arose, and on the stars
Lifted his curved lids, and kept them wide
Until it ceas'd; and still he kept them wide:
And still they were the same bright, patient stars.

(*Hyperion*, 1.350–53)

Here the meter serves a narrative purpose and also projects a lyric quality.

As we move across the stylistic spectrum we find numerous examples of blank verse written in what is often called a "middle" style—not particularly aiming for conversational effect but engaging in exposition, or developing an argument, or pursuing a path of meditation: in short, doing what various types of essays do. Thus, William Cowper, in 1785, expresses his detestation of cruelty to animals:

> I would not enter on my list of friends
> (Though grac'd with polish'd manners and fine sense
> Yet wanting sensibility) the man
> Who needlessly sets foot upon a worm.
> An inadvertent step may crush the snail
> That crawls at evening in the public path,
> But he that has humanity, forewarned,
> Will tread aside, and let the reptile live.
>
> (*The Task*, 6.560–67)

And Karl Shapiro, in 1945, complains of cruelty to poets:

> No one with half a dozen poems in print
> Can have failed to notice the competitive
> And not unseldom ugly mood of rime
> And criticism. We are not known for graces
> In modern art. A young and tender poet
> Perhaps must necessarily be led
> Barefooted over broken glass to make
> His introduction, but once installed the threat
> To person and reputation is not removed.
>
> (*Essay on Rime*, 1466–74)

This is not, quite, the sound of common speech, but of educated reflection— a sort of higher journalism made higher yet by the unobtrusive boost the meter gives it.

This sort of discursive style is the foundation of many long poems, and it is capable of modulating into something grander when the occasion calls for it. William Wordsworth's autobiographical poem *The Prelude* is based in the middle style, but it gathers intensity not only in certain narrative passages but also at points of philosophical conviction:

> Dust as we are, the immortal spirit grows
> Like harmony in music; there is a dark
> Inscrutable workmanship that reconciles
> Discordant elements, makes them cling together
> In one society.

(1.340–44)

Another passionate philosophizer in blank verse, Wallace Stevens, goes even further in pursuing argument through images:

> Life is a bitter aspic. We are not
> At the centre of a diamond. At dawn,
> The paratroopers fall and as they fall
> They mow the lawn. A vessel sinks in waves
> Of people, as big bell-billows from its bell
> Bell-bellow in the village steeple. Violets,
> Great tufts, spring up from buried houses
> Of poor, dishonest people, for whom the steeple,
> Long since, rang out farewell, farewell, farewell.

("Esthétique du Mal," XI, 1–9)

Both in narrative and in drama, style can be even more elaborate and intense, in keeping with more drastic or rarefied states of feeling. Then we get the great set pieces, like the soliloquies of Shakespearean tragedy, or the more memorable speeches of Milton's *Paradise Lost*, such as this one of Satan's, in which the fallen angel greets his new dwelling place:

> Farewell happy Fields
> Where Joy for ever dwells: Hail horrors, hail
> Infernal world, and thou profoundest Hell
> Receive thy new Possessor: One who brings
> A mind not to be chang'd by Place or Time.

The mind is its own place, and in itself
Can make a Heav'n of Hell, a Hell of Heav'n.

(1.249–55)

In the modern period, Yeats is notable for achieving the grand style in remarkably compact forms. "The Second Coming," his haunting apocalyptic vision,
is only twenty-two lines long. It ends:

The darkness drops again; but now I know
That twenty centuries of stony sleep
Were vexed to nightmare by a rocking cradle,
And what rough beast, its hour come round at last,
Slouches towards Bethlehem to be born?

(18–22)

At its most extreme, style in blank verse may sidestep human rationality
or even human consciousness. In Alfred Tennyson's monologue "Lucretius,"
the Epicurean philosopher goes insane when given an aphrodisiac by his un-
philosophically minded wife. In his delirium he is assailed by a nightmare vision of the atomistic cosmos of his creed:

A void was made in Nature; all her bonds
Cracked; and I saw the flaring atom-streams
And torrents of her myriad universe,
Ruining along the illimitable inane,
Fly on to crash together again, and make
Another and another frame of things
For ever [. . .]

(37–43)

Tennyson's great rival as a monologuist, Robert Browning, gives us a less-than-
human speaker in his adaptation of Caliban, Shakespeare's monster in *The
Tempest*. In these lines Caliban describes making moonshine and tells how
the product affects him:

Look now, I melt a gourd-fruit into mash,
Add honeycomb and pods, I have perceived,

Which bite like finches when they bill and kiss,—
Then, when froth rises bladdery, drink up all,
Quick, quick, till maggots scamper through my brain;
Last, throw me on my back i' the seeded thyme,
And wanton, wishing I were born a bird.

("Caliban upon Setebos," 68–74)

Even these fairly brief extracts demonstrate that the meter typically achieves its most memorable effects not in a single line but cumulatively. Here it may be useful to scan an extended passage, both to illustrate the point further and to introduce a few more technical terms that will be helpful in reading the following chapters.

The conclusion of Matthew Arnold's "Sohrab and Rustum" is an especially apt example of the cumulative power of blank verse. Set in ancient Persia, the poem tells of two warriors, a father and son whom circumstances have separated, who meet on the field of battle unaware of each other's identity. The father kills the son and, on learning who his opponent was, sinks down in despair beside the corpse on the bank of the Oxus River where their duel occurred. The closing lines shift attention away from the tragic antagonists to the grandly indifferent river in its ceaseless flow:

```
  /   x   x  / x  / x   /  x   /
But the majestic river floated on, |

   /  x  x   /   x   /   x   /  /   /
Out of the mist and hum of that low land, |

 / x  x  /  x  /  x    \    /     /
Into the frosty starlight, | and there moved, |

   x  / x      /    x   /     x  / x x  /
Rejoicing, | through the hushed Chorasmian waste, |

  /  x  x  / x / x    /     /  /
Under the solitary moon; | he flowed

   /   x   x   / x  /    /  / x /
Right for the polar star, | past Oranjè, |

   /   x    x    /    x   /    x   /   x /
Brimming, | and bright, | and large; | then sands begin

  x  /  x  / x x  /    x   /  x   /
To hem his watery march, | and dam his streams, |
```

```
 x    /   x   / x        /  x  / x x   /
And split his currents; | that for many a league

    x   /    x   / x    / x    /  x /
The shorn and parceled Oxus strains along

     x     /   x  /  x    / x  / x  /
Through beds of sand and matted rushy isles— |

 / x   x  / x    x    /       /   / /
Oxus, forgetting the bright speed he had

 /  x  /    /  x    / x /  x  /
In his high mountain-cradle in Pamere, |

  x  /    x  /x x   / x x    / x  /
A foiled circuitous wanderer— | till at last

   x  /    x   /  x  / x  /     x   /
The longed-for dash of waves is heard, | and wide

  x  / x x    /    x  / x / x      /
His luminous home of waters opens, | bright

   x    /  x    \    x    /  x  / x     /
And tranquil, | from whose floor the new-bathed stars

x  /    x   /  x /  x  / x /
Emerge, | and shine upon the Aral Sea.
```

(875–92)

Weak or secondary stresses are not frequent, although we find them used as they are by many other poets when a conjunction or a preposition falls in a stress position: only the third and the next-to-last lines offer instances. The full weight maintained on accented syllables over so great a stretch may contribute to the grave, stately movement. Arnold avails himself of metrical substitutions in several places—not only spondees (even arguably two in a row in "Oxus, forgetting the bright speed he had") but trochees and anapests as well. A trochee (/ x) in place of an iamb is actually the most frequent substitution in blank verse of all periods. It is especially common in the first foot of a line (so much so that it is often spoken of simply as a "reversed foot"). Seven of Arnold's lines open with a trochee. The anapest, which became a more widely accepted substitution in Arnold's century, is a trisyllabic foot (x x /) and hence lengthens the iambic pentameter line to eleven syllables. Arnold adds a ripple to the verse by following an iamb with an anapest in phrases like "Chorasmian waste," "his watery march," and "for many a league." Besides sustaining his single sentence for eighteen lines, which itself might suggest the forward movement of the river, Arnold deploys his metrical substitutions to suggest fluctuations in that movement. This is especially evident in the middle of the passage. Two lines, regular metrically but slow-moving because of consonant clusters—"The shorn and parceled Oxus strains along / Through beds of sand and matted rushy isles"—are followed by two spondee-loaded lines:

>   /   /   / /
> Oxus, forgetting the bright speed he had
>
>   /   /
> In his high mountain-cradle in Pamere.

This heavy accentuation dissipates immediately in the line that follows, which is crammed with additional *unstressed* syllables. Line 888, "A foiled circuitous wanderer—till at last," if we treat "foiled" as monosyllabic, still comes to twelve syllables; evidently we are to swallow the lightest syllables of "circuitous" and "wanderer." (We shall have more to say later on concerning such an effect, when terms such as "elision" and "syncope" take center stage.) By contrast with the weighty groupings of stress in the lines just before it, this one offers an unstable, skittery rhythm. There is nothing crudely imitative in these shifts—after all, one of the slower-moving pairs of words here is "bright speed." What these successive manipulations of stress accomplish is subtler— an auditory reinforcement of the movement described as the river proceeds, first quickly and unimpeded, then "shorn and parcelled" in its slower mean- derings. The idea of a progress that undergoes intermittent changes of pace and yet continues inexorably to its end is underscored. In a less vaguely metaphorical sense than usual, the meter may be said to provide the passage with an undercurrent.

Arnold's strikingly varied placement of pauses, which are marked here with a vertical bar (|), does much the same thing. This, too, is something to be discussed at length; here we may note that some of these pauses are more em- phatic than others, and that Arnold is over-solicitous, some might think, in his use of punctuation to signal them. The fluctuations between lines that are end-stopped (having a break in both sound and sense before the line follow- ing) and lines that are enjambed (running on without a pause into the next line) are unsymmetrical and unpredictable. The same is true of Arnold's use of the pause within a line (the term sometimes used for this, imported a bit

awkwardly from classical prosody, is the caesura). Just as with his variations
in accent, Arnold is using pauses to affect the pace of his phrases, and this,
too, suggests the alternately fluid and thwarted progress of the stream. While
most of the pauses come between feet, one can at times occur between the
syllables within a foot (as in lines 878 and 888). The pauses are unquestionably
meant to be noticed: though some are stronger than others, the only one that
seems so minimal that it need not be marked is after the comma in "Oxus,
forgetting the bright speed he had." Arnold may overdo the device: in a line
like "Brimming, and bright, and large; then sands begin," we may be irritated
by the profuse punctuation, which is so obviously putting on the brakes. (In
the following chapters pauses will not be marked in quotations unless they
are specifically discussed in the attached commentary. The careful reader,
though, is bound to notice their effect.) Like metrical substitution and enjambment, the caesura or pause is a crucial resource for the writer of blank
verse. These all are vital for creating the sort of flexibility and dynamism required to knit together the sorts of intricate patterns we find in passages extending over many lines.

It might be thought that such devices are elements of a grand style, given
the lofty air of the example. (The loftiness is unsurprising; Arnold was endeavoring to imitate the style of Homer.) In fact, as we shall see, these and ancillary features are part of the mechanics of blank verse regardless of its
qualities of diction and syntax. Here is the opening of Andrew Hudgins's high
school–era memory, "Oh, Say, Can You See":

> "Granddaddy owned half of Marengo County,"
> she said. First date. Last date. "Wow, half the county!"
> I said. But what I thought was this:
> Right now your daddy sells appliances,
> your mom's a keypunch operator. My dad?
> "He's in the service." She reeled off a list
> of generals, heroes, governors—the assorted
> effluvium of Southern history whom
> she had descended from. Well, whup-dee-do.
>
> (1–9)

Hudgins, like many contemporary writers of blank verse, takes a looser approach to the meter than does Arnold. But here, too, we find some technical

features worth noting. Several of these lines have a so-called feminine ending —an added unstressed syllable at the end that makes a regular pentameter line eleven syllables long. This is not a device used by Arnold, but we find it frequently in Elizabethan drama. An especially interesting line arguably of this sort is

x   /   x / x   / x / x   / (x)

your mom's a keypunch operator. My dad?

Here we see how the naturalistic demands of conversational style apply pressure to conventional scansion. "My," in a stressed position, receives yet more stress from the emphasis contrasting it with the preceding "your," and this heavy stress on "My" causes the following word, "dad," to sound comparatively less emphatic. The degree of stress shifting at the end of the line is debatable, but there is some amusement in the possibility that "dad" is a feminine ending. We spoke of Arnold's insistent use of the pause in his line "Brimming, | and bright, | and large; | then sands begin." Here, we notice the comic emphasis the triple pause gives to "she said. | First date. | Last date. | 'Wow, half the county!'" (There is even perhaps a fourth pause here, after "Wow," though it is not pronounced enough to mark.) Hudgins, too, has made some calculating use both of end-stopping and enjambment. The craftsmanship in such a passage is not as elaborate as Arnold's, but it is equally thoughtful in pursuing its more casual effect, and it works with the same metrical toolbox. The metrical profile of "Well, whup-dee-do," as it lies in its line, is the same as "the Aral Sea," and both provide equally satisfying senses of closure. The meter is a startlingly neutral medium, as indifferent to the words it propels as the Oxus River is to the flotsam it carries downstream. Its readiness to ferry both "high" and "low" vocabulary is one principal reason for its continuing and expanding use by poets.

IV

Although some part of the variety in uses of blank verse has been suggested by the discussion so far, the range is far greater. Our present topics—how blank verse operates expressively in poetry, and what purposes it can be made to address—are in need of thorough examination, which the following chapters aim to provide. Equally important is the history of blank verse. A survey of that history in fact enables a discussion of the meter's properties, for the story of blank verse is one of many poets' technical discoveries and refinements over the course of more than four centuries. The impact of any stylistic innovation, we find, is cumulative—like the expressive effect of a passage of blank verse.

The meter's history has been somewhat neglected by scholars in the modern and postmodern periods. The last book to attempt an overview of the topic, *Blank Verse,* by the English esthete and Italophile John Addington Symonds, was published in 1895, two years after the author's death.[10] It is in fact a compilation of three longish essays Symonds wrote tracking the major phases in the history of blank verse up to his own time. A fuller though also more dispersed treatment of the subject is found in sections at various points of George Saintsbury's *A History of English Prosody,* whose three hefty volumes appeared from 1906 to 1910.[11] This is a canonical work of literary history, of great usefulness still, as is the work of Symonds, even if present-day readers are unlikely to share some of the late Victorian tastes of these two authors. Other valuable studies of blank verse have tended to be more specialized, centering on a single poet, or a group of poets, or on a particular time period. *Milton's Prosody* by Robert Bridges (rev. ed. 1921) is one of the most influential.[12] Odd as it may seem, the blank verse of the twentieth century and beyond has never been chronicled as that of previous epochs has been. The third and fourth chapters of this book offer an outline, at least, of that unwritten history. The chapter that precedes them necessarily gives a précis of information available elsewhere, since a discussion of blank verse in the last three or four generations would be cryptic in many respects without the longer look backward that this provides. In these historical chapters we shall take advantage of numerous occasions for technical analysis of the meter in its successive stages of development.

The conviction governing this discussion throughout is that blank verse has continued to be a potent medium in the modern period and beyond. There is some disagreement about this, to judge from statements such as this one, which concludes the entry on blank verse in the latest edition of the *Princeton Encyclopedia of Poetry and Poetics* (1993): "The advent of free verse sounded the death-knell of this meter which was once and for long a powerful, flexible, and subtle form, the most prestigious and successful modern rival to the greatest meter of antiquity."[13] There is no doubt whatever that free verse put significant pressure on blank verse as well as on other fixed forms; but the "death" of the meter in the twentieth century is a rumor that a careful reading of twentieth-century poetry does not bear out. We shall return to this controversy in due course. But we had better begin at the beginning.

BEFORE THE TWENTIETH CENTURY

I

FOR REASONS no scholar has fully explained, English meter at the beginning of the sixteenth century was in grave disarray.[1] After the death of Geoffrey Chaucer in 1400, the language itself had undergone the shifts in grammar and pronunciation that made it Modern English: recognizable as our own language, however difficult its diction, usage, and spelling may sometimes make it for us to read. Concurrent with these changes and, some have argued, because of them, a startling awkwardness came to afflict English poets, especially when they attempted to write the decasyllabic line that Chaucer had handled with such suavity. In one hapless venture after another, the verse staggers, limps, or plunges ahead willy-nilly. In some late medieval poetry the "poetical imbecility" (C. S. Lewis's phrase) is so pronounced that only the presence of rhymes makes it clear that what we are reading was intended to be verse.[2]

The invention of blank verse in English is part of a larger story of the rescue of poetry from this state of prosodic anarchy. Here, too, some parts of the story remain mysterious. The poets who smoothed out the crimps in the decasyllabic line may not have been aiming at the accentual-syllabic line that we would call iambic pentameter. It is possible that they were trying simply to emulate the regular syllable count of verse written in Romance languages such as French and Italian—verse that is scanned without regard to accent. This is a question for specialists to wrangle over. English has so strong an accentual quality that the iambic meter, which is perceptibly close to natural speech rhythms, was bound to assert itself. It took many years, however, for poets to learn to use it with grace.

What came to be called blank verse in English began as an experiment, and not even a particularly promising one. Henry Howard, Earl of Surrey, undertook the first translation of Virgil's *Aeneid* into English, of which he completed versions of book 2 (the fall of Troy) and book 4 (the betrayal and death of Dido). Scholars date this work to around 1540. No doubt the translation circulated in manuscript, but it was not until several years after Surrey's unjust execution for treason in 1547 that any of it was published; book 4 appeared in an edition by William Owen in 1554, and Richard Tottel's edition of both books followed in 1557. The full title of Owen's edition suggests an attempt to forestall, or at least acknowledge, the puzzled reactions of readers: *The Fourth Book of Virgil, Intreating of the Love between Aeneas and Dido, Translated into English and Drawn into a Strange Meter by Henry late Earl of Surrey.* The "strange meter" of Surrey's translation was the first English blank verse.

"Strange" may have meant "foreign" as well as "unfamiliar." With the rise of vernacular literature, translators throughout Europe struggled with devising equivalents of Virgil's hexameters, which of course were unrhymed. Surrey evidently was familiar with Italian translations of Virgil which were in unrhymed lines of ten or eleven syllables, and he modeled his own lines on these. Nor was this the end of his indebtedness to precursors. Surrey consulted and liberally borrowed wording from Gavin Douglas's 1512 translation of Virgil into Scots, even as he declined to follow the example of Douglas's rhymed couplets. Douglas in fact provided some of Surrey's most vivid phrasing, but the absence of rhyme and the earl's attempts to satisfy the requisites of this "strange meter" brought a new sound into English poetry.

Surrey's partial *Aeneid* is a dignified work that now seems to have more historical than literary interest. By the end of Surrey's century, blank verse was to develop a flexibility and grace that were beyond his grasp. The noticeable stiffness in many of his lines suggests that he was feeling his way, more mastered by the meter than master of it. Here is his version of the death of Laocoön and his sons, attacked by serpents emerging from the sea "With gloing eyen, tainted with blood and fire: / Whoes waltring tongues did lick their hissing mouthes" (2:265–66).

And first of all eche serpent doth enwrap
The bodies small of his two tender sonnes:
Whose wretched limes they byt, and fed theron.
Then raught they hym, who had his wepon caught
To rescue them, twise winding him about,
With folded knottes, and circled tailes, his wast.
Their scaled backes did compasse twise his neck,
With rered heddes aloft, and stretched throtes.
He with his handes straue to vnloose the knottes:
Whose sacred fillettes all be sprinkled were
With filth of gory blood, and venim rank.

(2.269–79)

Given the turbulent physical movements, the grotesque violence being de-scribed, one might reasonably expect the verse to have more animation. Surrey is intent upon maintaining an unvaried count of ten syllables per line (some-times by dint of pronouncing the -ed in a word like "scaled"), and he is con-servative in shifting accents from their iambic pattern or in using the caesura with expressive effect. The most noticeable substitutions—trochees for the first and third iambs in "He with his handes strave to unloose the knottes"—are token departures from the meter's stolid march. Even when it has the promise of communicating horror or pathos, the vocabulary seems fixed in place rather than given added impetus by Surrey's blank verse.

Although Surrey's pioneering effort met with respect, it did not by any means inaugurate a vogue. For some years it remained a solitary artifact. Nicholas Grimald essayed a few short translations in blank verse (more wooden than Surrey's), which appeared in the famous anthology known as Tottel's *Miscellany* (1557). The next important chronological development was the first use of the meter in drama. This occurred in 1561–62 when *Gorboduc*, a tragedy by Thomas Norton and Thomas Sackville, was played at the Christmas Revels of the Inner Temple and soon afterward before Queen Elizabeth. Although *Gorboduc* is not a translation, the young courtiers who wrote it were aiming, like Surrey, to emulate the style of a classical author. In this case the author was Seneca, whose tragedies were translated and, as here, studiously imitated in the early years of Elizabeth's reign. As it had been for Surrey, the choice of blank verse here was an attempt to find a closer equivalent to the prototype's Latin than the customary rhymes of English poetry (dramatic as well as narrative) could furnish.

Gorboduc falls short of modern expectations for drama in so many ways that it may seem beside the point to criticize its verse. Characters do not engage in dialogue of the kind familiar to us from more naturalistic types of drama. Rather than conversing, they take turns declaiming. In keeping with classical convention, violence occurs offstage and is then reported by a horrified and loquacious eyewitness. The play is relentlessly didactic. By showing the gruesome consequences of a royal father's decision to divide his kingdom between his two sons (civil war breaks out; one son kills the other and is then killed by his mother for revenge, while the country descends into brutish lawlessness), Sackville and Norton hoped to impress upon their virgin queen the vital importance of settling the question of royal succession. Both men were members of Parliament, and their writing was shaped by classical standards for oratory as well as by those for drama. This in itself would be likely to produce a work more static than is suited to the theater, but the verse is so heavy-handed as to intensify the basic fault. Toward the end of the play Fergus, Duke of Albany, plans to usurp the throne:

> If euer time to gaine a kingdome here
> Were offred man, now it is offred mee.
> The realme is reft both of their king and queene,
> The ofspring of the prince is slaine and dead,
> No issue now remaines, the heire vnknowen,
> The people are in armes and mutynies,
> The nobles they are busied how to cease
> These great rebellious tumultes and vproares [...]
>
> (5.1.124–31)

Here are the typical flaws almost any extended passage exhibits. The lack of rhythmic variation is pronounced, and one notices the authors' tendency to redundancy, both to add unnecessary emphasis and, at times, to fill out a line. Phrasing like "slaine and dead" and "The nobles they" are sure signs of syllable counting. Verse like this could not hope to serve as an inspiring example for ambitious dramatists, though it provided an intriguing challenge by presenting so much to improve upon. Again, the response was slow in coming. Blank verse was at this point hardly a siren song for younger poets, and neither epic nor drama had as yet found a poet who could write iambic pentameter not merely with metrical regularity but with imaginative genius.

One poet of the period, George Gascoigne, who had collaborated on translating Euripides' *Jocasta* into blank verse, was the first to use the meter for a purpose neither dramatic nor narrative in his didactic satire "The Steel Glass" (1576). This exposé of Elizabethan vanities stitched together lists of worldly pomps for the reader's disapproval:

> Our bumbast hose, our treble double ruffes,
> Our sutes of Silke, our comely garded capes,
> Our knit silke stockes, and spanish lether shoes
> (Yea velvet serves, ofttimes to trample in)
> Our plumes, our spangs, and al our queint aray
> Are pricking spurres, provoking filthy pride,
> And snares (unseen) which leade a man to hel.
>
> (165–71)

The soon-predictable use of anaphora is tedious enough, but the almost unvarying placement of the caesura after the fourth syllable is more disaffecting still.[3] Gascoigne deserves notice for innovation in his application of blank verse to a new genre, but his work, like the others we have been discussing, is with reason more often cited than read. A more dynamic species of this experimental verse would have to emerge if it were ever to be more than a literary curiosity.

Enter Christopher Marlowe. Born in the same year as Shakespeare but destined to die young, Marlowe was the first playwright able to make blank verse an effective medium for drama. Beginning in the 1580s, he wrote the series of plays in blank verse which established it as the dominant form for drama in the next several decades. Although the effects he achieved with the meter were far less various than those which Shakespeare and other poets were to discover in his wake, he deserves great credit for taking the stiff, unpromising matrix presented by *Gorboduc* and transforming it into poetry of the highest order:

> Was this the face that launched a thousand ships,
> And burnt the topless towers of Ilium?

Sweet Helen, make me immortal with a kiss.
Her lips suck forth my soul: see where it flies.
. . . .
Oh, thou art fairer than the evening's air
Clad in the beauty of a thousand stars.
Brighter art thou than flaming Jupiter,
When he appeared to hapless Semele:
More lovely than the monarch of the sky,
In wanton Arethusa's azure arms,
And none but thou shalt be my paramour.

(*Doctor Faustus*, 5.1.97–100; 110–16)

Was this the meter that had clomped about in line on shackled line in *Gorboduc*? Marlowe had managed to breathe life into it. Of course, part of the beauty here is based in diction as well as in meter. Marlowe enriches the sound with patterns of consonance ("*t*opless *t*owers," "*m*ake *m*e i*mm*ortal," "*s*uck forth my *s*oul: *s*ee"), and of assonance ("*fair*er than the evening's *air*," "Arethusa's *a*zure *a*rms"). There is some precedent for this in *Gorboduc*, which makes use of alliteration, but Marlowe's sound patterns are more various and more effective for being less obtrusive. He also allows himself a greater rhythmical flexibility than any previous writer of blank verse had felt free to use. By later standards he is quite conservative. Yet it is remarkable how much a few carefully placed variations can do to dispel the curse of monotony. One sees this in a line like

x / x / x / / x x /
Her lips suck forth my soul: see where it flies.

The reversal of the fourth foot, after the perfectly regular procession leading up to it, emphasizes the erotic and spiritual ecstasy that occurs as the climax of this seductive vision. A few lines later on, the more common reversal of the first foot in "Clad in the beauty of a thousand stars" is welcome for the bit of variety it affords, but it becomes more interesting in conjunction with the same effect in the line following: "Brighter art thou than flaming Jupiter." The meter here, by varying its flow, gives a boost to the imagery: it is a way of making the light effect a little more dazzling. A subtler variation occurs in the earlier line:

```
    x   / x   /   x x  / x  / x /
Sweet Helen, make me immortal with a kiss.
```

Either an extra unstressed syllable is added to the third foot,

```
    x x    /
me immor-
```

making this iamb an anapest as scanned above; or we could consider this a form of elision, in which the longer vowel of "me" and the shorter first syllable of "immortal" are melded together. In either case, the variation lightens the movement of the line, and may even offer a subliminal reinforcement of the sense of it, as we see (or hear) "me," the speaker's self, fusing with "immortal," the condition he aspires to. Marlowe in such passages shows himself able to mold the meter expressively, which is what differentiates iambic pentameter that is poetry from iambic pentameter that is verse.

There is a heady air of discovery in this achievement. In the prologue to his first great theatrical success, *Tamburlaine the Great* (part 1), he promises the audience something very different from the jangling rhymed couplets they were accustomed to:

> From jigging veins of rhyming mother-wits,
> And such conceits as clownage keeps in pay,
> We'll lead you to the stately tent of war,
> Where you shall hear the Scythian Tamburlaine
> Threatening the world with high astounding terms [...]

>> (1–5)

And this in fact is what the ticket holders got in plenty, as the conquering hero sang his own praises:

> I hold the Fates bound fast in iron chains,
> And with my hand turn Fortune's wheel about;
> And sooner shall the sun fall from his sphere
> Than Tamburlaine be slain or overcome.

>> (1.2.174–77)

The prologue is precise in its description of what is to follow, for the difference in verse form, the absence of rhyme, is accompanied by a highly charged rhetoric ("high astounding terms"). Ben Jonson no doubt had such passages in mind when, in his great eulogistic poem on Shakespeare, he praised in passing "Marlowe's mighty line" (30).[4] Although Marlowe showed himself capable of toning down his style somewhat after *Tamburlaine* (*Doctor Faustus* and other later work shows him capably using the meter in dialogue that is more naturalistic), the showstopping speech is typically what we most remember. Both his characters and their emotions tend to lack facets. His greatest set pieces, like Faustus's final scene, begin at a high pitch and go higher; there is plenty of intensity but not always much subtlety.

Clearly, audiences found the plays thrilling, and playwrights found Marlowe's verse a captivating model to emulate. Marlowe's refinement of blank verse coincided with the rise of the professional theater, and his grand speeches for titanic characters gave actors the kind of roles they coveted. One can tell something is striking a chord when it excites ridicule. Thomas Nashe inveighed against "idiot Art-masters . . . who (mounted on a stage of arrogance) think to out-brave better pennes with the swelling bumbast of bragging blank verse . . . and the spacious volubility of a drumming decasyllabon."[5] "Bombast" (as we would spell it) is perhaps what Marlowe started with in *Tamburlaine,* but even in that play and certainly in later ones he transcended it, as Faustus's invocation of Helen serves to show. His lyric touches softened the austere march of the meter just sufficiently, we might say, to show what might be done with it. In his own practice, he never quite liberated himself in some respects. He is sparing (although, as we have seen, effective) in admitting metrical substitutions, and even more sparing in manipulating the caesura. Most noticeable of all is his subservience to the pause at the end of the line. Although he had too fine an ear to reproduce the yawn that seems to be hovering parenthetically at the end of each line in *Gorboduc,* Marlowe is still bound to a system in which the grammar and the meter coincide in a discernible pause at the pentameter's end. Very often this is punctuated, but the pause is there, enforced by the phrasing, even when the punctuation is not. Saintsbury is correct, if ponderously witty, in speaking of such lines by Marlowe and his circle as "end-*lopped* if not *stopped.*"[6] Writing of weaker examples, he deplores "[a] perpetual hobble, as it were, in the pace; an ever-officious obstacle and blocking in the wind-stroke or the oarage of poetry. In the worst examples of all, even more unpleasant metaphors suggest themselves; the verses positively *hiccup* in their abrupt severance of rhythm and meaning."[7] Marlowe is better than this, but if his work does not lapse into hiccups, neither does it achieve the ease of movement that characterizes the best dramatic poetry of the period. That was to be Shakespeare's accomplishment.

II

Comprehensive studies of blank verse in the Renaissance invariably cite Shakespeare's innovative work with the meter as crucial to its further development. As suggested above, his ability to overcome the naggingly evident pause at the line break that proved so persistent for his precursors is a point of major importance. Symonds writes: "Throughout [Shakespeare's]writings there is a subtle adjustment of sound to sense, of lofty thoughts to appropriate words; the ideas evolve themselves with inexhaustible spontaneity, and a suitable investiture of language is never wanting, so that each cadenced period seems made to hold a thought of its own, and thought is linked to thought and cadence to cadence in unending continuity."[8] And Saintsbury, who as we have seen was highly conscious of "the excessively integral character of the line"[9] in Marlowe, rhapsodizes: "It was Shakespeare, Shakespeare only, and Shakespeare himself not at first nor till after long, who thawed the ice, broke the bonds, and set the music finally in unhampered motion."[10] However quaint we find such effusiveness today, we are bound to agree with these critics' judgment. Shakespeare indeed "thawed the ice" in fashioning his lines. In his work we find ourselves reading for the first time iambic pentameter not by increments of a line or two at a time but by verse paragraphs that sustain themselves over unpredictable spans, paradoxically challenging as well as satisfying the demands of the meter. Shakespeare does this through technical dexterity applied in a number of ways.

The obvious term to invoke at this point is enjambment—the word prosodists use to denote the running-on in both sound and sense of one line into the next. Shakespeare certainly makes use of enjambment, increasingly in his later plays. In *The Tempest*, which may be his last, we find it in the opening lines of a famous speech of Prospero's:

> Our revels now are ended. These our actors,
> As I foretold you, were all spirits and
> Are melted into air, into thin air [...]

(4.1.148–50)

The enjambment here in the second line is especially conspicuous since the more typically unstressed conjunction "and" has been moved into a stressed position. In reading it we put more stress on the word than we would if we were reading a prose sentence: "These our actors, as I foretold you, were all spirits and are melted into air." And yet the line is not end-stopped, and the additional stress we place on the word is not one that encourages a pause: we are carried over into the third line without any sense of a hiatus. This analysis would suit numerous instances of enjambment in Shakespeare and later poets.

Shakespeare uses other strategies to bridge the line break as well. One of the most noticeable, and most influential among his contemporaries, is his frequent use of an additional unstressed syllable at the end of a line—the "feminine ending" that we discussed briefly in chapter 1. The first four lines of Hamlet's best-known soliloquy are eleven-syllable lines of this sort:

> To be, or not to be: that is the question:
> Whether 'tis nobler in the mind to suffer
> The slings and arrows of outrageous fortune,
> Or to take arms against a sea of troubles,
> And by opposing end them.

> (*Hamlet*, 3.1.56–60)

The feminine ending, like enjambment, blurs the boundary of the line end. Interestingly, it seems to supply a carryover effect whether or not lines are end-stopped, as this passage illustrates. In this regard it is more versatile than enjambment. As we see here, the end of the second line of the passage ("suffer") is enjambed, while those of the lines before and following are not: "question," "fortune," "troubles" are all set off by punctuation. Yet there is scarcely any difference in the flow of the passage from one line to the next in any case. What really brings us to a halt is the end of the sentence partway through the fifth line: "And by opposing end them." Only then is the momentum of the lines significantly checked. One may speculate that the feminine ending is a means of fooling the ear. If, as readers or listeners, we have the iambic pentameter pattern in our heads, the added unstressed syllable creates, for the briefest instant, the sense that we have passed over to the next line. Even if there is end-stopping, we overlook it, and once we are in the next line our attention is focused on what is ahead, not on the line break we failed to register. It is a

simple trick, but a remarkably effective one. Scholars who specialize in counting inform us that the percentages of enjambed lines and of lines with feminine endings in Shakespeare's plays increased markedly throughout his career,
and even more casual readers will notice his greater freedom in this regard
when comparing his earlier with his later plays.[11] Clearly, continuity was a
persistent aim of his, more daringly pursued as he went along.

Continuity is served in a more fundamental way in Shakespeare's verse
than the discussion thus far has indicated. Enjambment and the feminine ending are useful devices for overriding the end of a pentameter line. What is crucial, though, is not a particular technical device, however deftly used, but an
ear for extended, often asymmetrical patterns of sound, and a rhetorical control that can negotiate complex alliances between meter and grammar. As we
saw in the *Hamlet* passage above, it is the conclusive "And by opposing end
them" which brings the verse decisively to rest in the middle of a line, its participle breaking the balanced symmetry of two opposed infinitives ("to suffer,"
"to take arms"). It is syntax as much as meter that creates the flow of the passage. Speaking of flow, can there be a better example than Othello's description
of the relentlessness of his capacity for revenge when Iago hypocritically begs
him to soften his rage against Desdemona?

> Like to the Pontic Sea,
> Whose icy current and compulsive course
> Nev'r keeps retiring ebb, but keeps due on
> To the Propontic and the Hellespont,
> Even so my bloody thoughts, with violent pace,
> Shall nev'r look back, nev'r ebb to humble love,
> Till that a capable and wide revenge
> Swallow them up.
>
> (*Othello*, 3.3.450–56)

Here, of course, the extended simile as well as the extended syntax add
propulsion to the onflow of the meter to its end at the chilling period, making
for a remarkably unified effect.

Shakespeare had to work through numerous experiments to gain the co-
operation of sound and sense that is apparent here. We can see him on the way
to it in a famous passage from an earlier play, *Richard II*. John of Gaunt's eu-
logy on England begins

> This royal throne of kings, this scepter'd isle,
> This earth of majesty, this seat of Mars,
> This other Eden, demi-paradise,
> This fortress built by Nature for herself
> Against infection and the hand of war,
> This happy breed of men, this little world,
> This precious stone set in the silver sea [. . .]
>
> (2.1.40–47)

And the catalogue of superlative epithets continues for another ten lines until the grammar resolves itself to bring the sentence to its despairingly antithetical end:

> This land of such dear souls, this dear, dear land—
> Dear for her reputation through the world—
> Is now leased out—I die pronouncing it—
> Like to a tenement or pelting farm.
>
> (57–60)

The whole sentence with its long-delayed predicate is sustained over twenty lines. This kind of catalogue structure could be numbing; but here the richness of language and the variation in length of individual phrases works against the threatening beads-on-a-string effect. Still, compared with the passages from *Hamlet* and *Othello,* this one is stiffer both in movement and in overall conception: what it shows is that Shakespeare early on was working at the problem he eventually solved so brilliantly for himself and for his followers.

We have concentrated thus far on the endings of Shakespeare's lines. What about his treatment of meter inside them? The same willingness to experiment, increasing throughout his career, governs his approach to metrical substitutions. Any one of his greater verse passages exhibits a shrewd elasticity within the line as well as cunning attention to how lines are conjoined. Substitutions, and thoughtful use of the caesura, enhance the expressiveness of his language. Excerpts from two speeches of Macbeth's offer illustrations. In the first passage, a soliloquy, Macbeth is struggling with second thoughts about his forthcoming murder of Duncan.

> If it were done when 'tis done, | then 'twere well
> It were done quickly. | If th' assassination

Could trammel up the consequence, | and catch, |
With his surcease, | success; | that but this blow
Might be the be-all and the end-all— | here, |
But here, | upon this bank and shoal of time, |
We'd jump the life to come.

(Macbeth, 1.7.1–7)

Here Shakespeare deploys pauses to emphasize the halting perplexity of the fainthearted assassin. (In performance an actor might even add more pauses: one placed after "If it were done" in the first line would be natural enough.) It is impossible to read the lines quickly. They move slowly, plodding along as in the first line of monosyllables, and they move just as slowly through the polysyllabic entanglements of the tempted mind, which itself seems "trammeled" in knotty phrasing like "and catch, / With his surcease, success." The frequency of the pauses and the fitful way in which they move from one spot to another in each line suggest something the rest of the play bears out in regard to Macbeth's paradoxical character. He is at once ponderous and agitated in his planning and his reaction to events. In his fine book, *Shakespeare's Metrical Art,* George T. Wright comments that "iambic pentameter . . . usually conveys a sense of complex understanding, as if the speakers of such lines were aware of more than they ever quite say, or as if there were more in their speeches than even they were aware of."[12] This is certainly the impression given in the passage just quoted, and it is given with equal power in Macbeth's last great speech:

```
x  /  x   /  x  / x  / x  / (x)
Tomorrow, and tomorrow, and tomorrow

/   x   x  / x  /   x   / x  /
Creeps in this petty pace from day to day,

x  x  /  / x \ x  x /  x  /
To the last syllable of recorded time;

x  /  x  / x  /  x   / x  /
And all our yesterdays have lighted fools

x  / x / x  /  /  /  /  / (x)
The way to dusty death. Out, out, brief candle!

/   x x  / x   / x x  /   / (x)
Life's but a walking shadow, a poor player
```

```
      x   /   x   /   x   /   x  /   x   /
That struts and frets his hour upon the stage

      x    /  x  /    x   /   /  x x  /
And then is heard no more. It is a tale

     /     x x  / x    /  x   /     x   / (x)
Told by an idiot, full of sound and fury,

    /   x / x    /  x
Signifying nothing.
```

(5.5.19–28)

Here the use of the caesura and even of less marked pauses is sparing. The movement is one of an inexorable ongoing trudge. The metrical stress forced onto both the "and's" in the first line deepens the sense of wearying repetition in these plodding tomorrows. The passage is paradigmatic in the way it maintains iambic pentameter as a norm that is adventurously departed from but returned to in due course. The fourth and seventh lines are perfectly regular. Others have common trochaic substitutions, such as "Creeps in," "Life's but," "Told by," all at the beginnings of lines, and "It is," after the caesura in the eighth line. Some little joke may be in play in the line "To the last syllable of recorded time," which features an extra syllable awkwardly slipped in. The paired spondees in "Out, out, brief candle!" give the effect of an outcry, especially in contrast to the sequence of regular iambs and the pause preceding them. And the additional unstressed syllable of the feminine ending caps the drama with anticlimax: the excess of feeling drops back, more or less immediately, into futility. If we look back, we see that this effect has been foreshadowed in the first line, "Tomorrow, and tomorrow, and tomorrow." Together with the triple repetition of "tomorrow," this variation gives the line what prosodists would call a "falling rhythm," which is appropriate to the situation. Macbeth is on an intractable course, and it is one that leads not only onward but downward on "the way to dusty death."

Shakespeare can be breathtakingly free in this kind of expressive variation. When King Lear cradles the body of the dead Cordelia, his extremity of emotion is suggested by the savage and systematic wrenching of the meter:

> Why should a dog, a horse, a rat, have life,
> And thou no breath at all? Thou' lt come no more,
> Never, never, never, never, never.

(*King Lear*, 5.3.308–10)

Every foot is reversed in this line of "never's," and this seems emblematic of the play's brutal depiction of social and natural order turned upside down.

Shakespeare's blank verse would be remarkable enough had he confined himself to extended speeches of the sort we have been examining. But, of course, he also made the meter a far more effective medium for dialogue than it had been before. As with the longer speeches, he picked up hints from Marlowe and greatly expanded on them. One reason Shakespeare's plays continue to be staged is that even with the difficulties presented by a sometimes obscure diction and numerous obsolete usages, an audience is still able to hear the dialogue as actual speech supported by recognizable feelings. When Romeo gate-crashes the Capulets' masked ball, he is detected by Tybalt, who complains of his presence to his uncle Capulet, Juliet's father: "Uncle, this is a Montague, our foe" (*Romeo and Juliet,* 1.5.63). Capulet, in a magnanimous mood (it is still act 1), counsels the boy to ignore the trespass, to forget the feud for this one evening. "Take no note of him," he commands:

> It is my will, the which if thou respect
> Show a fair presence and put off these frowns
> As ill-beseeming semblance for a feast.
> *Tybalt:* It fits when such a villain is a guest.
> I'll not endure him.
> *Capulet:*   He shall be endured.
> What, goodman boy! I say he shall. Go to!
> Am I the master here, or you? Go to!
> You'll not endure him, God shall mend my soul!
> You'll make a mutiny among my guests!
> You will set cock-a-hoop. You'll be the man!
>
>   (1.5.73–83)

We notice how the meter, without any very remarkable contortions, is elastic enough to accommodate two very different tones—or rather, three, since that of Capulet changes once Tybalt's petulant self-righteousness kindles his anger. His geniality dissolves into offended, patriarchal sarcasm: "You'll be the man!" These are tones familiar to all of us; we hear them indulged in whenever generations lock horns. As in soliloquies, so in dialogue: Shakespeare's verse continues to be viable because of its ability to capture fluctuations of feeling and render them in depth.

Shakespeare's dialogue, like his speeches, generally moves, over the course of his career, from the static and artificial to the animated and natural. We see this in his occasional use of a device called stichomythia, inherited from Seneca. Stichomythia is dialogue in which a single line spoken by one character is answered by another character's single line that plays off the language of the first in some way. An extended passage of stichomythia can seem the verbal equivalent of a volley in tennis. In the fairly early comedy *A Midsummer Night's Dream,* we find Hermia and Helena discussing the misplaced affections of Demetrius, which, along with much else, will be redirected in the ensuing action:

> *Hermia:* I frown upon him, yet he loves me still.
> *Helena:* O that your frowns would teach my smiles such skill!
> *Hermia:* I give him curses, yet he gives me love.
> *Helena:* O that my prayers could such affection move!
> *Hermia:* The more I hate, the more he follows me.
> *Helena:* The more I love, the more he hateth me.
> *Hermia:* His folly, Helena, is no fault of mine.
> *Helena:* None, but your beauty: would that fault were mine!
>
> (1.1.194–201)

This is insistently artificial (made even more so by the use of rhyme in the first few exchanges). We appreciate the neatness by which the characters' conflict is defined in such a passage, but we are unlikely to become emotionally involved in such elegant badinage. Contrast this with the later use of the device in *Hamlet:*

> *Queen:* Hamlet, thou hast thy father much offended.
> *Hamlet:* Mother, you have my father much offended.
> *Queen:* Come, come, you answer with an idle tongue.
> *Hamlet:* Go, go, you question with a wicked tongue.
>
> (3.3.10–13)

In this case the artifice does not call attention to itself (we might say, in fact, that the blank verse does not call attention to itself *as verse*). Stylized as this is, with "Come, come" hurled back as "Go, go," with "idle tongue" returned as "wicked tongue," it does not flutter away from the tense emotions of the mother and son in their confrontation. It delves into them. The formal device actually touches on the raw nerve tormenting Hamlet throughout the play, for the word "father" means one person to him and another person to his mother. This is one of many possible examples of Shakespeare's knack for re-animating even the more stilted conventions of verse in the theater of his time.

Shakespeare's period was, of course, the greatest for the theater in English, and he was eventually joined and followed by a number of highly talented dramatists who learned from his development of iambic pentameter and added refinements of their own.[13] It would take a much longer book than this to study dramatic blank verse of the Renaissance in ample detail. (Fortunately, a great deal of critical literature is available on the subject.) Here we can touch on only a few points in regard to Shakespeare's colleagues (or sometimes rivals). Ben Jonson, Francis Beaumont and John Fletcher, Thomas Middleton, John Webster, Cyril Tourneur, and John Ford are a few of the noteworthy verse dramatists of the time. Symonds devotes considerable attention to characterizing the blank verse of such playwrights, and is able to single out individualizing stylistic traits for each. Such analyses bear out George T. Wright's comment: "It is characteristic of this meter that strong poets of every period have not merely learned to use it efficiently, refining their knowledge of it into a skill which they come to manipulate almost instinctively, but that they wrestle with it, compel it to perform new work, and tune it to their own distinctive energies."[14]

Shakespeare's continued experimentation was an unusually successful form of this "wrestling." As we have seen, many of his rhythmical tactics discovered more elasticity than rigidity in the pentameter line. To see that this was not the only way for a poet to "tune" the verse we need look no further than Ben Jonson, who typically maintains the metrical pattern with few discrepancies. This cooler, seemingly more classical approach results, in Jonson's best blank verse, in lines that are taut without being stiff. Especially in great comedies like *The Alchemist* or *Volpone,* we feel that the firmness of the verse is a distancing device geared to moral satire. Rather than encouraging emotional involvement with the characters, it frames them for us as they reveal themselves to ethical scrutiny. An over-the-top character like Sir Epicure Mammon, one of the alchemist's dupes, seems all the more extravagant in his self-indulgent fantasies because their lushness contrasts with the containing severity of the verse. Projecting what the alchemist's elixir will bring him, he imagines a kind of Playboy Mansion for himself:

> I will have all my beds blown up, not stuffed:
> Down is too hard. And then mine oval room
> Filled with such pictures as Tiberius took
> From Elephantis, and dull Aretine
> But coldly imitated. Then, my glasses
> Cut in more subtle angles, to disperse
> And multiply the figures as I walk
> Naked between my succubae. My mists
> I'll have of perfume, vapored 'bout the room,
> To loose our selves in; and my baths like pits
> To fall into; from when we will come forth,
> And roll us dry in gossamer and roses.
>
> (*The Alchemist*, 2.2.42–53)

The colossal egotism of the speaker ripples along, supported by rhythms whose smoothness displays without distraction the unchecked self-satisfaction of what is being said.

At the other end of the stylistic spectrum is John Webster, who goes even further than the later Shakespeare in his metrical manipulations. Aiming not at satire but at horrific melodrama in tragedies like *The White Devil* and *The Duchess of Malfi*, Webster wrenches his lines to communicate raw extremes of emotion. Sometimes it is difficult to read them as blank verse at all. His most famous line, from *The Duchess of Malfi*—"Cover her face: mine eyes dazzle: she died young" (4.2.267)—is piercing as poetry, but it is hard, if not impossible, to scan it as iambic pentameter. A longer passage from the same play shows how startling Webster's liberties can be:

> Sure, he was too honest. Pluto, the god of riches,
> When he's sent by Jupiter to any man,
> He goes limping, to signify that wealth
> That comes on God's name comes slowly; but when he's sent
> On the devil's errand, he rides post and comes in by scuttles.
>
> (3.2.242–46)

Symonds, attempting to explain such anomalies, looks to performative possibilities: "Scansion in the verse of Webster is subordinate to the purpose of the speaker; in writing it he no doubt imagined his actors declaiming with great variety of intonation, with frequent and lengthy pauses, and with considerable differences in the rapidity of their utterances."[15] Perhaps. But interpolated pauses could do little to make the straggling last two lines of the speech above sound anything like blank verse. Webster is, of course, not always this extreme. His noticeable aberrations are frequent enough, however, to have made him famous for metrical license. The term "Websterian" is applied by some prosodists to blank verse that intentionally indulges in blatant metrical infractions. Such verse, after languishing as a Jacobean curiosity for over two centuries, supplied intriguing models for T. S. Eliot and other modernists (see chapter 3). In the generally placid pond that is versification, some ripples take a very long time to reach the shore.

Blank verse reigned triumphant on stage until the outbreak of civil war closed the public theaters in 1642. The Cromwellian regime kept them shuttered until the Restoration in 1660. While the meter was reaching its peak as a dramatic medium, its earliest use in epic, Surrey's Virgil translation, was not much remembered and certainly not imitated. The other early, scant attempts at blank verse narrative or satire moldered in obscurity. It was to be one of those Cromwellians, John Milton, who restored blank verse to epic, giving rise to an even wider range of possibilities for this protean meter.

III

Milton's imprint on the history and practice of blank verse is so deep as to mark off an epoch. In the centuries after Milton, any poet seriously engaged with the meter has been obliged to look closely at his accomplishments, and this has intimidated as many as it has inspired. *Paradise Lost* was so successful in making blank verse an institution that it is with some effort that we remind ourselves that Milton's choice of the meter for a long epic poem was regarded by himself and by others as revolutionary. Verse narratives in English had typically been written in rhymed couplets or in various kinds of stanzas. (Think of Chaucer, Edmund Spenser, or, to descend a step, Giles Fletcher.) As long as blank verse was so firmly associated with the stage, it was not, apparently, thought of as available for other purposes. Milton's own first use of the meter was in a dramatic piece, the masque *Comus* (1639). During the Commonwealth period, while the theaters were closed, Milton was largely occupied with political and religious controversy and with diplomatic correspondence in his position as Secretary of Foreign Tongues to the Council of State. With the Restoration in 1660, the theaters were once more open and Milton, having narrowly escaped prosecution for treason, was out of a job. At least he had the time now to write the epic poem he had contemplated for years. His decision to write it in blank verse was, at this time, both innovative and contrarian. Certainly the meter was familiar to readers from its earlier use in the theater. But in the theater, tastes had changed, and blank verse was no longer the preeminent form. It was being challenged both by younger poets like John Dryden who urged the superiority of heroic couplets to unrhymed verse and also, increasingly, by prose. In the theatrical context blank verse was viewed as outmoded; in the context of narrative poetry there was next to no tradition of it. Milton claimed that his use of it in epic poetry was "the first in English," indicating that he was unaware of, or had forgotten, Surrey's *Aeneid.*

When *Paradise Lost* was first published in 1667, the absence of rhyme was widely seen as a striking eccentricity. The second edition in 1674 was prefaced by an explanation (solicited from Milton by his publisher) of "why the Poem Rimes not." In his brusque paragraph headed "The Verse," Milton typically mounts his defense by going on the attack. Situating his unrhymed verse with its classical forebears, he lambastes rhyme as the device of a "barbarous Age" (i.e., the Middle Ages):

> The measure is *English* Heroic Verse without Rime, as that of *Hom*er in *Greek*, and of *Virgil* in *Latin;* Rime being no necessary Adjunct or true Ornament of Poem or good Verse, in longer works especially, but the Invention of a barbarous Age, to set off wretched matter and lame Meter; grac't indeed since by the use of some famous modern Poets, carried away by custom, but much to thir own vexation, hindrance, and constraint to express many things otherwise, and for the most part worse than else they would have exprest them.[16]

He goes on to ally himself with "*Italian* and *Spanish* poets of prime note" as well as "our best *English* tragedies" in perceiving that "true musical delight . . . consists only in apt Numbers, fit quantity of Syllables, and the sense variously drawn out from one Verse into another, not in the jingling sound of like endings, a fault avoided by the learned Ancients both in Poetry and all good Oratory." And he concludes with a sentence that epitomizes several of his salient traits: his self-confidence and elitism, his love of tradition, and (somewhat contradictorily) his ardor for innovation: "This neglect then of Rime is so little to be taken for a defect, though it may seem so perhaps to vulgar Readers, that it rather is to be esteem'd an example set, the first in *English,* of ancient liberty recover'd to Heroic Poem from the troublesome and modern bondage of Riming." Among the writers of blank verse up to this time, no one had ventured to make a case for it with this kind of polemical zeal.

Milton's blank verse in *Paradise Lost* is challenging to describe (and even more, to imitate) because it exhibits so much painstaking control of minute detail while achieving an effect of vastness and profundity—something far different from lapidary refinement.[17] Few artists have accomplished so fruitful a marriage of force with finesse. These characteristics are hinted at in his own description of "the measure" as consisting, on the one hand, in "apt Numbers, fit quantity of Syllables," and, on the other, in "the sense variously drawn out from one verse to the other." Care for the first set of criteria insures structural firmness within the line; attention to the latter gives the verse amplitude, as individual lines follow a branching logic extending in "periods," as rhetoricians would say, or in paragraphs of cumulative density. Each of these factors requires some discussion.

Milton's line, if we come to it after immersion in the relaxed versification of Webster or even the late Shakespeare, is likely to seem metrically austere. Feminine endings are much less frequent than in dramatic verse; in *Paradise Lost,* interestingly, they are more often to be found from book 9 on than in earlier books. That is to say, they show up more often following the Fall of Adam and Eve. It is possible, as some commentators have suggested, that Milton meant this metrical relaxation to serve as a coded reference to the climax of his narrative: just as the original order of the cosmos is disrupted by sin, so is the meter deflected in its march. This might be more persuasive if the endings were totally absent earlier in the poem. In any case, Milton uses the tactic affectingly in Adam's lament:

> O might I here
> In solitude live savage, in some glade
> x / x \ (x)
> Obscur'd, where highest Woods impenetrable
> To Star or Sun-light, spread thir umbrage broad,
> And brown as Evening [. . .]

> (9.1084–88)

"Impenetrable," besides lacking stress on its final syllable, has only a faint stress on the one before that, so that there is an effect of slippage: these, apparently, are woods in which one could lose one's footing (as the meter does, and as Adam and Eve have done in another sense). Even in this brief passage, and even in the stand-out line, we sense a tighter grasp on the prosody than is typical of theatrical blank verse.

Tighter, yes—but not to the point of monotony. Milton allows himself a wide range of metrical substitutions. Especially common is the inversion of the first foot:

> /   x
> Taught by the heav'nly Muse to venture down
>
> (3.19)

But Milton substitutes a trochee for an iamb in other positions when it suits his purpose:

> /   x
> But past who can recall, or done undo?
>
> (9.926)

> /   x
> Of *Eve*, whose Eye darted contagious Fire
>
> (9.1036)

> /   x
> Draw after him the whole Race of mankind
>
> (3.161)

It is harder to find a trochee in the final position, but arguably it is there in

> /   x
> Yet Chains in Hell, not Realms expect: meanwhile
>
> (6.186)

Another reader might hear this final foot as a spondee, and that is a substitution certainly to be found elsewhere:

> /   /
> And wisdom at one entrance quite shut out.
>
> (3.50)

And sometimes, when a spondee is placed earlier in the line, it is led up to by a pyrrhic:

> *Leviathan,* which God of all his works,
>
> ```
>  x / x   /  x   x    /     / x      /
> ```
> Created hugest that swim th' Ocean stream.
>
> (1.201–2)

(Notice the deliberate awkwardness here: accents are swept out of position in much the same way that the enormous bulk of the whale displaces tons of seawater.) Some of the most famous lines in *Paradise Lost* are even more heavily freighted, such as the summary description of Hell:

> Rocks, Caves, Lakes, Fens, Bogs, Dens, and shades of death
>
> (2.621)

The last two feet are perfectly regular, which reestablishes the meter for readers unable to hear the catalogue of monosyllables as iambs. But iambs they are, although a heavier than usual emphasis falls on the "unstressed" syllables, and the commas visually reinforce this. What seems to save these syllables as iambs, oddly, is rhyme. The rhyme-sound of "Fens" and "Dens" sets the second and third feet in a paired balance. The rhyme gives just enough extra force to the accent to keep "Lakes, Fens" and "Bogs, Dens" from being spondees. The over-lapping patterns of assonance (long *a*'s and short *e*'s) help to knit together the monosyllabic items of the list with the more expansive (and conventionally metrical) final phrase. If we experiment by substituting synonyms that lack these sound patterns, we see how much less persuasively iambic the line becomes:

> Crags, Clefts, Pools, Swamps, Mires, Lairs, and shades of death

Here the first six words of the line are much less amenable to being grouped as iambs, and the line is not only heavy but *halting* in a way that Milton's is not. His experiment may test the limits of iambic pentameter, but it manages (just barely) to stay within them.

The most complex aspect of Milton's metrical practice within single lines is his use of various forms of elision. Any page of *Paradise Lost,* except in a drastically (and unwisely) modernized edition, will display its share of apostrophes; some pages are pepper'd with them. Milton, like others of his period, punctuates to mark suppressed vowel sounds, as in past tenses or past participles, as illustrated in the previous sentence. Another common use of the apostrophe is to mark an elision of two words, the first ending and the second beginning with a vowel. The definite article is most often treated this way:

> Who durst defy th' Omnipotent to Arms
>
> (1.49)

We quickly become accustomed to "th' Eternal," "th' Ethereal," and so on. "Th' Horizon" is more surprising, and we may be puzzled to come upon a seeming discrepancy like "the Hemisphere," or "the Heav'n." Milton in such cases elides the article or not, as it suits him. He is similarly variable in the kind of elision within a word ("syncope" is the term many prosodists use for this) that "Heav'n" displays: in some lines the word will appear as "Heaven," presumably because two syllables rather than one were needed. Although such inconsistencies may be puzzling at first sight, scanning the line in question usually provides an explanation. The harder cases concern unstressed or lightly stressed syllables which are not replaced by apostrophes but which, if counted, make their lines too long. As we have seen, Milton has no qualms about the added terminal syllable of a feminine ending, although he is sparing in its use. But what about lines like these?

> Extol him equal to the highest in Heav'n
>
> (2.479)

> Of sorrow unfeign'd, and humiliation meek
>
> (10.1104)

> Of all our good, sham'd, naked, miserable
>
> (9.1139)

All these lines are long. The first has eleven syllables if we read "Heav'n" as monosyllabic. The second has twelve and the third eleven. According to one analysis, we have in each case an unmarked elision to take into account. The meter remains reasonably regular in the first line if we half-swallow the second syllable of "highest." In the second line Milton may wish us to pronounce the second "i" in "humiliation" as a *y*-sound, which gives the word four syllables rather than five; and we may be asked to do a similar melding of the end of "sorrow" and the beginning of "unfeign'd" if we insist on a decasyllabic line. In the last line the word to be crimped would be "miserable"—pronounced, not at all preposterously, as "mis'rable." This is one explanation of such anomalous lines. A rival one is that Milton at such points is allowing himself a kind of metrical substitution—an anapest for an iamb—that some scholars view as an innovation dating to later times in nondramatic verse.

In the early part of the twentieth century, Robert Bridges argued forcefully for the presence in Milton of the kinds of elision described above. His book *Milton's Prosody* makes the case with an exhaustingly punctilious array of examples. George Saintsbury, in his massive *History of English Prosody,* argued just as forcefully for Milton's use of anapests in such instances. Following their dispute through all its forking paths reminds an onlooker of how strangely vehement arguments over prosody tend to be. In this case the quarrel seems especially futile, since it centers around Milton's intentions, which we are unlikely ever to know, and the practices of printers of that era, which were far from uniform. The two theories both "explain" the metrical phenomena reasonably. For a reader, though, it may not matter much whether Milton was unusually adventurous with elision (Bridges) or a pioneer in admitting an occasional anapest into his blank verse (Saintsbury). What we *hear* in such lines is a willingness to play with the possibilities of packing an extra light syllable into a line that in this poet's practice is usually stricter than that of the dramatists.

We have still to consider what Milton meant in referring to "the sense variously drawn out from one Verse to another." More than any other poet, Milton makes us aware of the crucial importance of considering blank verse not in isolated lines (except for specialized purposes, as we have just been doing) but in extended passages. He is a master of enjambment and of the varying placement of pauses within his lines. (The term "caesura" does not seem to apply very well in describing Milton's practice, since he sometimes uses more than a single pause within a line.) These masterly fluctuations in pacing, together with the expressive shifts of stress and patterns of assonance, give his work a richly orchestrated rhythmical character. Add to this his extraordinary control of extended syntax, and we have the major elements of

Milton's blank verse over longer stretches. (Milton's vocabulary, of course, is the *most* immediately noticeable element of his poetic style; but since here we must focus on meter, we must treat diction somewhat narrowly, in relation to particular metrical effects.) We have seen how Shakespeare led the way in moderating the emphatic line breaks to which earlier blank verse was prone, and concurrently in sustaining an extended sentence structure over several lines at a time. Milton takes these tactics of dramatic verse and expands on them for his own epic requirements.

Milton's versecraft in extended passages has been widely studied; here, a few examples must suffice.[18] Some of the most obvious expressive manipulations occur in descriptions of motion. The verse becomes imitative when Satan attempts to make his way across the realm of Chaos to invade the newly created earth.

> At last his Sail-broad Vans
> He spreads for flight, and in the surging smoke
> Uplifted spurns the ground, thence many a League
> As in a cloudy Chair ascending rides
> Audacious, but that seat soon failing, meets
> A vast vacuity: all unawares
> Flutt'ring his pennons vain plumb down he drops
> Ten thousand fadom deep, and to this hour
> Down had been falling, had not by ill chance
> The strong rebuff of some tumultuous cloud
> Instinct with Fire and Nitre hurried him
> As many miles aloft: that fury stay'd,
> Quencht in a Boggy *Syrtis,* neither Sea
> Nor good dry Land, nigh founder'd on he fares,
> Treading the crude consistence, half on foot,
> Half flying: behoves him now both Oar and Sail.

> (2.927–42)

For most of the passage Milton's enjambments emphasize what at first seems Satan's freedom of movement but soon is revealed as vulnerability to elemental forces. His ascent in the opening four lines, with no end-stopping and only two light pauses marked by commas, seems irresistible. But the steady rise is

rudely interrupted as Satan hits an air pocket. At first Milton slows the pace
with closely spaced pauses:

>   rides
> Audacious, | but that seat soon failing, | meets
> A vast vacuity: |

From here on the self-confidence implied by the enjambments turns into
something more like helpless vertigo. After the especially strong pause following "vacuity," the bottom drops out and the verse again accelerates, only this
time the direction is downward:

>   all unawares
>   / x   x / x   /   /   / x /
> Flutt'ring his pennons vain plumb down he drops
> Ten thousand fadom deep

(Notice how the spondee of "plumb down" acts like a lead weight suddenly
added, as the action goes from fluttering to plummeting.) After being buffeted
back up by the tumultuous updraft, Satan manages to find a dubious sort of
footing in a swamplike area. The verse, from the phrase "that fury stay'd" to
the end of the passage, now end-stops every line as well as marking pauses
within each line, and the movement, no longer airborne in either direction,
becomes a hard slog through the "crude consistence" of the mire.

    Milton uses his expressive technique in many ways less obviously mimetic
than this. Sometimes a metrical substitution will herald a change in tone or
atmosphere. When the Creator prepares to bring into being our universe, he
rides his chariot into the midst of the same Chaos that Satan had such trouble
crossing, commanding, "Silence, ye troubl'd waves, and thou Deep, peace"
(7.216). The final spondee with its assonance receives cosmic attention—and
certainly the attention of the reader prepared to witness a new world being
made. In other passages we notice how the pauses, so effectively deployed or
withheld in an action passage like that of Satan's voyage, can be equally effective in dialogue, where they imply qualities of personality or feeling. The final
lines of Eve's speech to her husband just before their expulsion from Paradise
—the last speech assigned to any character in the poem—will illustrate:

In mee is no delay; | with thee to go, |
Is to stay here; | without thee here to stay, |
Is to go hence unwilling; | thou to mee
Art all things under Heav'n, | all places thou, |
Who for my wilful crime art banisht hence. |
This further consolation yet secure
I carry hence; | though all by mee is lost, |
Such favor I unworthy am voutsaf't, |
By mee the Promis'd Seed shall all restore.

(12.615–23)

Eve may no longer have the innocence of an unfallen being, but the short phrases marked off by pauses in her opening lines suggest the directness and simplicity of moral insight. The punctuation is precisely directive, for the pauses marked by semicolons and periods are more emphatic than those marked by commas. The pauses highlight the alternatives ("with thee," "without thee") of her easy choice, and they help to balance the pronouns against each other, so that we are reminded that henceforth Eve and Adam must be each other's only Paradise. But this simple view of things, focusing on their relationship, opens out at the end of the passage to a broader vision. Simultaneously, the verse extends its increments. The midline pauses diminish and, in the last two lines, disappear as Eve reveals that she shares in Adam's prophetic knowledge of the ultimate salvation of their offspring:

though all by mee is lost,
Such favor I unworthy am voutsaf't,
By mee the Promis'd Seed shall all restore.

Although the characters in Milton's poem do not speak with anything like the naturalistic quality of stage characters, his finely calibrated versification gives their words dramatic power. The effect is more ceremonious, more ritualized than that of most theatrical verse but equally capable of connecting language to emotion. In this, as in so many other ways, *Paradise Lost* proved to be a hard act to follow.

IV

Milton's influence on the later development of blank verse was enormous, but its full impact was delayed for a time by shifts in literary fashion. When theaters reopened at the Restoration, blank verse was no longer the dominant form it had been on the stage. One of the odder literary anecdotes of the time tells of Dryden seeking Milton's permission to turn *Paradise Lost* into a rhymed opera—which the older poet graciously granted. For a time heroic couplets were the vogue in theater, and their popularity in other kinds of poetry continued much longer. When, in the eighteenth century, poets increasingly made forays into blank verse, much of the work was stiff or pallid. To later readers, such poems have seemed intimidated by the gigantic shadow cast by *Paradise Lost*. Nevertheless, several of them were lavishly appreciated in their time.

These eighteenth-century works suggest that poets following Milton saw opportunities in the meter that ranged beyond either epic or drama. James Thomson's *The Seasons* (1730) collects four long poems of nature description following the course of a year, capping these with a "Hymn" to the Creator of these varied scenes. With some geographical and philosophical digressions, the work offers images of British rural life and landscape that appealed mightily to several generations. Reprinted fifty times in its own century and still widely read in the next, *The Seasons* seems important today for expanding the use of blank verse beyond narrative to descriptive and meditative purposes. Thomson's style is not one that readers today would find winning. In his monumental *The Influence of Milton on English Poetry*, Raymond Dexter Havens remarks that "if there is a pompous, contorted way of saying things, Thomson is likely to hit upon it. . . . Calling things by their right names and speaking simply, directly, and naturally, as in conversation, seems to have been his abhorrence."[19] A few lines on the end of Autumn show the justice of this criticism:

> When Autumn scatters his departing gleams,
> Warned of approaching Winter, gathered, play
> The swallow-people; and, tossed wide around,
> O'er the calm sky in convolution swift,
> The feathered eddy floats [. . .]

>   ("Autumn," 836–40)

What Thomson and many other eighteenth-century writers borrowed from Milton actually had more to do with obvious traits of diction and syntax than with handling of meter. What is Miltonic here is the Latinate vocabulary and the preference for inverted word order ("in convolution swift"). Scarcely anything, though, of Milton's skill with pauses and enjambment has been absorbed. The sense, such as it is, is not variously drawn out to any great extent. Like other attempts at blank verse in this period, Thomson's lines often sound like couplets lacking rhymes, and this stiffness of movement, together with the ponderous or sometimes simply odd diction ("swallow-people," it turns out, is Thomsonese for "birds"), makes for hard going. Even less ingratiating than this, and equally famous in its time, is Edward Young's gloomy series of religious meditations, *Night Thoughts* (1742).[20] Havens, never one to mince words, comments bluntly, "It is Young's good fortune that he is little read."[21] The long and noble tradition of Christian meditation on mortality is not enhanced by Young's lack of subtlety:

> While Man is growing, Life is in Decrease;
> And Cradles rock us nearer to the Tomb.
> Our birth is nothing but our Death begun;
> As Tapers wast, that Instant they take Fire.
>
> (Night V, 717–20)

Young, also, had written copiously in couplets before turning to blank verse; even more evidently than Thomson, he lacks Milton's ease of movement. The terrific popularity of *Night Thoughts* over several decades seems to be evidence of an unaccountable masochism on the part of the reading public.

Looking back on blank verse in the century after Milton's death, we can find few works of more than antiquarian interest. Two positive points, however, emerge from these musty bibliographical annals. One is that, especially after Thomson's great popular success, the meter was being used ever more often by poets chafing against the tyranny of the couplet. A second is that these efforts, clumsy or tasteless or wrongheaded as they may have been, showed that the meter could be applied to many different modes of poetry. Parody or burlesque, philosophical speculation, religious meditation, descriptive sketches, and didactic treatises—all these took their places alongside epic and drama in the blank-verse repertoire. (The first stirrings of this modal expansion predate

Thomson. In 1701 John Philips published his celebrated parody of Milton, "The Splendid Shilling." Philips went on to write the first major, serious poem in the meter after Milton, *Cyder* (1708), which deals with orchards and cider making in a Miltonic style. It was widely read, and widely praised.) We are not used, nowadays, to reading essays in verse, and poems like Mark Akenside's *The Pleasures of Imagination* or Thomas Warton Jr.'s "The Pleasures of Melancholy" are unlikely to attract us. Yet later poets working in iambic pentameter owe these and others·like them a debt for so busily exploring the startling adaptability of the meter.

Readers who are left yawning by Thomson or actively irritated by Young may find William Cowper a relief. There are numerous Miltonic turns of phrase in *The Task* (1785), and yet in reading it we are more likely to notice anticipations of Wordsworth than reverberations of Milton. Cowper accomplished some new things in this discursive poem in six books, a celebration of rural life. He managed much more smoothly than his immediate precursors to integrate precise description with generalizing discussion. When he writes of the way city fashions creep in to corrupt the simplicity of the country, he does it by means of a sharply observed vignette of a farm girl tricked out in inappropriate attire:

> Her head adorn'd with lappets pinn'd aloft
> And ribands streaming gay, superbly raised
> And magnified beyond all human size,
> Indebted to some smart wig-weaver's hand
> For more than half the tresses it sustains;
> Her elbows ruffled, and her tott'ring form
> Ill propp'd upon French heels; she might be deemed
> (But that the basket dangling on her arm
> Interprets her more truely) of a rank
> Too proud for dairy-work or sale of eggs.

(4.539–49)

Here the extended syntax flows freely, unhaunted by the ghost of the couplet. Notably, too, the vocabulary is scaled down; Cowper avoids the ludicrous effects of earlier poets (even, sometimes, Milton himself) who apply Miltonic diction to mundane subjects. Cowper can be even plainer. His lines on the woodman's dog, out with his master on a winter day, have even more liveliness and conversational ease:

> Shaggy and lean and shrew'd, with pointed ears
> And tail cropped short, half lurcher and half cur
> His dog attends him. Close behind his heel
> Now creeps he slow, and now with many a frisk
> Wide-scampering snatches up the drifted snow
> With iv'ry teeth, or ploughs it with his snout;
> Then shakes his powder'd coat and barks for joy.
>
> (5.45–51)

"Now creeps he slow" ought to sound stilted, and the line would be metrically the same if Cowper had written "Now slow he creeps." Somehow the uncommon word order has the effect of emphasizing the slowness of the dog's gait, which then shifts into the contrasting movement in the lilt of "many a frisk."

Even when his diction is decidedly Miltonic, Cowper sometimes (admittedly not always) is able to give it a surprising freshness. Here is a view of cattle patiently awaiting fodder on the morning after a snowstorm:

> The cattle mourn in corners where the fence
> Screens them, and seem half petrified to sleep
> In unrecumbent sadness.
>
> (5.26–29)

This is Miltonic, certainly, but in an intriguingly domesticated way. The assonances ("mourn," "corners," "Screens," "seem," "sleep") deepen the tone, and the combination of "half petrified" and "unrecumbent," which runs the risk of ponderousness, unexpectedly succeeds in bringing vividness to the scene. It highlights the patient stillness of animals after a hard night, standing upright and waiting to be fed. *The Task* is too quiet and rambling a poem, probably, for modern tastes; but it is far more readable than many others of its time, and it has undoubted importance in having shown how the volume of Milton's verse could be turned down to make it suitable for less-than-epic occasions.[22] This discovery was soon exploited by William Wordsworth and Samuel Taylor Coleridge.

V

The nineteenth century gave us romantic blank verse and Victorian blank verse; each of these includes poetry of the highest order. The story here, even more than at several points before, is of multiplying applications, broadening scope.

The first important romantic writers of blank verse, Coleridge and Wordsworth, continued the relaxation of style we noted in Cowper, seeking a conversational tone that Milton's grand rhetoric could not supply. Coleridge wrote a number of pieces that have come to be called "Conversation Poems," from the subtitle he gave to one of them. In these, Coleridge demonstrates that blank verse allows for naturalistic gestures that mimic the spontaneity of speech. When he begins one poem ("This Lime Tree Bower My Prison") with the words, "Well, they are gone," we feel that poetry has ventured into a new neighborhood. The conversational note is even more pronounced in Wordsworth, who famously asserted that a poet is "a man speaking to men,"[23] and, in a passage that numerous critics (including Coleridge) took issue with, "that there neither is, nor can be, any *essential* difference between the language of prose and metrical composition."[24]

Wordsworth's focus, and that of his opponents in this debate, is on diction, and thus differs from our own. It is interesting, though, how difficult it is to keep diction and meter distinct from one another in discussing his work. Part of what we are calling the conversational effect in Wordsworth relies on an embrace of ordinary vocabulary and an avoidance of the ornate. But in his blank-verse poems a deliberately unshowy approach to the meter may be just as important, though less immediately noticeable. Not to be noticed *as meter*, in fact, seems to be a primary aim of Wordsworth's blank verse. A kind of transparency is sought, and sometimes achieved in the best of his descriptive passages. "The Old Cumberland Beggar" opens with a view of the old man seated at the side of the road, eating "the dole of village dames."

> And ever, scattered from his palsied hand,
> That, still attempting to prevent the waste,
> Was baffled still, the crumbs in little showers
> Fell on the ground; and the small mountain birds,
> Not venturing yet to peck their destined meal,
> Approached within the length of half his staff.

> (16–21)

The pictorial clarity, the precision of such a phrase as "the length of half his staff," are characteristic; and as they go beyond their poetic precursors, they point ahead to even more photographic qualities in later periods. Certainly here the meter, while serviceable, is unobtrusive. It has an even, unemphatic movement. In fact, some of the accents are about as unemphatic as, in an iambic poem, they could manage to be:

```
    x  / x   / x   \   x  / x   /
And ever, scattered from his palsied hand,
    x  / x /   x \ x /   x   /
That, still attempting to prevent the waste
```

Wordsworth's willingness to place prepositions like "from" and "to" in stress positions has bothered metrical precisionists. Of course, he was hardly the first poet to do this. The Shakespeare line discussed in chapter 1—"The caterpillars of the commonwealth"—is one of a multitude of lightly stressed lines to be found in his plays; and here it is worth reiterating that in many iambic pentameter lines the differing levels of accent in spoken English are audible, and that such lines have always been accepted as regular. Granted, a large proportion of them in a poem tends to dilute the rhythmic energy. That Wordsworth should do this in two successive lines, and indeed in the same position (the third foot) in each line, suggests that he was not overwhelmingly concerned with the dangers of midline slackening.[25]

Wordsworth relaxes the meter in a less dubious way in the penultimate line:

```
    x  / x x   / x  /   x  / x    /
Not venturing yet to peck their destined meal
```

By this time the taste for elision encouraged by Milton had waned, and the poets of the nineteenth century (as Saintsbury notes with delighted approval) allowed themselves the liberty of trisyllabic substitution—an anapest for an iamb, as in the second foot of this line. This tactic speeds and lightens a line without weakening it and, along with the customary trochaic substitutions, helps prevent monotony.

Those who dislike Wordsworth's blank verse generally object to what they call its prosiness. Saintsbury (a Shelley devotee) declares that "[p]assage after passage of the *Prelude* is either intentional burlesque or sheer prose."[26] The slackness of rhythm, when the language itself is dull, undoubtedly gives such critics of that poem plenty of ammunition. Lines like

> An idler among academic bowers,
> Such was my new condition, as at large
> Has been set forth [...]

(8.503–5)

are likely to be read only in academic bowers, if at all. One must be careful, though. Some of Wordsworth's nudgings of poetry in the direction of prose are not merely adequate as poetry but fresh and eloquent. One may think of the climactic line from "Michael," in which it is told how the old shepherd, grieving for his lost son, sat by the unfinished sheepfold he began when the boy went off to seek his fortune:

> and 'tis believed by all
> That many and many a day he thither went
> And never lifted up a single stone.

(464–66)

In the perfectly iambic, conversational last line we feel the terrible weight of those unlifted stones.

Wordsworth's handling of the pause is usually inconspicuous, especially if compared with Milton's bravura technique. His syntax, too, is less brilliant than Milton's, since his extended sentences often seem to blur rather than highlight their successive points. He was in the habit of composing his poems while walking for miles through the country. This fact has, predictably, given rise to gibes at his "pedestrian" style. It is true that there is often a steady, processional movement to his lines, so that his verse seems to have not just a characteristic pace but a stride all its own. This evenness of movement can add to the proselike quality, though again the effect is finally determined by the language. Wordsworth and Coleridge both write fine passages of blank verse in a more elevated style when the occasion calls for it. Poems like Wordsworth's "Tintern Abbey" and Coleridge's "Frost at Midnight" glide upward in style as they move from frames of personal narrative to inset meditations. The grander mode, at its most effective, is much less stylistically (and metrically) intricate than Milton's, but it achieves nonetheless an exalted tone. The romantics' objects of faith—Nature and the Imagination—may have taken the place of Christian ones, but the feeling in such passages is no less religious. Blank verse, which served these poets well in focusing closely on material reality, proved capable of expressing the spiritual insights that were romanticism's chief contribution to culture. When Coleridge writes in "The Eolian Harp":

> O! the one Life within us and abroad,
> Which meets all motion and becomes its soul,
> A light in sound, a sound-like power in light,
> Rhythm in all thought, and joyance every where [. . .]
>
> (26–29)

or when Wordsworth in "Tintern Abbey" describes "that serene and blessed mood"—in which

> the breath of this corporeal frame
> And even the motion of our human blood
> Almost suspended, we are laid asleep
> In body, and become a living soul:
> While with an eye made quiet by the power
> Of harmony, and the deep power of joy,
> We see into the life of things
>
> (43–49)

—we see how the verse that was so sturdily employed for rustic narratives needed only a slight formal tightening to be equally appropriate for metaphysical speculation.

Some of the first romantic poets' most important contributions to the development of blank verse were generic rather than stylistic. For most of the eighteenth century the presumption had been that poems in blank verse would be sizable—more often than not book-length. Coleridge and Wordsworth set the fashion for a variety of shorter forms: poems of philosophical or religious musing, descriptive sketches of persons or places, brief narratives (Wordsworth's "Michael" is less than five hundred lines), poems of personal address (verse letters, not a new form in itself but new in the intimacy of the tone and content). Many of the types of short poems we now take for granted were pioneered by these poets, and for many of them blank verse was the chosen medium. In many of these, as in Wordsworth's book-length *The Prelude,* the autobiographical content and the apparently straightforward presentation of the poet's "I" were equally influential. Whatever else many of these short pieces may be, the undisguised, active presence of a poet-narrator in them gives them the feeling of diary entries. The unobtrusive prosody of Wordsworth's blank verse aided in this effect of naturalness; readers who had experienced earlier poetry as a grand performance for which they were the audience suddenly met with poetry which, it seemed, they were just happening to overhear. This brings the discussion of these poets back to where it began, with poetry as conversation.

Poetic style often seems to behave like a pendulum. The second generation of romantics, Byron, Shelley, and Keats, all wrote interesting poems in blank verse; but—perhaps fearing the threat of prosiness—they tended to shape their lines in a more formalized manner. The material they dealt with was correspondingly more rarefied, distant from the rustic scenes the earlier romantic poetry depicted so reverentially. Nature, of course, is a powerful presence for them, but there is less of a balance in their work between the mundane and the visionary than there was for Wordsworth. Paradoxically, although their poems are often more intensely sensuous in imagery, they can seem less of this world than the older poet's calmly observed rural scenes. Both in style and substance they take a step back from the problematic, naked immediacy of Wordsworth's manner. This may produce works of consummate art—but that they are works of art we are reminded anew with each luxuriant line.

The domestic themes and settings of Wordsworth were not for them. Characters and descriptions tend toward the exotic or mythopoeic, even toward the bizarre. Byron used blank verse sparingly, for melodramatic works such as the drama *Manfred* that do not show him at his best. The short apocalyptic piece "Darkness" is impressive, though the handling of the meter has little of the energy he brought to rhyming forms. Shelley used blank verse more extensively—in his historical tragedy *The Cenci,* in his imposing *Prometheus Unbound* (where it is interspersed with numerous rhymed lyrics), and in the early narrative *Alastor, or The Spirit of Solitude.* Mary Shelley, in her note to this piece, writes: "The versification sustains the solemn spirit which breathes throughout; it is peculiarly melodious."[27] Some of Shelley's imagery in this account of a visionary poet's communings with Nature could be described as Wordsworthian; but the verse has a more Miltonic cast in lines like "Dim tracts and vast, robed in the lustrous gloom / Of leaden-coloured even" (556–57). An extended sentence beginning a few lines further on could have taken every one of its images from Wordsworth, and yet it shows how different the ultimate effect of such a scene can be when the verse is differently shaped and paced:

> A pine,
> Rock-rooted, stretched athwart the vacancy
> Its swinging boughs, to each inconstant blast
> Yielding one only response, at each pause
> In most familiar cadence, with the howl
> The thunder and the hiss of homeless streams
> Mingling its solemn song, whilst the broad river,
> Foaming and hurrying o'er its rugged path,
> Fell into that immeasurable void
> Scattering its waters to the passing winds.
>
> (561–70)

Here the expressive use or withholding of the pause gives the lines an animated, even agitated quality appropriate to the description. We notice how the initial trochee and the substituted anapest in the middle of the line gives extra speed to

> /   x   x   /   x x   /   x   /   x   /
> Foaming and hurrying o'er its rugged path.

Other interesting displacements are here as well, in the strange line

> /   x   x   /   x x   /   x   /   /
> Yielding one only response, at each pause[28]

which seems to achieve only the most precarious balance with its odd (wind-driven?) jumble of stresses; or the smoother-sounding

/ x x x   / x \   x   / x   /
Scattering its waters to the passing winds

—a hendecasyllable, in which we may read "Scatt'ring" if we are ardent for ten syllables and fond of elision. This would make the line regular except for the initial trochee. The relatively lighter stress on "to," however, unsettles the line either way, and it seems the meter may be miming the "scattering" process of water pouring over a precipice. Compared with even the most intense passages in Wordsworth, the sound effects are more excessive, and to some readers they may seem feverish.[29]

Keats wrote what many have considered the most beautiful blank verse of the century in his unfinished epic *Hyperion* and the also unfinished reworking of it, *The Fall of Hyperion.* The opening lines of *Hyperion,* a mythological poem whose plot was to center on the fall of the Titans and their supplanting by the Olympian gods, depict Saturn, the deposed Titan monarch, enmeshed in the trauma of his fall. The intelligence of Keats's absorption of Milton (especially of Milton's quieter lyric touches) shows in every line:

> Deep in the shady sadness of a vale
> Far sunken from the healthy breath of morn,
>   /   /
> Far from the fiery noon, and eve's one star,
>   /   /   /   /
> Sat gray-hair'd Saturn, quiet as a stone,
> Still as the silence round about his lair;
> Forest on forest hung about his head
>   /   /
> Like cloud on cloud. No stir of air was there,
> Not so much life as on a summer's day
>   /   /
> Robs not one light seed from the feather'd grass,
>   /   /
> But where the dead leaf fell, there did it rest.
>   /   /
> A stream went voiceless by, still deadened more
> By reason of his fallen divinity
> Spreading a shade: the Naiad 'mid her reeds
>   /   /
> Press'd her cold finger closer to her lips.

(1.1–14)

The spondees, or feet that are arguably spondees, are numerous. Keats's language, which brilliantly conveys a pervading sense of stillness, is reinforced by the additional weight these substitutions give to his lines. In the fourth line the additional emphasis is extraordinary, for in the first two feet we have not only the additional accents but also a kind of pun in the repetition of "Sat" in "Saturn." The implication is that Saturn's immobility and his identity are one and the same. While the spondaic substitutions are the most noticeable feature, they are by no means the only impressive manipulation of sound. Keats emulates Milton's elaborate patterns of pause, alliteration, and assonance throughout, as well as the more usual trochaic substitutions. As in any accomplished blank verse, individual variations yield their full effects not simply in regard to single lines but in the context of those preceding and following. The last sentence of the passage begins:

> A stream went voiceless by, still deadened more
> x / x \ x / x x / x /
> By reason of his fallen divinity
> Spreading a shade

The middle line stands out in contrast to the more usual movement of the phrases surrounding it. It not only *looks* shrunken, compared with the visible length of lines around it: it is metrically disintegrating, because of the relatively light stress on "of" soon followed by

> / x x / x /
> fallen divinity

in which the two words with abutting unstressed syllables collapse into each other. If one chooses to read "fallen" as a virtual monosyllable ("fall'n"), the expressive point is the same. Just as the spondees emphasize Saturn's motionless trance, the unexpected lightening of this line mirrors his new and astounding fragility.

Keats was unable to sustain this style to his own satisfaction for long. *Hyperion* was abandoned, partway into book 3. When he attempted the theme again, under the title *The Fall of Hyperion: A Dream*, the verse was not quite as imbued with Milton. The impressive weight of the passage examined above gives way, in the later version, to something less marmoreal. In place of the omniscient narrator Keats supplies a poet-dreamer who is both actor and narrator of the first part of the poem, the framing of the vision of the Titans' fall. Consequently, the new opening has a more personal tone and a more rapid movement:

> Fanatics have their dreams, wherewith they weave
> A paradise for a sect; the savage, too,
> From forth the loftiest fashion of his sleep
> Guesses at Heaven; pity these have not
> Trac'd upon vellum or wild Indian leaf
> The shadows of melodious utterance.

(1.1–6)

This version also was to be abandoned.[30] Both fragments, with their differing styles of blank verse, supplied potent models for later poets. Except, perhaps, for *The Faerie Queene* (which is of course on a completely different scale), these are the greatest unfinished poems in English.

The early deaths of Byron, Shelley, and Keats left their successors, the Victorian poets of midcentury, an open field. Throughout the rest of the century, blank verse was used more widely than ever and with a generally higher level of technique. Poets found the meter protean in its ability to carry descriptive, meditative, narrative, or dramatic burdens in lengths of all sorts. As with Shakespeare's fellow dramatists, the better romantic and Victorian poets each put a personal stamp on the meter. Anyone studying the blank verse of the period would wish to give some attention to a host of poems we must regretfully pass over: not only numerous ones by poets already discussed in some detail, but works like Walter Savage Landor's "Iphigeneia" and "To My Child Carlino," or Matthew Arnold's "A Dream," or Elizabeth Barrett Browning's *Aurora Leigh,* to name only a few more. D. G. Rossetti's fervid monologue "A Last Confession" is striking but in the end less impressive than his vivid description of early (1849) railway travel, "Antwerp to Ghent."[31] Fanciers of the outré may wish to look up "How the Abbey of Saint Werewulf Juxta Slingsby Came by Brother Fabian's Manuscript," by Sebastian Evans—a piece of comic (or would-be comic) medievalism. But here we have space only to glance at the work of the two most influential Victorian writers of blank verse, Browning and Tennyson.

Both Browning and Tennyson wrote voluminous blank-verse sequences (Browning's *The Ring and the Book* and Tennyson's *The Idylls of the King*), but their creation and refinement of brief dramatic monologues had more far-reaching influence. Perhaps daunted by the challenge left by Keats's epic fragments, they turned to the monologue, in which such narrative as there was would be filtered through the voice of a speaker, and the chief emphasis would be on that speaker's personality as revealed by his utterance. In their best efforts there is great vividness of character, concentrated or distilled by the compactness of the design.

Blank verse allows great leeway for naturalistic turns, as Renaissance dramatists demonstrated. It can closely approach the style of everyday speech, while retaining the ability to elevate itself when a less colloquial tone is fitting. In a play we discover what a character "sounds like" not from a single speech but from all of them, and not simply from speeches but from dialogue. Browning and Tennyson, in writing these shorter poems, gave themselves much less scope for disclosing multiple facets of a character. With a single speaker, a single "situation" (the occasion of the monologue), and not much space, they needed to make a virtue of economy and project the essence of a character without indulging in what could prove to be distracting complications. This is not to say that the characters they created lack all complexity, but there generally is (perhaps has to be) a focus in these poems on one element of personality, or on a few closely overlapping ones. Each speaker has a distinctive, soon recognizable voice that expresses his inner truth, sometimes more than he could imagine. As in its earlier dramatic uses, blank verse offers supreme flexibility to poets attempting to fashion such voices.

Of the two great monologuists, Browning is the more naturalistic. "Fra Lippo Lippi" presents the painter-monk on his ramblings, chatting up the night watch:

> 'Tell you, I liked your looks at very first.
> Let's sit and set things straight now, hip to haunch.
>
> (43–44)

In "Mr. Sludge, 'The Medium,'" the fraudulent spiritualist is alternately belligerent and craven upon having been found out:

You'll tell?

        Go tell, then! Who the devil cares

What such a rowdy chooses to . . .

                Aie—aie—aie!

Please, sir! your thumbs are through my windpipe, sir!

Ch—ch!

                                (14–18)

In "The Bishop Orders His Tomb at Saint Praxed's Church," the corrupt, dying prelate snarls out worldly vanity (and malevolence toward his predecessor):

And so, about this tomb of mine. I fought

With tooth and nail to save my niche, ye know:

—Old Gandolf cozened me, despite my care;

Shrewd was that snatch from out the corner South

He graced his carrion with, God curse the same!

                                (15–19)

All of these are rogues, running a gamut from more to less likable; each is speaking in iambic pentameter, and each sounds very much like himself. Browning's expressive energy begs for staging by some great character actor who would simper, wheedle, or growl as each passage seems to invite. In the third extract, the line

     /   x   /   /   x   / x   / x   /

    Shrewd was that snatch from out the corner South

seems, with its combination of harsh consonants and reversed or augmented accents (trochee followed by spondee), an auditory distillation of envy and rapacity. The Bishop cannot help admiring opportunistic greed so like his own. Such poetry makes dramatic immediacy its primary goal—and often enough achieves it.

Tennyson's practice is cooler. While he, also, aims to define his characters and their situation through individualized voices, his style tends to be loftier. If Browning's Renaissance painters and assorted scoundrels sometimes have the broad grotesquerie of cartoons, Tennyson's sometimes seem to have stepped out of a Greek frieze. This less lapel-grabbing manner aims to be classical in its reserve (although sometimes it seems equally to have its source in Victorian notions of propriety). In any case, it is a stance that complements Tennyson's consciously melodious verse. Eschewing Browning's more blatant reaches for verisimilitude (sentence fragments, slang, sputterings), he makes his voices memorable through lyric sonorities that underpin each speaker's emotions and perceptions in an intuitive but persuasive way.

In "Tithonus," the eponymous speaker, granted immortality but not eternal youth, laments his condition to his lover, the dawn goddess Aurora, in a tone of lyric despair that is sustained throughout the poem. The famous opening lines show how ably and economically Tennyson can establish a mood by means of sound:

> The woods decay, the woods decay and fall,
> The vapours weep their burthen to the ground,
> Man comes and tills the field and lies beneath,
> And after many a summer dies the swan.
> Me only cruel immortality
> Consumes: I wither slowly in thine arms,
> Here at the quiet limit of the world,
> A white-haired shadow roaming like a dream
> The ever-silent spaces of the East,
> Far-folded mists, and gleaming halls of morn.

> (1–10)

The opening four lines are basically regular and end-stopped, except for the extra lilt of line 4 (provided by one of those anapests that so enraptured Saintsbury). This graceful steadiness makes the contrasting movement of the next phrases all the more poignant:

> / / x /x / x / x /
> Me only cruel immortality

> x / / / x / x \ x /
> Consumes: | I wither slowly in thine arms

Both the enjambment and the caesura after the colon throw considerable emphasis onto "Consumes," while the spondees on the pronouns stress the

mismatch of divine and human that has led to this process of endless disin-
tegration. The reader will also have noticed the many assonances that enrich
the overall sound of the passage. Tennyson uses this kind of emotional sound-
painting as well in his other well-known poem of this sort, "Ulysses." The hero
exhorts his veteran crew to join him for a last, fatal voyage:

> The lights begin to twinkle from the rocks: |
>   x /   /   /   x /   /   /   x   /
> The long day wanes: | the slow moon climbs: | the deep
> Moans round with many voices. Come, my friends,
> 'Tis not too late to seek a newer world.
>
>   (54–57)

If we think of the way Keats used spondees in *Hyperion,* we might expect them
to make a line slower. They often do so. Here, though, the context of Ulysses'
eagerness to cast off and the calculated pause after each colon suggests something other than languor. In fact, with the line chopped and punctuated as it
is, we hear impetuosity, restlessness, the speaker's straining against the passage
of time. It is as if those weighty phrases (absolutely symmetrical in meter) are
obstacles needing to be shunted aside so that Ulysses can respond to the siren
song of the deep.

Tennyson is not always so orchestral. In other monologues and, even
more, in narrative poems, he employs blank verse in a much more matter-of-
fact style. "Dora," for instance, was meant to imitate Wordsworth, and it is plain-
spoken indeed, ending with lines as unconcerned as many of Wordsworth's with
their lack of melody:

> So these four abode
> Within one house together; and as years
> Went forward, Mary took another mate;
> But Dora lived unmarried till her death.
>
>   (164–67)

But Tennyson's distinctive legacy as a verse technician is the more musical
blank verse. Indeed, some of his best-known passages in the form are deliberate experiments that bend it in a lyric direction: "Tears, Idle Tears" is often

spoken of (and reasonably) as a song. Such passages can of course be gorgeous, but compared with Milton and Keats in this regard, their opulent music may seem more florid, less suggestive. Of course, not many poets would fare much better in such a comparison.

The nineteenth century saw the emergence of an American poetry that won readers in England as well as at home. Blank verse, from this period on, can be seen as a transatlantic phenomenon. Many of the themes of English romanticism found echoes in American poetry; in particular, a Wordsworthian veneration of nature had its counterpart in descriptive pieces, and for these, blank verse proved to be a dependable vehicle. The American blank verse was, in its relative lack of ornament and its pared-down rhetoric, close also in style to Wordsworth. Coming to it after poets like Shelley, Keats, and Tennyson, one is especially struck by the lack of ostentation in its management of sound. William Cullen Bryant's "Thanatopsis" has often been described as the first great American poem. It is a graceful piece, written with taste and skill, but a reader who values patterns of assonance would find in it little Keatsian resonance. It must be one of the most placid meditations on mortality ever written: Bryant cheerfully offers as a comforting reflection the idea that the earth is a gigantic tomb. It may be that a more flamboyant approach to sound would sort ill with the composure in Bryant's calmly flowing lines.

> To him who in the love of Nature holds
> Communion with her visible forms, she speaks
> A various language; for his gayer hours
> She has a voice of gladness, and a smile
> And eloquence of beauty, and she glides
> Into his darker musings, with a mild
> And healing sympathy, that steals away
> Their sharpness, ere he is aware.
>
> (1–8)

As we see here, metrical variations are scarce and discreet. The trisyllabic feet in lines 2 and 3 seem to add smoothness to an already smooth progress. Bryant has other blank-verse poems—"Inscription for the Entrance to a Wood" and "A Winter Piece," for example—that offer the same modest enjoyment. Some of Wordsworth's strength has gone out of the style; its attractive mildness verges on gentility. The straightforward diction, though, was a quality nurtured on this side of the Atlantic even as English poetry after Wordsworth grew more ornate.

John Greenleaf Whittier is another poet of the time who offers some fine examples of this plain, unassuming vocabulary in blank verse. His "Abraham Davenport," a pithy moral anecdote, is genuinely bracing in its mixture of good sense and spiritual hardihood.

Of course, numerous pieces in conventional modes by lesser-known poets swell the century's roster. The reclusive Frederick Goddard Tuckerman, best known for some of his sonnets and his ode "The Cricket," wrote narratives in which the presences of Wordsworth and Tennyson can be discerned, sometimes transposed a bit awkwardly to settings in western Massachusetts. The pensive "The Stranger" and the melodramatic "Mark Atherton" are examples. An avid amateur botanist, Tuckerman is overly generous in sharing his researches with the reader. At the century's end, Trumbull Stickney, who died young of a brain tumor in 1904, wrote dramatic pieces with exotic settings whose mannered diction strains too hard to evoke the charms of antiquity. "Oneiropolus" succeeds better than the rest: the meter is expertly handled, but the style is discouragingly fusty, setting this work apart from the growing trend toward plainness in American blank verse over the course of the century. Stickney's gifts are more evident in some of his lyrics.

The blank verse of those two occasional poets, Thoreau and Emerson, is more interestingly jagged. Thoreau did not write many pieces in the meter, and some of his noticeable departures may be unintentional lapses. The opening of "Winter Memories" presents one such puzzle:

> Within the circuit of this plodding life
> There enter moments of an azure hue,
> Untarnished fair as is the violet
> x x / x /   /   x   /   /   x
> Or anemone, when the spring strews them
> By some meandering rivulet [...]

(1–5)

The iambic pattern is almost too regular in the first three lines, and it becomes so again in line 5. Did Thoreau deliberately seek the lurch the meter takes in line 4? The lack of other such effects in the rest of the poem makes this unlikely. His better-known "Smoke" has variations that seem more obviously aimed at:

>   /   /   /   x / x / /
> Light-winged Smoke, Icarian bird,
> Melting thy pinions in thy upward flight,
> Lark without song, and messenger of dawn,
> Circling above the hamlets as thy nest;
> Or else, departing dream, and shadowy form
> Of midnight vision, gathering up thy skirts;
> x /   /   / x   \   x /
> By night star-veiling, and by day
> / x x   x   /   x   / x   /   x /
> Darkening the light and blotting out the sun;
> Go thou my incense upward from this hearth,
> And ask the gods to pardon this clear flame.

Thoreau seems to be experimenting with compensating for absent syllables with additional accents. The first line is short—eight syllables, or nine if we are meant to pronounce "winged" as two. The number of speech stresses is six, as if to make up, or more than make up, for the detriment. The more regular second line is needed to give us a clearer sense of what meter we are reading. The later short line, also eight syllables, bunches stresses at the beginning, breaks a foot with a comma, and sidles back into the iambic pattern by way of a forced stress on "and." The line immediately following this is long by one syllable and regular except for substituting a dactyl (oddly) for the first iamb. Some readers will find these touches awkward. Such weighty lines may be incongruous with their lighter-than-air subject. The most favorable way to construe them is as sequences of rhythm overriding the structure of this or that single line—as Thoreau's attempt to achieve an elasticity in the meter that many another poet has pursued. A more graceful use of enjambment might have served the purpose less problematically.

Emerson's metrical liberties are sometimes traceable to literary models. In "Hamatreya," he recasts Milton's experiments in homely New England terms. Where Milton fills a line with resounding proper nouns—"Damasco, or Morocco, or Trebisond" (*Paradise Lost*, 1.584)—Emerson offers "Bulkeley,

Hunt, Willard, Hosmer, Meriam, Flint" (1). For Milton's famous one-line survey of the landscape of Hell, he substitutes "Hay, corn, roots, hemp, flax, apples, wool and wood" (3). As with Bryant and Thoreau, there does not seem to be much striving after symphonic (or even merely euphonic) effects. Yet a number of his blank-verse pieces retain their interest: "The Snow-Storm" and "Days" are the best known, although "Seashore," which depicts the ocean speaking to the poet, has fine moments:

> I with my hammer pounding evermore
> The rocky coast, smite Andes into dust,
> Strewing my bed, and, in another age
> Rebuild a continent of better men.

(34–37)

This is eloquent but not self-consciously musical, and this sober style set the tone for the earliest notable writers of blank verse in the next century, Edwin Arlington Robinson and Robert Frost. (It is fascinating to speculate on the blank verse that Poe might have written, for he was far more preoccupied with sound than his great contemporaries were. But Poe was an indefatigable rhymer. Emerson referred to him cattily as "the jingle man.") On the spectrum ranging between speech at one end and music at the other, American blank verse was decidedly oriented toward speech—and, it might be added, toward speech that was sparing of histrionic flights. The tone, both in the emotional and the acoustical sense, was restricted. But the twentieth century was to widen the range of tonal coloring in such poetry well beyond that of the sturdy utterances of Emerson and his peers.

BLANK VERSE AND MODERNISM

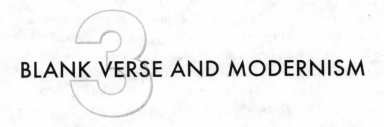

I

AT THE END of the nineteenth century it would not have occurred to many writers in England or in America that blank verse was a form in need of justification or defense. This was to change within a few decades. When Robert Frost, in 1935, contributed a preface to Edwin Arlington Robinson's posthumous book-length poem *King Jasper,* he began by noting with approval the older poet's resistance to modernist stylistic trends: "Robinson stayed content with the old-fashioned way to be new."[1] By this time the battle lines were firmly drawn: on one side were experimental modernists who believed that versification itself must undergo revolutionary changes to achieve poetry of lasting value in the twentieth century, and on the other were traditionalists like Frost and Robinson who dissented from this premise. For Robinson, Frost, and some three generations of twentieth-century poets who agreed with them, blank verse was still an appealing form, however retrograde a taste for it appeared to the avant-garde. Robinson's taste for it, as a browse through his *Collected Poems* will show, was more than ample: "gargantuan" might be the better word. Although in the latter phase of his career blank verse was no longer the almost automatic choice for long poems that it had become by 1900, Robinson stubbornly clung to it. Much of the bulk of his *Collected Poems*— a volume of close to 1,500 pages—consists of numerous, mostly narrative, poems in blank verse.

Robinson's blank-verse poems are of many sorts, some of which have evident nineteenth-century models. He wrote Browningesque monologues for speakers drawn from history: "Ben Jonson Entertains a Man from Stratford," "Rembrandt to Rembrandt," "Toussaint l'Ouverture," and others. Treading uncomfortably in the footsteps of Tennyson, he wrote a trilogy of lengthy Arthurian romances: *Merlin, Lancelot,* and *Tristram* (which surprisingly became a best seller). Other pieces derive from biblical sources: "Lazarus," "Sisera," "Nicodemus," and "The Three Taverns," which last concerns St. Paul. He also wrote a good many narratives, variously realistic, allegorical, or fantastic, for which he invented his own plots and characters. Some of these are brief, discrete episodes or vignettes, while others are longer and more complex in structure: the former have the character of short stories, the latter of short novels.

Time has not been tolerant of much of this work. The book-length poems in particular have not aged well. Robinson's position in American poetry is secure, depending not only upon old chestnuts like "Richard Cory" but upon equally adept rhyming poems that are subtler: "Eros Turannos," "Hillcrest," "For a Dead Lady," and many excellent sonnets. These achievements have prompted many a reader to approach his longer works with an open mind, only to fall back in eventual disillusionment. There are several reasons for this. The most basic one is that nearly all these poems are too long for what they are saying. Yvor Winters, who admired Robinson more than he did most other modern poets, was correct in commenting that "Robinson too often seems to work on the principle that five mediocre lines are as effective as one good one."[2] Even if one has the patience to put up with what Winters elsewhere calls "the great Robinsonian vice of uncontrolled loquacity,"[3] there are further obstacles to enjoyment. "The old-fashioned way to be new" usually proves to be an old-fashioned way to be old-fashioned in the case of Robinson's realistic verse novels, which make use of the paper-thin characters, contrived plots, and melodramatic denouements of the popular fiction of his period. The disabling feature of works like *Roman Bartholow* or *The Glory of the Nightingales* is their failure to create and sustain narrative interest. It is almost beside the point to note that the verse in them is undistinguished, because they would not be effective fictions if written in prose.

David Perkins casts Robinson as a leading example in discussing the plight of narrative poetry in the modern era. Already by Robinson's time, he observes, there was no audience for an attempt to write novels in verse. The reader of fiction is put off because it is poetry; the reader of poetry, because it lacks the intensity he seeks. And because these pressures of appreciation are felt most of all by poets themselves as they write, their intentions are divided and they fail to accomplish either. It is extremely doubtful that, had Robinson been writing prose, he would have allowed himself the fatal excess of reflection that clogs his plots or the too-easy melodrama of the plots themselves.[4]

This is a persuasive argument, though it should be noted that, *theoretically,* another poet might have succeeded where Robinson failed, since talent in the right hands is ultimately stronger than any *Zeitgeist.* It should be acknowledged, also, that some of these longer poems have their moments. There are passages of rarefied beauty in the Arthurian trilogy—particularly in *Lancelot*—though the overall effect is probably too sedate for current tastes. *Avon's Harvest,* perhaps because it follows the well-defined patterns of a ghost or horror story, succeeds better than the more realistic poems; while it has little intellectual depth, it effectively conveys eeriness. Most of Robinson's longer narratives, though, seem to have run afoul of the hazards David Perkins has described. They are museum pieces.

It is a relief to turn to some works for which no apologies need be made. Robinson did write some fine pieces in blank verse, all of them shorter than the ill-starred narratives so far discussed, that are better both conceptually and line by line. Just as the form is more concentrated, the verse is tauter. Frequently the longer poems deserve Winters's criticism of "a defect of Robinson's blank verse which becomes noticeable whenever the subject is not adequate to support great poetry: a mechanically repetitious beat, marked by heavily endstopped lines."[5] But one would not say this of the fine monologues for Rembrandt and Ben Jonson, or of narratives—atypically and effectively brief—such as "Isaac and Archibald" and the lesser-known "Aunt Imogen" and "Tasker Norcross." Robinson's blank verse in these is hardly innovative, but it is fluent and well-turned. Except for characterizing touches in some of the monologues, he mostly avoids mannered phrasing. When he uses more complex diction the effect is to concentrate attention on a difficult thought. For instance, in "Rembrandt to Rembrandt" the painter, his reputation in decline, muses on his wife's good fortune in having died before his reverses; otherwise, he speculates,

> She might, like many another born for joy
> And for sufficient fulness of the hour,

Go famishing by now, and in the eyes
Of pitying friends and dwindling satellites
Be told of no uncertain dereliction
Touching the cold offence of my decline.

(112–17)

Certainly this is not a sentence to be rapidly skimmed, but the syntax is not especially knotty and the meaning is plain enough. Unhurried, meditative, the poem moodily probes questions of artistic self-doubt and unappreciated genius as the painter pursues a colloquy with his self-portrait. The greater part of the poem is plainer than the passage just quoted, and all the grander for it, as in the closing lines in which Rembrandt, assured of posthumous fame, exhorts himself to

    accommodate your greatness
To the convenience of an easy ditch,
And anchored there with all your widowed gold,
Forget your darkness in the dark, and hear
No longer the cold wash of Holland scorn.

(324–28)

Plainer even than this is the lucid, open style of reminiscence in the New England idyll "Isaac and Archibald." The narrator recalls his boyhood friendship with two old farmers, and in particular going with one to visit the other on a scorching summer day:

We walked together down the River Road
With all the warmth and wonder of the land
Around us, and the wayside flash of leaves,—
And Isaac said the day was glorious;
x / x \ x / x x / /
But somewhere at the end of the first mile
I found that I was figuring to find
How long those ancient legs of his would keep
The pace that he had set for them.

(22–29)

Here the style is nicely gauged to glide from the lyricism of the landscape description to the humor of the wearying boy's dismay at his elderly companion's vigor. Nothing momentous happens in this narrative, and yet in some ten pages Robinson captures the now-vanished rural life of New England indelibly, as well as conveying memorable insights regarding childhood, old age, and friendship. There is no obvious metrical "fingerprint" here or elsewhere in his work. The little disruption of the two last feet of the one line scanned here may hint both at the boy's flagging pace and at the length of the long, hot march.[6] But usually the verse is unobtrusive, favoring an even, rhythmic stride. This piece will remind the reader of Wordsworth and, in subject matter if not in rhythm, of Robinson's younger contemporary, Frost.

As this discussion may already have suggested, Robinson's contribution to the development of blank verse was one not of technique but of topical diversity. Leaving aside the quixotic book-length poems (which is exactly what readers do), one finds a number of memorable shorter pieces of many kinds. Only a few of these are well known: "Isaac and Archibald," "Ben Jonson Entertains a Man from Stratford," and perhaps "Rembrandt to Rembrandt." Others deserve at least as much notice. "Aunt Imogen," "Tasker Norcross," and "Lazarus," a second set of three, are compelling and are quite different thematically and tonally from each other. As a narrative and dramatic poet Robinson has more variety than Frost, although in some cases his material seems less firmly under control. He is in his blank-verse poems as he is in general, a poet periodically meriting rediscovery.

The second great modern poet of New England, Robert Frost, scarcely needs to be rediscovered, although critical views of his work over the years have undergone several phases of refocusing.[7] Frost first became famous for the blank-verse poems that make up nearly all of his second collection, *North of Boston.* By the end of his long life, however, his rhymed lyrics had taken precedence over all but a few of them in both the critical and popular mind. Why did this happen? The habits of most anthologists may in part explain it, for their bias is most often toward shorter poems and, of course, Frost's work offered many attractive examples from which to choose. There was also, in regard to the blank-verse poems, a shifting consensus as to which ones most repaid attention. Many of the early popular favorites, such as "Mending Wall" and "Birches," were to be shunted aside after a few decades by Randall Jarrell and other critics who stressed the more harrowing elements of Frost's imagination as these are dramatized in pieces like "Home Burial" and "A Servant to Servants." A curiously binary view of the poet came to be implied, as if his practice veered, emotionally and thematically, between extremes—one dark and acidic, the other sunny and maple-sugary. This was inaccurate and unhelpful, since the shadings of human experience in Frost's narrative and dramatic poems cover a broad spectrum, and within many poems a number of tonal shifts may be observed. The tragedy of "Home Burial," it is true, is undiluted, but it is far more typical of Frost (and this is an index of his modern temper) to mix tragedy with comedy, as in "The Witch of Coös" or "The Housekeeper." That the humor in these cases is gruesome or bitter simply adds to the dramatic complexity. All this may seem a digression from prosody, but in fact it is intrinsic to the issue: Frost's theory and practice of versification grew out of his efforts to make his verse expressive of a wider range of tones and feelings than he found treated by his predecessors.

Before Frost formed any theories of his own, he learned about versification as most poets do, through dutiful apprentice work. In his earliest blank verse that survives, the style is a generic late-nineteenth-century one. Written in 1891 when he was in high school, "A Dream of Julius Caesar" recounts a vision of the heroic specter:

> His toga streaming to the western wind,
> The restless fire still gleaming in those eyes,
> Just as before the Roman Senate, years
> Agone, he stood and ruled a people with
> His mighty will, Caesar, first conqueror of
> The Roman World.
>
> (40–45)

Recalling this poem many years later, Frost said that it, and his subsequent youthful poems in blank verse, were attempts to write in "a form suggested by the eclogues of Virgil . . . luckily (I consider it) in no vain attempt to Anglicize Virgil's versification, dactylic hexameter."[8] As one can see from the boy's enjambments, he had yet some technical points to master. But he was a diligent student. The blank-verse poems written later the same year are smoother; he thought enough of the much briefer "Caesar's Lost Transport Ships" to be tinkering with it as late as 1897. Its closing lines have genuine authority, and the meter is now firmly under control:

Each one alone went leaping down the world
With no sail set, deserted on the deck,
And in the hull a tremor of low speech.
And overhead the petrel wafted wide.

(9–12)

It is clear that Frost, had he continued in this vein, could well have produced a mass of blank verse similar to Robinson's—that is, observing the established norms of iambic pentameter without conspicuous prosodic experimentation. By the time he became known to the public, though, it was precisely his challenging of the norms that distinguished his work in the form.

Frost in his later years took up the traditionalists' banner with such vigor in opposing free verse that it is always a little startling to recall the revolutionary aspects of his style and the theories it embodied. In writing and rewriting the New England eclogues of *North of Boston,* he crystallized his thinking about what he called "sentence-sounds," or "sentence tones," or "the sound of sense." In his correspondence from the *North of Boston* period, he contrasts himself to Swinburne and Tennyson, and more broadly to "the assumption that the music of words was a matter of harmonised vowels and consonants. . . . I alone of English writers have consciously set myself to make music out of what I may call the sound of sense."[9] Examples he offers elsewhere make it clear that what is conveyed by the sound of sense is the full gamut of expressible feeling, much of which earlier poetry has slighted: "You can get enough of those sentence tones that suggest grandeur and sweetness everywhere in poetry. What bothers people in my blank verse is that I have tried to see what I could do with boasting tones and quizzical tones and shrugging tones (for there are such) and forty eleven other tones. All I care a cent for is to catch sentence tones that haven't been brought to book."[10]

The importance Frost places upon this sort of expressiveness governs his approach to meter. He is among poets one of the most conscious of the difference between rhythm and meter and the relation of the two that results in poetry. Frost worked out for himself, in an unusually intense way, a sense of how rhythm and meter play off against each other. If one wished to draw illustrations from a single poet, Frost would be an obvious source. He nearly always brings his discussions of the sound of sense around to its ramifications for versification. Two more passages from his letters flesh out the argument:

An ear and an appetite for these sounds of sense is the first qualification of a writer, be it of prose or verse. But if one is to be a poet he must learn to get cadences by skillfully breaking the sounds of sense with all their irregularity of accent across the regular beat of the metre. Verse in which there is nothing but the beat of the metre furnished by the accents of the polysyllabic words we call doggerel. Verse is not that. Neither is it the sound of sense alone. It is a resultant from those two. There are only two or three metres that are worth anything. We depend for variety on the infinite play of accents in the sound of sense. The high possibility of emotional expression all lies in this mingling of sense-sound and word-accent.[11]

My versification seems to bother people more than I should have expected—I suppose because I have been so long accustomed to thinking of it in my own private way. It is as simple as this: there are the very regular preestablished accent and measure of blank verse; and there are the very irregular accent and measure of speaking intonation. I am never more pleased than when I can get these into strained relation. I like to drag and break the intonation across the metre as waves first comb and then break stumbling on the shingle. That's all, but it's no mere figure of speech, though one can make figures enough about it.[12]

It is curious that Frost, having expounded these ideas so elaborately in his letters, did not offer as detailed a treatment of them in formal prose. He seems to have resisted making a definitive statement of them. Yet it is clear that he is following the same line in "The Figure a Poem Makes," the preface to his *Complete Poems* (1949):

All that can be done with words is soon told. So also with meters—particularly in our language where there are virtually but two, strict iambic and loose iambic. The ancients with many were still poor if they depended on meters for all tune. It is painful to watch our sprung-rhythmists straining at the point of omitting one short from a foot for relief from monotony. The possibilities for tune from the dramatic tones of meaning struck across the rigidity of limited meter are endless.[13]

So much for the theory. How well does Frost's mature blank verse bear it out? Most readers will agree that Frost practices what he preaches. The distinction he makes between strict iambic and loose iambic meter in the passage just quoted is useful to keep in mind in regard to his blank verse. Frost certainly wrote rhyming poems that are strict (or strict enough) in their use of iambics, but it is hard to find anything consistently strict in his blank verse: the meter is loose simply in its varying counts of syllables from line to line even apart from the expressive emphases imposed by speech rhythms on the metrical frame. Frost is capable of writing regular lines when he chooses, as in the opening of "Birches":

> When I see birches bend to left and right
> Across the lines of straighter darker trees,
> I like to think some boy's been swinging them.

> (1–3)

Or the end of "An Old Man's Winter Night":

> One aged man—one man—can't keep a house,
> A farm, a countryside, or if he can,
> It's thus he does it of a winter night.

> (26–28)

But lines as regular as these are outnumbered in their respective poems by ones that are less so; and it is rare to find passages much longer than these that do not feature some pronounced variations.

Frost's usual procedure is to embed his regular lines among ones that are noticeably jagged. "The Wood-Pile" begins:

> x / x x x / x / x / /
> Out walking in the frozen swamp one gray day,

> x / x / / x x / x /
> I paused and said, 'I will turn back from here.

> / / x / x / x x / x /
> No, I will go on farther—and we shall see.'

> x / x / x / x / x /
> The hard snow held me, save where now and then

> x / x / x / x / x /
> One foot went through. The view was all in lines

> / x x / x / / /
> Straight up and down of tall slim trees

```
    x   /  x /  x   /  x   /  x   /  (x)
Too much alike to mark or name a place by

   /  x  x   /  x   /  x  /  x   /
So as to say for certain I was here

    x   /    x   /  /  x   x   /  x  ·  /
Or somewhere else: I was just far from home.
```

(1–9)

The first line is long (eleven syllables) and sounds even longer than it is because it is so heavily stressed. This scansion, allowing one pyrrhic and one
spondaic substitution, is tentative. A plausible case could be made for an accent on "Out" (thus balancing the spondee at the end with one at the beginning of the line); and there could doubtless be a partial one on "in," since it is
in the stress position and is relatively stronger than the syllable preceding it.
Such a scansion, though, would make this an even more overweight line by
iambic standards:

```
    /    /  x  \  x  /  x    /     x    /   /
Out walking in the frozen swamp one gray day
```

Spondee resisters could make the line reasonably regular by reading the first
foot as iambic and by reading "gray day" as a feminine ending (but an unusually heavy one):

```
   x   /  x  \  x  /  x    /     x    /  (x)
Out walking in the frozen swamp one gray day
```

Even readers who know the poem well may find themselves hesitating among
these possibilities, and this is often the case with Frost's expressive variations.
Often it is clear that a line is irregular, but deciding *how* it varies from the norm
can be a challenge. Frost's own trust in the sound of sense makes his poetry
effective *as sound,* but at times conjectural to scan. In this case the difficulty
for a reader is increased because, this being the first line of the poem, no metrical norm has been established. We find regular iambic pentameter in lines
4 and 5 (two in a row!) and of course standard variations such as trochaic substitutions. (For instance, lines 2 and 9 feature an identical twist: a third-foot
trochee following a pause.) But line 1 is not the only one to feature less conventional metrical variations. Line 6 ("Straight up and down of tall slim trees")

is only eight syllables long. The last two feet have lost their unstressed syllables. Here we might remember with some amusement Frost's comment, "It is painful to watch our sprung-rhythmists straining at the point of omitting one short from a foot for relief from monotony."[14] Under the aegis of the sound of sense, the poet here omits not one "short" but two. None of this compromises the excellence of "The Wood-Pile," but it does make the poem, like many more of Frost's, a problematic model of blank verse.

Another New England poet, Robert Francis, who as a young man was strongly influenced by Frost, developed doubts over the years about his mentor's blank verse. In a memoir of Frost he discusses his preference for the older poet's rhymed lyrics over his blank-verse poems. Frost, he asserts,

> knew as well as anyone the need for constantly shifting the stresses in an iambic line for grace and expressiveness and flexibility; but in making these shifts to accommodate speech rhythms he not infrequently lost the iambic beat altogether, so that the line falls into a rocking rhythm with only four feet, and can be made to fit the iambic pattern only by forced reading. . . . Whoever reads by ear as well as by eye—and how else should poetry be read? —will be disturbed by this "crumbling" effect in many of the longer poems, and will encounter many of the too regular plodding lines. Frost's fondness for monosyllables aggravates his problem, for it is polysyllables that most clearly establish and sustain a meter.[15]

Francis illustrates his comments by scanning the opening the lines of "A Servant to Servants," but the same somewhat fitful forays into irregularity and back out from it are what we have been analyzing in "The Wood-Pile." The point about monosyllables is a shrewd one: Frost's restrictive idea of a conversational idiom undoubtedly had consequences for versification. Francis's analysis is a thoughtful statement of the case that can be made against the master's liberties.

Is there a case to be made for them? There is, if we are receptive to Frost's esthetic premises. The alternation, to which Francis objects, between "'crumbling'" lines and "plodding" ones may fulfill one of Frost's aims by highlighting a deliberate roughness in his art. This is the side of Frost that rebels against the smooth musicality of Swinburne and Tennyson. Late in his life, Frost came up with a homely metaphor for the relation of rhythm and meter: a donkey pulling a cart. "For some of the time the cart is on the tugs and some of the time on the hold-backs. . . . [T]he one's holding the thing back and the other's pushing it forward."[16] The interesting thing about this metaphor is the apparent equality of its two terms: neither rhythm (the donkey) nor meter (the cart) is mightier, and Frost imagines their maintaining a condition of constant tension, alternating dominance.

Frost's blank verse relies on these startling recurrent contrasts in movement in order to be what he wished his writing to be: dramatic. The sound of sense is a dramatic concept, and if one believes with Frost that "[e]verything written is as good as it is dramatic,"[17] one will go to great lengths to hitch up some of those unruly rhythmic donkeys. As Frost puts it, "A dramatic necessity goes deep into the nature of the sentence. Sentences are not different enough to hold the attention unless they are dramatic. No ingenuity of varying structure will do. All that can save them is the speaking tone of voice somehow entangled in the words and fastened to the page for the ear of the imagination. That is all that can save poetry from sing-song, all that can save prose from itself."[18] The implied defense for rhythmic overridings of meter is that they project in a lifelike way "the speaking tone of voice"; yet they are not free of artificial constraints. They are "fastened to the page" by the forms in which they are "entangled." Again the implied idea is one of continuous struggle, tension, tug-of-war. If this quality "goes deep into the nature of the sentence," then presumably Frost is simply acknowledging this fact of nature by writing as he does.

Frost's preoccupation with "drama" is continuous. It is unsurprising that some of his noticeable bendings of meter come from the mouths of fictive speakers. The witch's son in "The Witch of Coös" describes the march of the skeleton in lines that disarrange the meter so as to suggest the ongoing precariousness of the thing:

> It left the cellar forty years ago
> And carried itself like a pile of dishes
> Up one flight from the cellar to the kitchen,
> Another from the kitchen to the bedroom,
> Another from the bedroom to the attic,
> Right past both father and mother, and neither stopped it.
> Father had gone upstairs; mother was downstairs.
> I was a baby: I don't know where I was.

> (28–35)

The veerings in and out of audible iambic meter convey more than the wobbliness of the skeleton: they supply much of what we infer about the son's character. His childish naivety shows in his pleasure in the step-by-step pattern he recounts ("Up one flight . . . Another . . . Another"), in his relish in the grotesque image of the walking skeleton carrying itself "like a pile of dishes," and in his belated acknowledgment that all of his information is secondhand. In the sequence

<pre>
    x / x   \   x / x \ x / (x)
Another from the kitchen to the bedroom,
    x / x   \   x / x   \ x / (x)
Another from the bedroom to the attic,
    /   /   /   / x x   / x x / x   /   /
Right past both father and mother, and neither stopped it
</pre>

the cart is holding the donkey back in the first two lines, while in the third the donkey lurches forward with it. This little prosodic display of contending forces serves to deepen simultaneously the imagery, characterization, and aural effect of the poem.

Some of Frost's most interesting effects arise from voices overlapping each other in dialogue. Here are some lines from "The Fear":

> The woman spoke out sharply, 'Whoa, stand still!'
> I saw it just as plain as a white plate,'
> She said, 'as the light on the dashboard ran
> Along the bushes at the roadside—a man's face.
> You *must* have seen it too.'
>   'I didn't see it.
> Are you sure—'
>   'Yes, I'm sure!'
>   '—it was a face?'
>
>   (8–13)

Although Frost occasionally italicizes words (as he does here with "*must*") he more often leaves it to the reader to divine the proper emphases, guided by the sound of sense. There are often a range of possible readings, more and less dramatically charged. Take the line broken in three parts by the woman's interpolation. One obvious reading careens away from iambics:

        x   x   /
        Are you sure—'

                    x   x   /
                    'Yes, I'm sure!'

                            /   x   x   /
                            '—it was a face?'

But if we attune our ears to Frost's speakers, we may find it plausible to trust the iambic pattern. This makes sense especially if the man is contrasting his perceptions with the woman's. "I didn't see it," he insists:

        x   /   x
        Are you sure—'

                    /   x   /
                    'Yes, I'm sure!'

                            x   /   x   /
                            '—it was a face?'

An interesting dynamism emerges in this second scansion, since the woman's interruption breaks the second iambic foot in two: that is, it makes her snapped retort even *more* of an interruption. The other speaker's emphases may be heard as skeptically putting the woman on the spot: Are you really able to swear to it? Couldn't it have been something else that you saw? A performer (or performers) reading the poem aloud would be obliged to choose one of these options (or another more eccentric); but in reading the poem to ourselves it is likely that we will hear what Frost wants us to hear, the patterns of speech rhythms and those of meter consorting in "strained relation." To a degree, we will sense one pattern superimposed on the other, and which one we should consider dominant may be largely a matter of personal taste in negotiating the curious elasticity of Frost's monosyllabic lines.

It is equally easy to find examples of this kind of Frostian dramatic shaping of verse in poems that are not dramatic or even narrative in the usual sense. Shifts in meter give animation to landscape. In "Birches," the ice-coated trees begin to thaw, and

<pre>
  /   x /   /   /   x   x   / x   /
Soon the sun's warmth makes them shed crystal shells,

 / x x   x / x /   x   \   x   /   /
Shattering and avalanching on the snow-crust—

  x   / x   / x   /   x   / x /
Such heaps of broken glass to sweep away

  x   /   x / x   /   x /   x   / (x)
You'd think the inner dome of heaven had fallen.
</pre>

(10–13)

The shattering of the ice is figured in the shattering of the iambic pattern in the first two lines, and the metrical regularity of the next two (not slavish regularity: the two scansions are not identical) mirrors the tidying-up that is being contemplated ("Such heaps of broken glass to sweep away"). The slight ruffling of the meter of the last line by the presumed elision of "heaven," followed by the feminine ending, harks back in a milder way to the disorder earlier described, which may not be so easily banished. These sorts of expressive manipulations of meter are frequent in Frost; given his "dramatic" aims, he sometimes went further with them than would please the exact prosodist. Another result, ironically, was that less-than-studious readers were sometimes under the impression that Frost was writing free verse, which he abhorred. In a comment for an anthology that in 1942 reprinted "The Death of the Hired Man," he felt obliged to conclude with this plaintive sentence: "By the way, it's in blank verse, not free verse."[19]

A final point may be made about dramatic values in Frost. Diction is not our subject, except as it affects versification. It is worth noting, though, that much of Frost's success in verse dialogue derives from his tact in adjusting levels of diction. No matter how easy it may be to construct conversational sentences in iambic pentameter, an extended dialogue passage is bound to seem artificial in places. As we have seen, Frost's dialogue functions sometimes as an economical way to advance a story line ('Are you sure—' / 'Yes, I'm sure!'). When his characters go deeper into the matter at hand, there is typically an unobtrusive heightening of the style. One of Frost's most famous passages is this exchange of definitions from "The Death of the Hired Man":

> 'Home is the place where, when you have to go there,
> They have to take you in.'

> 'I should have called it
> Something you somehow haven't to deserve.'

(118–20)

Homely as the vocabulary remains, there is a ritual gravity that informs the counterpoised statements, each a distillation of experience. We may wonder if New England farm couples really talked in this fashion, but when we are reading the poem we do not question the appropriateness of such pronouncements. They have the ring of folk wisdom. At a more intense pitch of eloquence, the plain style, with only discreet heightenings of diction, invokes a tone that transcends village proverbialism. Frost's last major blank-verse poem, "Directive," attains an oracular or scriptural note and assimilates it to a compelling description of an abandoned upland farm reverting to wilderness:

> Back out of all this now too much for us,
> Back in a time made simple by the loss
> Of detail, burned, dissolved, and broken off
> Like graveyard marble sculpture in the weather,
> There is a house that is no more a house
> Upon a farm that is no more a farm
> And in a town that is no more a town.

(1–7)

Unnamed as the narrator remains, the quality of the voice is highly dramatic. We infer a speaker whose own life-quest has qualified him to serve, as he offers to do, as the reader's "guide." He is someone who has sufficiently acquainted himself with life's joys and sorrows to be, as the poem's closing words put it, "whole beyond confusion." Intriguingly, a much larger proportion of lines in this poem are metrically regular than is usual with Frost; the variations, such as they are, are mostly standard (a number of feminine endings, for instance). In this case the poet seems to have judged that the voice of his seer-narrator was best supported by a metrical movement that would progress smoothly and inexorably, rather than one recurrently subject to roughness.

Although this discussion of Frost began with some comparisons to Robinson, differences between the two poets outweigh similarities. In some respects Frost was more adventurous than his fellow New Englander, in others less. Robinson's placid acceptance of iambic pentameter is at odds with Frost's practice of restless experimentation, yet in range of subject matter the younger poet is the more conservative. New England was only one of several settings for Robinson the narrative poet; but for Frost in all but a few poems it is the essential background and, often enough, foreground. The major exceptions to New England narratives (or shorter New England descriptive pieces) in Frost's blank verse are satirical or didactic poems that have not worn well: "Build Soil" is one dispiriting example. The two biblical "masques"—*A Masque of Reason* and *A Masque of Mercy*—are written as plays but are unstageable even as closet drama; like many modern works derived from the Bible, they seem the depleted offspring of a robust original. Such miscalculations were less frequent for Frost than they were for Robinson. Staying cautiously on his own turf, Frost enjoyed a remarkable number of successes.

The compact narratives of *North of Boston* were followed by several more in the same vein: not only well-known pieces like "The Witch of Coös" but its overlooked companion, "The Pauper Witch of Grafton," and others like "The Bonfire," "The Ax-Helve," "A Fountain, a Bottle, a Donkey's Ears and Some Books," and "Snow." Frost never attempts anything on the scale of Robinson's verse novels or Arthurian poems. His longest blank-verse narrative, "Snow," occupies fourteen pages in his *Complete Poems,* and most of the others are nowhere near as long. His shrewdness in husbanding his resources (and in gauging his readers' attention span) has saved a greater proportion of his work from receding into obscurity. Frost is capable of brilliant elaboration in the longer pieces, as in these lines from "Snow" that describe, from within a snow-bound house, the top of a drift pressed against a windowpane:

> 'It looks as if
> Some pallid thing had squashed its features flat
> And its eyes shut with overeagerness
> To see what people found so interesting
> In one another, and had gone to sleep
> Of its own stupid lack of understanding,
> Or broken its white neck of mushroom stuff
> Short off, and died against the window-pane.'

(159–66)

But his bias, and his genius, is for compression. One of his finest narratives, "'Out, Out—'" takes only thirty-four lines to tell of a boy's death in a farm accident, its brevity emphasizing better than any extended commentary the bleak view of existence summed up in the taciturn conclusion:

> No one believed. They listened at his heart.
> Little—less—nothing!—and that ended it.
> No more to build on there. And they, since they
> Were not the one dead, turned to their affairs.
>
> (31–34)

This kind of extremely pared-down narrative—running less than a page—has proven one of the most durable models Frost left for later poets. ("The Vanishing Red," at twenty-nine lines, is another example of such effective brevity.) The twentieth century's love of speed encouraged all sorts of abbreviations and accelerations in poetry (imagism is an extreme example), and Frost, however antimodernist he sometimes professed to be, partook of the trend. The very brief descriptive poem in blank verse goes back to Wordsworth and other romantic poets; but narrative so streamlined was a twentieth-century form. If Frost was not its sole progenitor, he was certainly one of the first to write notable poems of this kind, as well as many equally notable, equally brief descriptive pieces. The traditional connection of blank verse to longer forms, loosening since the romantic era, pretty much gave way as Frost and other twentieth-century poets applied the meter to poems of less than a page. What was once the meter of epic was now licensed for lyric, and soon enough would be certified to deliver epigrams.

II

Most readers know the story of how Robert Frost, nearing forty and unable to make headway as a poet in America, moved with his family to England in 1912. There he found a publisher for his first two books, the second of which was the innovative blank-verse collection *North of Boston*. He also made the acquaintance of a number of English poets who found many of his ideas and interests compatible. Frost had only a few fleeting contacts with W. B. Yeats, the dominant poetic presence of the time. Accounts of their meetings, arranged by their mutual friend Ezra Pound, make amusing reading. One gets an impression of two battleship-sized egos steering warily to avoid collision. However unsatisfactory as social experience, the coming together of the two poets was emblematic of an emerging force reshaping poetic style on both sides of the Atlantic. Frost's insistence on the primacy of speech and the centrality of dramatic qualities in poetry had its counterparts in British poetry before World War I. The rejection of the musicality of High Victorian and Pre-Raphaelite verse in favor of a more conversational or even colloquial style was the first phase of modernism in poetry; it was a discipline Yeats had begun to impose on himself by the time he met Frost, and his style grew more angular still as he advanced into middle age. These two poets should have had much to talk about, and it is too bad that their difficult personalities held them mutually aloof.

Yeats's early poems in blank verse are languorous in rhythm, swathed in the misty atmospherics of the Celtic Twilight. The speaking style of the lovers no longer in love in "Ephemera" is firmly ensconced in the nineteenth century, and the lyric melancholy is reinforced by the placid, rather Keatsian verse:

> Pensive they paced along the faded leaves,
> While slowly he whose hand held hers replied:
> 'Passion has often worn our wandering hearts.'

> (10–12)

Line 11 is remarkably slow even by the early Yeats's standards: the word "slowly" is followed by five aspirated monosyllables in a row, naturally putting the brakes on enunciation. Of course, such features are unsurprising in a piece whose earliest version appeared in Yeats's first collection in 1889. But the slow and ceremonious style had staying power. It informs later narratives drawn from Irish legend—"The Old Age of Queen Maeve" (1903) and "The Two Kings" (1913)—and the "Dramatic Poem" called *The Shadowy Waters* (1906). The high estheticism of early Yeatsian blank verse is echoed in that of near contemporaries like Arthur Symons and T. Sturge Moore. Yeats was a tireless reviser, and his alterations of these pieces show that he was attempting to disencumber his lines from what he came to think of as "embroidery." But sharpening diction in such cases does not greatly animate the lethargic movement of the verse. Yeats's turn toward speech values and more vivid emotions declared itself most clearly in shorter poems.

"The Second Coming," published in 1920, is by far the most celebrated of Yeats's poems in blank verse. Yeats's response to the Russian Revolution and the world war that overlapped it has succeeded in communicating apocalyptic dread even to the majority of readers who, it is safe to say, are unfamiliar with the esoteric sources of the poem's ominous symbols. The handling of the meter in this poem is dramatic in Frost's sense, its customary pattern being hard pressed to restrain the rhythmic jolts of agitated emotion. Excited feeling is also suggested by enjambment, which like the metrical bendings also underscores the imagery:

> The blood-dimmed tide is loosed, and everywhere
> The ceremony of innocence is drowned;
> The best lack all conviction, while the worst
> Are full of passionate intensity.

(5–8)

Neither "the blood-dimmed tide" nor the malign purposes of "the worst," these enjambments suggest, can be contained; they both spill over from one line to the next. It is in the poet's vision "out of *Spiritus Mundi*" which is the poem's climax that we find the flow of the meter subtly but unmistakably hobbled as the fearful sight is disclosed:

```
x  / x    /  x    / x x   /   x    /
The Second Coming! Hardly are those words out

  x  x  / / x    /  x   / x x   ./ (x)
When a vast image out of Spiritus Mundi

  /  x  x  /    /   x  x  /   x  x   / (x)
Troubles my sight: somewhere in sands of the desert

x  /   x  / x  / x  x   x  /   x x  /
A shape with lion body and the head of a man,

x  /    /  x   / x x  \  x  /
A gaze blank and pitiless as the sun,

x  / x  x   /    /    x  / x  /  (x)
Is moving its slow thighs, while all about it

  /   /  x  \  x x /  x   / x  /
Reel shadows of the indignant desert birds.
```

(11–17)

There is something like a stuttering effect, especially in lines 13–15, owing to the spondees and the insertion of so many additional unstressed syllables. The slow, fitful coming to life of the figure, the movement of its "slow thighs," is portrayed in the meter's limping. The famous last lines of the poem disrupt meter similarly to allude to the motion described:

> x   /   /   /   x   /   x   /   x   /
> And what rough beast, its hour come round at last,
>
> /   x   /   x   /   x   /   x   x   /
> Slouches towards Bethlehem to be born?

> (21–22)

The final line is problematic—no doubt intentionally. If one accepts the scansion just offered, the line is all trochees but for a final iamb, an extreme way of emphasizing a falling rhythm before (at the last step, as it were) curtailing it. But the prosodic status of "towards" is questionable. The word can be pronounced as a single syllable or as two syllables with the accent on the second rather than the first. The first option gives us

> /   x   /   /   x   /   x   x   /
> Slouches towards Bethlehem to be born

—a nine-syllable line combining disparate feet: trochee, spondee, iamb, anapest. Reading "towards" as two syllables, we may choose a different scansion:

> /   x   x   /   /   x   /   x   x   /
> Slouches towards Bethlehem to be born

—which is an odd mixture of trochees and iambs. There is no obviously preferred solution to this kind of metrical conundrum; different readers will hear the line in different ways. But in any one of these examples, and perhaps in the indeterminacy that bedevils each and all, Yeats creates a movement that is oppressively weighty and yet precariously tottering, a sound-equivalent of the shambling gait of the bestial Antichrist. Yeats rarely risks his overall iambic movement as radically as Frost does, but by this point in his career he was fully capable of localized drastic manipulation of it for much the same aim as Frost's—dramatic expressiveness.

Any discussion of Yeats's pursuit of the dramatic must take account of his verse plays, but we shall defer that topic to the next section of this chapter. Here it may be worthwhile to point out that our comparison of Yeats with Frost goes only so far. While Yeats worked hard and successfully to make his language less ornate, it rarely approaches the level of colloquialism that is the norm in Frost. It creates an effect of conversation when Yeats so intends, but it is typically what he called in a late poem "high talk." Someone whose models of discourse were such men as his own father, Oscar Wilde, and his friends in the Rhymers' Club could hardly be expected to converse in the manner of a New England farmer or of one of those Irish peasants who appear sporadically in his work (Lady Gregory usually had to correct Yeats's forays into dialect). His language can be blunt, but it is not that of the common man, and Yeats did not wish it to be. Another difference between Frost and Yeats is in tonal range. While Frost avowed an interest in pursuing a great variety of tonal shadings in his "sentence-sounds," Yeats concentrated on feelings that were, to use a frequent word of his, "passionate." It was the extremes of emotion, particularly as these are found in tragedy, that tended to occupy him, and consequently even many of his less-imposing poems are strangely imbued with poignancy or vehemence. For Yeats's purpose, blank verse proved to be as malleable a medium as it was for Frost and other conservative modernists, but what resulted was poetry more elevated and rarefied—this even after the evolution of his style.

Yeats deprecated rhetoric. According to his well-known dictum, out of his quarrel with other men a man makes rhetoric, while out of his quarrel with himself he makes poetry. One has to take this with a large grain of salt. "The Second Coming" is one of the more rhetorical poems ever written, and Yeats's work bristles with audience-swaying tactics, perhaps the most obvious of which is his addiction to the kind of question we call rhetorical. It may be that in discussing Yeats's speech effects we should look more to oratory and the classic theater for models than to ordinary conversation. With this in mind, we may nevertheless find among Yeats's blank-verse poems several which, if not exactly relaxed, are less histrionic than "The Second Coming." The curious dialogue poems "Ego Dominus Tuus" and "The Phases of the Moon" set forth Yeats's spiritualistic findings—his theories of the antithetical self and of the historical cycles he called "gyres"—much more engagingly than the prose treatise *A Vision*. "Shepherd and Goatherd," in eclogue form, is an elegy for Robert

Gregory. Much less known than Yeats's other poems on the same subject, it has affecting moments despite its braving of anachronism. The intriguing narrative "The Gift of Harun Al-Rashid" allegorizes Yeats's marriage and celebrates his wife as medium and muse. Yeats also wrote blank-verse poems of lyric or epigrammatic brevity. Such pieces as "In the Seven Woods" and "A Prayer on Going into My House" publish the poet's alienated (and sometimes alienating) moods with lapidary precision. The first of the sequence of "Supernatural Songs" ("Ribh at the Tomb of Baile and Aillinn") narrates the sort of mystical vision that earlier works like "Ego Dominus Tuus" didactically discuss. As many of his contemporaries did, Yeats found the meter highly accommodating.

In his own time, and even more obviously in retrospect, Yeats was a towering figure in the British poetry scene before World War I. Other poets who are still read with pleasure and interest today, such as Hardy and De la Mare, wrote little blank verse and hence are beyond the range of this discussion.[20] Some notice must be taken, though, of Yeats's slightly younger British contemporaries. Often loosely grouped together as "Georgian" poets, many of these shared Yeats's dramatic interests and, conforming to what still seemed to many an unbreachable convention, wrote much of their work—stage plays or dialogue poems—in blank verse. Even in England, poets like Wilfrid Gibson, Lascelles Abercrombie, and Gordon Bottomley are now unremembered or, at best, faded names. Their writing is not without energy or intelligence, but it has dated badly. They now serve the melancholy purpose relegated to bygone minor poets: to illustrate poetic trends that have since been absorbed or superseded. Gibson specialized in short dialogue poems—playlets, one might say—dealing with the privations of the working class. His collection *Daily Bread* (1910) pursues the theme with scant subtlety: few of these poems of three or four pages lack a fatal factory accident or something equally dire. The blank verse allotted to the thinly realized characters does nothing to add dimension to them, being consistently flat and undifferentiated. Abercrombie also wrote sometimes of humble folk, but he was more bookish, and his work ranges beyond the proletariat in many longer pieces. He wrote in more complex (though not necessarily more effective) forms. Sometimes he undertook to combine narrative and dialogue within a single poem, but rather than interweaving the two he simply set chunks of speech and of story side by side in awkward alternation. Unlike Gibson's determinedly demotic style, Abercrombie's can be toplofty, especially when dealing with historical characters. In "Vashti," loosely derived from the Old Testament Book of Esther, the Persian queen rebukes her husband King Ahasuerus's lubricity:

> Lovest thou me, or dost thou rather love
> The pleasure thou hast in me? This is not nice,
> Believe me. They're more sundered, these two loves,
> Than if all the braving seas marcht between them.

(I, 42–45)

The king responds in kind: "What, shrinking from thine own delightsomeness?" (I, 46). Placing either of these poets' work next to *North of Boston* can only enhance one's rating of Frost's skill and tact in regard to style and dramatic form. Gordon Bottomley ranks a step above Gibson and Abercrombie by virtue of one blank-verse poem, "The End of the World," that has been often and deservedly anthologized. In verse finely handled, Bottomley renders the title event from the viewpoint of a couple stranded in an isolated farm house. In this rural English apocalypse, the world's end is accomplished through a snowstorm that never stops (an idea that, decades before the atomic bomb, seems to presage scenarios of "nuclear winter"). The nicety of detail and the matter-of-fact tone work to evoke an authentic chill, as day after day of storm goes by:

> When snow slid from an overweighted leaf,
> Shaking the tree, it might have been a bird
> Slipping in sleep or shelter, whirring wings;
> Yet never bird fell out, save once a dead one—
> And in two days the snow had covered it.

(29–33)

Both in its content and its grim restraint, this is an unusual poem for 1907. If Georgian poetry had produced more work of this quality, it would more readily find readers today.

One English poet of the period who *is* still widely read is Edward Thomas. Thomas's career as a poet was crucially stimulated by Robert Frost. Before the two men met, Thomas had supported his family precariously with his prose writings: biographies, travel books, pieces on country life, much reviewing.

Frost encouraged him to write poems on some of the same scenes and subjects he had treated in prose. The long tradition of English nature poetry lies behind Thomas, of course, but one feels that Frost's example was decisive in shaping his style. The premise of many a Thomas poem is the same as in Frost: the poet writes of what he saw on his walk or reports his talks with those he met on the way. It is the idyll or eclogue, updated and adapted to England's bleaker climate. Thomas has Frost's conversational ease and his inclination to understatement as well as much concrete detail gleaned from sensitive observation. Also like Frost (and decidedly unlike Gibson and Abercrombie), he habitually practices compression, and the absence of padding in his poems heightens their intensity of feeling beyond what might be expected of a manner so quiet and unstudied. As to versification, Thomas's pentameter lines are not subject quite as frequently as Frost's to expressive flexing, but there are enough variations to suggest that in this regard also the English poet sought to emulate his American friend.[21] In his famous poem "Rain," the meter is regular in many of the lines, which makes the isolated shifts more striking. The first line is clearly designed to stand out from the rest of the sentence it introduces:

>   /   / x   /   / x x x /   /
> Rain, midnight rain, nothing but the wild rain
> On this bleak hut, and solitude, and me
> Remembering again that I shall die
> And neither hear the rain nor give it thanks
> For washing me cleaner than I have been
> Since I was born into this solitude.
>
>   (1–6)

One has to get through lines 2 and 3 before a clear sense of the meter is established. In line 1 there is not only what seems like one too many accented syllables but the additional weight given by the commas to the words they follow. Even without the title, this wrenching of prosody makes it clear what word is paramount. The end of the poem is just as striking in a subtler way. The poet meditates on his sympathy for all the living and the dead whom "the rain rains upon," a "helpless" feeling like that of one "broken reed" standing in the water among others equally broken:

Myriads of broken reeds all still and stiff,
Like me who have no love which this wild rain
Has not dissolved except the love of death,

```
x  /  x  /  x    /  x  /  x    /
```
If love it be for what is perfect and

```
 x  /  x  /  x  /  x  /  x  /
```
Cannot, the tempest tells me, disappoint.

(14–18)

The plodding ("perfect") regularity of the meter in the last two lines might be expected to dissipate a little the shock of the preceding phrase "the love of death." Actually, it deepens the shock, by imposing a sense of inexorability. The surprising enjambment following the unexpected but incontrovertible metrical stress on the word "and" carries the reader on to the last line with its delayed predicate. Unlike the commas in the opening line, these seem to wave us along to the bleak knowledge of life implied by the final word, the perception that there is of all things only one that cannot disappoint. This grim conviction nestles so comfortably within the metrical pattern that its full effect is something like a delayed explosion.

However Frostian some of Thomas's inspirations may have been, even these few lines show that he adapted Frost's program to his own poetic voice. He is not as insistently monosyllabic as Frost, and his fondness for the well-placed anapest and other modifications gives some of his lines a lighter, speedier movement. Here are some typical lines from "March" that illustrate such features:

```
     x    /  x  /  x  /    x  x  /   /  (x)
```
While still my temples ached from the cold burning

```
  x  /  x   /   x   /  x   /  / x
```
Of hail and wind, and still the primroses

```
   /  x  x  /   x   / x   / x  /
```
Torn by the hail were covered up in it,

```
   x  /  x    /    x   /   x  x  /   /
```
The sun filled earth and heaven with a great light

```
   x  x  /  x  /  x  x   /     x   x   /   /
```
And a tenderness, almost warmth, where the hail dripped,

```
  x  /  x   /  x  /   x   /  x  /
```
As if the mighty sun wept tears of joy.

(4–9)

The variations in the opening pair of lines (pyrrhic, spondee, and feminine ending in line 4, and an odd terminal trochee in line 5) correspond to the turbulence of the weather suitably enough, but we should be wary of identifying a particular variation with a particular imagery. Except for the extrametrical unstressed syllable, the pattern of "from the cold burning" is repeated in "with a great light" and "where the hail dripped." Without being crudely schematic, the frequent rhythmic fluctuations suggest the mysterious grandeur and startling suddenness that such a shift of weather displays. If Thomas's less orthodox lines here are notably free, it is equally notable that line 6 (regular save for the initial trochee) and line 9 (absolutely regular) serve as anchors for the more free-floating lines that precede or follow them. Thomas took up poetry later than most, and had only a few years in which to write it before his death in World War I. Some have viewed his metrical deviations as rough spots caused by an incomplete mastery of technique. This may be the case in a few instances, but in general his handling of verse is easily explicable as a personal adaptation of Frost's expressive theory. Of the modest amount of poetry Thomas wrote, there are other memorable poems in blank verse: the understated war poems "Fifty Faggots" and "As the Team's Head-Brass" and country vignettes such as "The Path," "Wind and Mist," "Old Man," "The Unknown Bird," and "Up in the Wind" are representative.

The First World War, which killed not only Thomas but many other talented writers, put an end to the vague movement called Georgian poetry. The darker view of human possibilities provided by trench warfare made the earlier poetry seem outmoded: more fairly in some instances than in others, Georgian poets were identified with nostalgic escapism. But the war brought prominence to a new wave of poets who made war their subject. Two of these, Siegfried Sassoon and Robert Graves, wrote significant poems in blank verse.

Sassoon's battle poems are so devoted to shocking verisimilitude in their descriptions that their prosody may not claim much notice from readers. A piece like "Counter-Attack" is intent above all to document such sights as a trench filled with the dead bodies of the speaker's fellow soldiers:

> x   /   x   /   x   /   x   / x   /
> And trunks, face downward, in the sucking mud,
>
> / x   x   /   x   /   x   /   x   /
> Wallowed like sodden sand-bags loosely filled;

```
x   / x / x / x   / x  /
```
And naked sodden buttocks, mats of hair,

```
/     / x /   / x x  / x x    /
```
Bulged, clotted heads slept in the plastering slime.

```
x    / x / x /    x / x x  /
```
And then the rain began,—the jolly old rain!

(9–13)

Here there is nothing as thoroughgoing as some of Thomas's metrical bends, though there is an emphatic heaviness to the stressing in the first three lines (even some of the unstressed monosyllables like "face" and "bags" seem heavy for their positions). The penultimate line substitutes three different feet—spondee, trochee, anapest—for three of its iambs, which might seem to give special emphasis to the close of the horrific catalogue. And yet the final line, with only one substitution—a terminal anapest—is climactic in a more surprising way. In "the jolly old rain" it is not only the word choice but the incongruous lilt of the anapest that provides a hint of repressed hysteria.[22]

This poem actually occupies a middle ground in regard to expressive variation. Sassoon elsewhere makes good use of the unruffled metrical paradigm to attain a prophetic note, as in the vision (and beat) of an endless march that concludes "Prelude: The Troops":

> And through some mooned Valhalla there will pass
> Battalions and battalions, scarred from hell;
> The unreturning army that was youth;
> The legions who have suffered and are dust.

(23–26)

At the other extreme, at the end of "Repression of War Experience," metrical disturbance parallels mental disturbance as a shell-shocked veteran, safe at home, suffers a flashback:

> Hark! Thud, thud, thud,—quite soft . . . they never cease—
> Those whispering guns—O Christ, I want to go out
> And screech at them to stop—I'm going crazy;
> I'm going stark, staring mad because of the guns.

(35–38)

The virtually unscannable "Thud, thud, thud" and the shattered meter of the final line have their appropriate effect. Yet even in a piece like this one most lines are regular, with occasional standard variations. In so far as the meter is bent in response to the pressure of feeling, it recalls the histrionic voice effects of Browning rather than the more varied and nuanced ones of Frost. If Browning had seen service on the western front, he might have written such a piece as this. Sassoon was hardly an innovator, but he was shrewd in applying traditional stylistic resources to an unheralded situation, offering compelling glimpses of horrors no poet of his generation could have foreseen. Although Sassoon survived the war by many years and wrote prolifically on many subjects, his later poetry never aroused the same interest that his trench poems had. One later piece, "Villa d'Este Gardens," is attractive and notable for the lighter pace of its blank verse, aided by numerous, gracefully handled feminine endings.

Robert Graves also survived his combat experience by many years. Unlike Sassoon, he managed to outgrow his initial labeling. He is now more likely to be identified with romantic and mythological themes than with the horrors of war. (At times during his career his prose writings—historical novels such as *I, Claudius* and revisionary mythographies such as *The White Goddess*— threatened to overshadow his poetic work of whatever kind.) Graves's war poems include a number that rely on Sassoonian shock effects. His finest war poem (and one of the finest war poems of the twentieth century) was written twenty years after the war ended. "Recalling War" is distinguished not only for its reflectiveness and stern avoidance of sentimentality but for its memorably taut blank-verse lines. The speaker, whose "Entrance and exit wounds are silvered clean" (1), recalls that time when

> Natural infirmities were out of mode,
> For Death was young again: patron alone
> Of healthy dying, premature fate-spasm.

(17–19)

The sardonic appropriation of the tone of a breakfast-food advertisement in "healthy dying" is typical. Rather than the overpowering emotion Sassoon dramatized in "Repression of War Experience," there is in this poem a manner altogether cooler. Graves's speaker is well enough able to recall "The inward scream, the duty to run mad" (37), but time has given memories of battle the eerie quality of a child's dream. The poem ends:

> Machine-guns rattle toy-like from a hill,
> Down in a row the brave tin-soldiers fall:
> A sight to be recalled in elder days
> When learnedly the future we devote
> To yet more boastful visions of despair.
>
> (42–46)

Graves's other blank-verse poems are often equally accomplished. His mastery of the meter encompasses humor and satire, as in "Front Door Soliloquy," "Welsh Incident," and "The Hung Wu Vase." He also is, when he chooses, a Gothic fantasist. "Down" is a harrowing nightmare poem, while "The Pier-Glass" unforgettably pictures its doomed heroine as she lives out her abandonment in her "lost manor," compelled to pay nightly visits to an empty bedroom:

> Empty, unless for a huge bed of state
> Shrouded with rusty curtains drooped awry
> (A puppet theatre where malignant fancy
> Peoples the wings with fear).
>
> (8–11)

Graves's eccentric and intense involvement in the study of myth and ancient lore informs many of his poems: those in blank verse include "Theseus and Ariadne," "The Broken Girth," "*Non Cogunt Astra*," and "The Beds of Grainne and Diarmuid." Most numerous of all (too numerous, in fact, to list) are the poems he wrote on the nature—often on the vagaries—of love between man and woman. Many of these pieces, especially those from his later years, have an epigrammatic trenchancy that distances but does not muffle their emotion.

As with many good poets working extensively in blank verse, Graves put an individual stamp on the meter. It is clear from poems like "The Pier-Glass" and "Recalling War" that he was capable of punctilious prosody when he chose. Frequently, though, he modifies the verse with individual mannerisms. In many poems he intersperses shorter lines among regular pentameters to vary the movement. Sometimes this marks an important turn in argument or provides closure. In "Frightened Men," for instance, two of the last five lines are short. The speaker has been musing on the contrast between the mysterious "feline race" of women and "mouse-quiet" men such as himself. He concludes:

> The worst is when they hide from us and change
>   x /   x / x / x / x
> To something altogether other:
> We meet them at the door, as who returns
> After a one-hour-seeming century
>   x x /   / x /
> To a house not his own.
>
>   (16–20)

Line 17, stopping short of a final accent, no doubt enacts the disorienting otherness of the "change," and this feeling is intensified by the more severe truncation and shifting of stresses in the final line. It is not as easy to posit a thematic reason for some crimped lines in other poems. In the symbolic landscape of "The Climate of Thought," the poet concludes with these features:

> Wind, sometimes, in the evening chimneys; rain
> On the early morning roof, on sleepy sight;
>   /   /   x / x / x   / x
> Snow streaked upon the hilltop, feeding
>   x /   /   x x / x   /
> The fond brook at the valley-head
> That greens the valley and that parts the lips;
> The sun, simple, like a country neighbour;
> The moon, grand, not fanciful with clouds.
>
>   (16–22)

This kind of occasional clipping of lines so that they fall short by a syllable or an iamb is frequent enough to seem like a sort of nervous tic when it lacks an obvious expressive purpose. It is not an unprecedented device by any means; short lines are not hard to find in dramatic verse, and many poets have occasionally allowed themselves license in this regard. But it is a favorite arrow in this poet's quiver, part of what makes Graves sound like Graves. His approach to versification is not as daring as Frost's, but he was pliant and expressive in his rhythmic effects, and in pursuit of these he clearly regarded the standard pentameter line as malleable.

Different as they are in extent and aural quality, the deliberate roughenings of the iambic pentameter line that we see in Frost, Yeats, Thomas, and Graves are related in aim. The common aim was to move away from the elaborately musical effects of Tennyson and Swinburne to something convincingly like speech. For conservative modernists such as these, meter was something to be stretched—sometimes to the breaking point—but it was not something to be discarded. It remained the recognizable foundation of highly disparate voice exercises. In at least the first few decades of the twentieth century, "the old-fashioned way to be new" satisfied these and other poets who were stirred by dramatic values in poetry even when they were not writing for the stage.

III

To enlarge on our mention of dramatic values, this seems a convenient place for a brief discussion of modern verse drama. It can be brief for at least two reasons. First, our subject is not twentieth-century verse drama in general but plays from that period written in blank verse: a more restricted field. Second, the level of achievement and enduring interest of much of this work is disappointingly low.

One wonders what went wrong. When, as we have seen, so many early twentieth-century poets—English, Irish, American—shared an enthusiasm for poetic drama, how is it that the list of still viable plays in verse by them is so embarrassingly paltry? It is easy enough to grope for reasons. Prose was by this time so firmly established on the stage that verse drama had an uphill climb in commending itself to the public or to theater professionals. There were problems of expectations—those which the audience brings with it to a play, and those which a playwright ventures to have of the audience. With infrequent exceptions (it is rarely recalled that W. S. Gilbert wrote *Princess Ida* in blank verse), the poetic drama of the nineteenth century was not popular in its orientation, and later poets wishing to write in verse for a broader audience had to combat the assumption that they were engaged in endeavors that were academic or recherché. And if poets were content (as was Yeats, in his later dramatic writing) to forgo the popular audience, there was often a difficulty in justifying theatrical productions of texts not designed for mass consumption. The strength and prevalence of so many undoubtedly dramatic qualities in poems of various lengths offered serious competition to verse expressly intended for the theater. Plays cost money—lots of money—to produce, and are not as easily disseminated as a poem like Frost's "Home Burial." Given all these obvious stumbling blocks, perhaps the wonder is not that so few poets excelled in writing verse for the theater but that so many persisted in trying it.[23] In John Davidson's strange didactic play *The Theatrocrat* (1905) there is a striking moment in which a contemporary actor clearly states the challenge faced by poet-playwrights of the new century:

> Only once it seems
> A people has a theatre. Drama leaps
> To instant being, power, supremacy;
> From "Gorboduc" to "The Tempest" fifty years;
> And nothing since. Nor can it come again,
> Imagination being an outcast now,
> Unsceptered, unrefreshed, unclad, unknown
> In palace, hut, or hermitage: no home;
> A wandering bedlam.
>
> (3.338–46)

When Davidson two years later committed suicide, the commercial failure of nearly all his plays was thought to have contributed to his despair.

Blank verse, for the would-be playwright, offered some specialized challenges. The most obvious was the break in the chain of tradition. Because theatrical blank verse had ceased to be a living medium in the mid-seventeenth century, it had not evolved as it otherwise likely would have done, adapting itself to changes in idiom over time. Because the finest models were frozen in time, later poets had either to ape an antiquated style or somehow find an equal eloquence in the language of their own time. While nondramatic blank verse had broken free of Milton's influence to advance in numerous new directions, Shakespeare remained the dominant, inescapable model for stage poetry. And what poet feels comfortable vying with Shakespeare? Moreover, thinking of the problems posed by models, we should not forget the other end of the spectrum. Many of the brave or foolhardy poets who did choose to work in blank verse created plays that more often than not were undistinguished, and sometimes memorable in only unflattering ways. Better writers may be discouraged from using a literary form if their weaker contemporaries are unimaginatively plugging away at it: in their search for a style they will hunt for something they can assure themselves is free of stale, inherited gestures. Iambic pentameter, of course, was not to blame for the clichéd verbal style of many poet-playwrights; but there is no doubt that it acquired a certain stigma through association. Particularly once experimental modernism took hold, in the years after World War I, theatrical blank verse was viewed by younger poets as outmoded.

Even at the peak of its resurgence, blank verse for the modern stage was not without detractors. Bernard Shaw rarely missed an opportunity to rail against "the devastating tradition of blank verse" for "giving factitious prestige to the platitudes of dullards, and robbing the dramatic style of the genuine poet of its full natural endowment of variety, force and simplicity."[24] Shaw was only partly facetious when he wrote in his preface to *The Admirable Bashville* (a play that offers a parody of Shakespearean blank verse):

> It may be asked why I have written The Admirable Bashville in blank verse.
> My answer is that I had but a week to write it in. Blank verse is so childishly
> easy and expeditious (hence, by the way, Shakespear's copious output), that
> by adopting it I was enabled to do within a week what would have cost me a
> month in prose.[25]

Shaw's strictures are applied with a broad brush, but there is no doubt that they were warranted by some notably hapless works. The first few decades of the century thronged the stage with iambics in England and Ireland. Undaunted by the challenge laid out by Davidson in *The Theatrocrat*, one versifier, the completely and deservedly forgotten Stephen Phillips, wrote fourteen plays, many of which were hugely successful with the public. Phillips had a knack for targeting the lowest common denominator in his audience; this may have assured him popularity in his time but did nothing to compensate for his conspicuous lack of poetic talent. His style is crudely imitative and his prosody is mediocre when not inept. Phillips's reputation was well on its way to oblivion when he died in 1915; certainly his work was not a good advertisement for blank verse on the modern stage. The most modest sampling of such writing makes Shaw's gibes appear understated.

Both Lascelles Abercrombie and Gordon Bottomley achieved some celebrity as writers of verse plays, though their audience was a more restricted one than the unparticular crowds who applauded Phillips. We need not add much here to what has already been said of Abercrombie's verse, which was at best serious and thoughtful but which has not worn well. There is some historical interest in the apparatus surrounding his published poetry and drama. In a preface to a 1930 collected volume of his poems and plays, Abercrombie mulls over the distinction between plays in verse and what he calls "dramatic poems." Much as the nineteenth century did, he sees the difference stemming from whether the work is meant to be performed or not. "The plays were written to be performed; they were written in verse because that is the medium proper to the kind of drama they attempt; they were written in blank verse because nothing else can combine so effectively the flexibility of speech-rhythm with the formality of metrical pattern."[26] This seems a typical capsulization of the views more traditionally minded poets maintained in the face of emergent modernism when they pondered the lure of the theater. Abercrombie's plays in blank verse have some good writing in them, but they suffer from the same uncertainty of diction one finds in his poems. *Deborah,* set in a fishing village, opens with a simple-minded woman lamenting the epidemic that has recently struck: "There is no help for us; we are left alone, / Left in the power of the flying thing / That hates our lives [. . .]"(1.1–3). A few lines more, and she is interrupted by a man: "Now hold your crying tongue, daft-witted thing; / We're thrang enough without you clamorous" (1.7–8). It is hard to imagine actors delivering such confected peasant dialogue with conviction.

Bottomley was an ardent advocate for poetic drama. He gained favorable critical attention, if not wide popular exposure, for several of his plays. One of his specialties was what we nowadays would call a "prequel." *Gruach* portrays the first meeting and courtship of Shakespeare's Macbeth and Lady Macbeth. *King Lear's Wife* deals with the earlier history of that dysfunctional royal family. As willing satellites, works like these are bound to be outshone by their great originals. Yet one must credit Bottomley not only with audacity but intelligence and skill. He is a smoother stylist than Abercrombie, and in plays like these he handles diction shrewdly, avoiding language that is either overly quaint or anachronistically modern. (It could be objected that this sort of tact in bypassing pitfalls is a negative virtue, and that is just, to an extent.) The emphasis of these plays is on character. Bottomley presents the familiar Shakespearean figures at youthful, formative moments to show the quickening within them of those flaws and appetites that the famous tragedies display full-blown. In the following lines from *Gruach,* Bottomley's Macbeth is pondering the attractions of his future wife:

> A spirit of power that shakes my mind is here
> In this resourceful woman: she is as still
> As the white heat of a straight, half wrought sword
> That does not palpitate yet along its edge
> Lives quiveringly [. . .]

(1.504–8)

These plays, like most of Bottomley's, are a good deal shorter than any Shakespeare play. Other plays by Bottomley, like some of Yeats's later plays, are no more than a few pages—a feature which among many others suggests a practical difficulty in mounting performances. If these works survive, it is more likely to be on the page than on the stage. Bottomley's settings range from ancient to modern times; sometimes he used the history and lore of Scotland in his drama much as Yeats used those of Ireland. His prose testifies to his admiration for Yeats as a dramatist, and some of his staging techniques follow those developed by Yeats in the twenties, when, influenced by the Japanese No drama, the Irish poet sought a more stylized mode of presentation.[27]

Yeats was clearly the impetus for many of these British experiments with poetry in the theater. In his own dramatic writing, blank verse proved to be a diminishing factor as time went on. The verse of his early plays is similar in texture to his early blank-verse lyrics: ceremoniously slow, unabashedly eloquent in an often decorative way. The last lines of his first play, *The Countess Cathleen* (1892), are characteristic. Oona, the countess's foster mother, mourns her heroically self-martyred daughter:

> Tell them who walk upon the floor of peace
> That I would die and go to her I love;
> The years like great black oxen tread the world,
> And God the herdsman goads them on behind,
> And I am broken by their passing feet.

(5.268–72)

Much as he did in regard to his lyrics, Yeats grew impatient with this languorous style. In later work he was frequently willing to vary rhythms strikingly within a play by shifting from blank verse to prose, or to verse, sometimes rhymed, in other meters. The blank verse, when still used, was more urgent in movement as it was less prettified in diction. In *Calvary* (1920), Lazarus accosts Christ on his way to be crucified, and upbraids his Savior for having stolen death from him:

> Alive I never could escape your love,
> And when I sickened towards my death I thought,
> 'I'll to the desert, or chuckle in a corner,
> Mere ghost, a solitary thing.' I died
> And saw no more until I saw you stand
> In the opening of the tomb; 'Come out!' you called;
> You dragged me to the light as boys drag out
> A rabbit when they have dug its hole away;
> And now with all the shouting at your heels
> You travel towards the death I am denied.
>
> (55–64)

This is the tauter verse of *Calvary* and "The Second Coming," published in the same year, and it is the better for that as a dramatic medium. When all is said, though, blank verse was not central to Yeats's achievement as a dramatist. It was one of many tools he employed, and he made less use of it as he refined his theatrical aims. Fine passages of blank verse are to be found in *On Baile's Strand, Deirdre,* and other dramas, but in some of Yeats's most performable plays the part it takes is negligible or nonexistent. For instance, the early *Cathleen-ni-Houlihan* and the late *The Words upon the Window-Pane* are in prose, and his penultimate and perhaps finest play, *Purgatory,* uses a variable verse line that is usually shorter than pentameter. Yeats's theatrical experiments led him far beyond a view privileging blank verse as the obvious and essential form for verse drama, although he no doubt shared such a view with his contemporaries in his youth.

While Yeats moved beyond a predisposition to blank verse in the course of his career as a dramatist, many later poets never harbored such a predisposition in the first place. Probably the most prominent verse plays following

Yeats's were those of T. S. Eliot, and these are all in meters other than iambic pentameter. W. H. Auden's dramatic writings contain a few speeches in blank verse, but are typically a mélange of many verse forms. Christopher Fry's several verse plays won widespread attention at midcentury. Although they could be said to have a basis in iambic pentameter, they expand or crimp the line so frequently that "blank verse" seems not to be a usefully descriptive label. As the century wore on, verse drama of all sorts waned in England.

The theater of this period in the United States was even less hospitable to blank verse than Britain's, with few exceptions, most of which are now uninspiring. In the early years of the century Percy Mackaye wrote numerous verse dramas of a highly conventional sort, favoring exotic settings or historical themes that entailed much theatrical spectacle. *Jeanne d'Arc* and *A Thousand Years Ago* (a version of the Turandot story) are examples. His verse is unremarkable, and like other poets of the time who were drawn to the antique, his language dips into quaintness with a kind of naïve pleasure, unruffled, it would appear, by the revolution in diction which modernism was concurrently bringing to poetry. Mackaye's star has long since set. His indefatigability, though, is a wonder to contemplate. Vastly expanding on Bottomley's "prequel" stratagem, Mackaye in his old age wrote a sequence of four blank-verse dramas under the title *The Mystery of Hamlet King of Denmark,* relating the events preceding Shakespeare's tragedy. More than 650 pages, the work was (almost unbelievably) performed in 1949 in Pasadena. As David Perkins notes, it was "the longest presentation in the theater since the productions of ancient Athens."[28] One may surmise that this occasion did little to increase the public's demand for blank verse on the American stage, in Pasadena or elsewhere.

Among American playwrights-in-verse, Maxwell Anderson was the most successful, perhaps because he had a clearer sense of the limits of an audience's patience. Anderson, like Mackaye, wrote historical dramas—would-be warhorses like *Mary of Scotland* and *Elizabeth the Queen.* While some of these pleased the public, he aroused more critical interest by his attempts to treat contemporary themes in verse, in such plays as *Winterset* and *Key Largo.* In the thirties Anderson wrote fervently of his desire for American theater to "outgrow the phase of journalistic social comment and reach occasionally into the upper air of poetic tragedy."[29] He was convinced that "the best prose in the world is inferior on the stage to the best poetry."[30] For all his aspirations, though, he was not the playwright equipped to provide the best poetry or anything like it.

The poetry of Anderson's plays has been described as "a loose sort of blank verse."[31] This is a charitable way to categorize it. Even passages that are less "loose" than most are only haphazardly observant of the meter. At the end of *Elizabeth the Queen* the monarch sends her young lover Essex to his execution, lamenting:

> I could be young with you, but now I'm old.
> I know now how it will be without you. The sun
> Will be empty and circle round an empty earth . . .
> And I will be queen of emptiness and death . . .
> Why could you not have loved me enough to give me
> Your love and let me keep as I was?

> (3.487–92)

The collapse into prose of the last two lines is typical. The rhythmic handling is much cruder than we find in, for example, Christopher Fry, who is often equally free in altering line length. Anderson at least did not subject his audience to moth-eaten diction in these plays—there are not too many "prithees" to stumble over—but his idea of poetic eloquence, as we can see here, is not much different from soap opera dialogue. In *Winterset*, when his gangster character rants, the attempt to reconcile a low character with poetically vivid expression causes a strain. Railing at the city skyline from his vantage point in a riverside hobo-camp, the recently released convict declares, "By God, what life they've left me / they shall keep me well! I'll have that out of them—/ these pismires that walk like men" (1.1.12–14). Anderson's verse, it becomes apparent, has no essential organic connection to the plays it encumbers. Many of his dramas, with their pseudoprofundities excised, had an even wider display as Hollywood films; verse so mushily fashioned was no match for the rewrite men. It is hard to imagine Shakespearean drama with its poetry removed, but Anderson's audience-pleasing scenarios were highly transposable to the other medium. It is unlikely that many viewers of films like *The Private Lives of Elizabeth and Essex* or *Key Largo* are aware that they originated as verse plays. Their destiny as star vehicles for Bette Davis and Humphrey Bogart was there from the start, in the easily dispensable verse that never greatly complicated their box office appeal. It is fair to say that adaptation into films improved them.

If Anderson's approach to blank verse was to loosen it at will, that of most other theater poets in America from the thirties on has been to substitute other verse forms for it. Not that there were many of these: as the century passed its midpoint, enthusiasm for verse drama flagged. Archibald MacLeish's obtuse updating of the Book of Job, *J. B.,* was, like Eliot's *The Cocktail Party,* an unlikely popular hit. It is written in unrhymed lines of four beats—a sort of blank tetrameter. The trilogy of verse plays by Robert Lowell, *The Old Glory,* adapts stories by Hawthorne and Melville into one-act plays, all in free verse. Blank verse has been distinctly underemployed in the theater in recent decades. Discussing plays written after World War II breaks with this chapter's chronology; but with so meager a field to consider, this seems allowable, if untidy.

For an exception that proves the rule, one may point to the lonely distinction of William Alfred's play, *Hogan's Goat,* first performed in 1965 and published the following year. Set in the Irish-American community in Brooklyn in 1890, the play is a tragedy in the traditional sense without ever seeming academic. Alfred's materials—love and betrayal, corrupt politics, the immigrant experience—are familiar, but his handling of them is remarkably fresh. The complementary energy of language and versification stands out. Here are some lines in which the protagonist, Matthew Stanton, recalls his voyage as a boy in steerage to America:

> I slept six deep in a bunk short as a coffin
> Between a poisoned pup of a seasick boy
> And a slaughtered pig of a snorer from Kildare,
> Who wrestled elephants the wild nights through,
> And sweated sour milk. I wolfed my meals,
> Green water, and salt beef, and wooden biscuits,
> On my hunkers like an ape, in a four-foot aisle
> As choked as the one door of a burning school.

(1.61–68)

If we compare this with Anderson's invertebrate prosody, we see that Alfred has handled the metrical leeway customarily given to dramatists far more responsibly. The verse admits plenty of anapestic substitutions (two in one line in "And a slaughtered pig of a snorer from Kildare") and imitative emphases, as in the last line:

```
x   /   x  x  /   /  x x  /  x      /
```
As choked as the one door of a burning school.

Yet the verse never loses its spine. The rhythmic variations, just as much as the thoughtfully selected diction, support a style of speech appropriate for such characters in such a time and place. Alfred's play had no lack of audience appeal (in its opening run it made a star of Faye Dunaway); but somehow it achieved its popular success without sacrificing its literary substance, which significantly depends on prosodic discipline. The play is a reminder of what it is possible to do with blank verse in the theater—and what, in the last century, has been done in few instances and with diminishing frequency.[32]

IV

In "Canto LXXI," in the midst of musings on his usual mélange of historical, economical, and personal data, Ezra Pound inserts a parenthetical line recalling his and T. S. Eliot's challenge to traditional versification: "To break the pentameter, that was the first heave" (53). The language suggests a demolition project.[33] Pound wrote his share of pentameters before he set about breaking them. Many of his youthful lyrics are rhymed, but some employ blank verse with what might be called a post-Pre-Raphaelite prettiness. The brief "Erat Hora" begins:

> "Thank you, whatever comes." And then she turned
> And, as the ray of sun on hanging flowers
> Fades when the wind hath lifted them aside,
> Went swiftly from me.
>
> (1–4)

In slightly later, more interesting poems such as the "The Tomb at Akr Çaar" and "Portrait d'une Femme" we find him departing from the form in mild ways, by shortening lines or admitting occasional rhyme. For the most part, though, he maintains an iambic movement. Even some of the apparent shortenings of lines turn out to be matters of lineation rather than of meter. At the close of "Portrait d'une Femme" Pound attempts to emphasize the final line with a deep indentation:

> No! there is nothing! In the whole and all,
> Nothing that's quite your own.
>   Yet this is you.
>
>   (28–30)

Whatever jaggedness there is here is a purely visual effect, since "Yet this is you" smoothly supplements the preceding line to fill out a pentameter. Such pieces suggest that Pound could have written mature blank verse to good effect if he had not turned decisively to free verse, in practice and in polemics, as he championed the emerging imagist movement beginning a few years before World War I.

When Pound makes significant use of iambic pentameter in a piece from the mid-'teens, "Near Perigord," one sees not merely rhythmic manipulations but wholesale breaking of the meter:

> Tairiran held hall in Montagnac,
> His brother-in-law was all there was of power
> In Perigord, and this good union
> Gobbled all the land, and held it later for some hundred years.
> And our En Bertrans was in Altafort,
> Hub of the wheel, the stirrer up of strife [. . .]
>
>   (15–20)

The standard iambic pentameter is there in the last two lines of the passage. Earlier there is a gradually expanding range of modifications. Line 15 is missing its first unstressed syllable. Line 16 might be classed as a sort of awkward hexameter or an awkwardly loosened pentameter. Line 17 has had its final stressed syllable amputated. And line 18? "Gobbled all the land, and held it later for some hundred years" has no identifiable metrical identity. This, it seems, was one of the more provocative results of Pound's espousal of his program for imagists, one item of which states: "As regarding rhythm: to compose in the sequence of the musical phrase, not in the sequence of the metronome."[34] It is perhaps less than fair to seize on this example, since this poem features a hybrid rather than a purely imagist style. One must grant that some of Pound's imagist free verse comes a lot closer than these lines to "the sequence of the musical phrase." Yet the extreme disruption of a standard meter is useful to exhibit; here we can witness Pound throwing the metronome out the window, although he then retrieves it. The alternation between adherence to meter and its disruption continues throughout the poem, a sort of tug-of-war. Pound here is clearly treating the meter antagonistically.

T. S. Eliot shared this sense of antagonism in the early years of his friendship with Pound, and he was to have an even more potent influence than Pound did on his younger contemporaries. This was an influence furthered as much by Eliot's criticism as by his poetry. Pound in his prose had a tendency to make even his more thoughtful positions sound cranky. Eliot's prose manner, by contrast, was reassuringly academic even when promoting revolutionary views. He sounded not like a street-corner ranter but like a Harvard-educated oracle. Pound gave the free-verse movement much of its energy, but it was Eliot who supplied it with intellectual respectability. His important article "Reflections on *Vers Libre*" (1917) contains passages that can be read as an apologia for what Pound is doing to meter in "Near Perigord" and (as we shall see) for what Eliot does in some of his own poems. Eliot in fact cites some later lines from "Near Perigord" and praises them for "the constant suggestion and skilful evasion of iambic pentameter."[35] In the generalizing passage leading up to this, he argues against his Victorian precursor: "Swinburne mastered his technique, which is a great deal, but he did not master it to the extent of being able to take liberties with it, which is everything."[36] Eliot goes on to assert that "the most interesting verse which has yet been written in our language has been done either by taking a very simple form, like the iambic pentameter, and constantly withdrawing from it, or taking no form at all, and constantly approximating to a very simple one. It is this contrast between fixity and flux, this unperceived evasion of monotony, which is the very life of verse."[37]

Eliot found examples of such "evasion of monotony" not only in work of his contemporary Pound but in that of Jacobean dramatists, especially Webster. As we noted in the previous chapter, Webster's strange handling of pentameter lines was likely to be viewed as an eccentricity or a fault rather than as a virtue before his rehabilitation by Eliot. Eliot wrote many astute essays about Elizabethan and Jacobean drama, but his finest tribute to Webster is imitative rather than interpretive: the dramatic monologue "Gerontion," written in 1919. Some of Eliot's earlier pieces drop in and out of iambic pentameter, often with rhyme. But it is in "Gerontion" that we find the first major illustration of his prosodic theory in regard to blank verse. In the disorienting conflation of historical periods that is so typical of modernism, Eliot's character speaks in lines whose form and verbal texture have a Websterian flavor even as they address modern issues: the decadence of Western civilization and the loss of traditional religious belief. The poem contains numerous lines that avoid the iambic pattern and fall short of or overshoot the pentameter length; for example:

> I was neither at the hot gates
> Nor fought in the warm rain
> Nor knee deep in the saltmarsh, heaving a cutlass,
> Bitten by flies, fought.
>
> (3–6)

In its passages of densest argument, however, the Websterian style settles into a less fitful though still unpredictable movement. One can find lines that are regular blank verse, but those are immediately followed by ones that obviously are not—the "withdrawing" from the metrical standard that Eliot thought desirable. Gerontion complains of "History," personified as a deceiving female: "She gives when our attention is distracted" (38)—a regular blank-verse line with a feminine ending. But if we read the line in context, its regularity is isolated among lines of a notably non-iambic character. Here is the complete sentence:

> Think now
> She gives when our attention is distracted
> And what she gives, gives with such supple confusions
> That the giving famishes the craving.
>
> (37–40)

The unquestionably iambic pentameter lines in the poem are few enough that a reader unaware of Eliot's prosodic ideas might think them accidental. Knowing of his aims, however, we are continually aware of how extraordinarily calculating his manipulations are. If it is difficult to find lines that are perfectly regular iambic pentameter, it is easy to find ones that could be made to conform to the pattern without altering the sense. The Websterian movement of Gerontion's accusation of Christ comes at the emotional high point of the poem:

> I that was near your heart was removed therefrom
> To lose beauty in terror, terror in inquisition.

> (56–57)

It would have been easy enough (not better, but easy enough) for Eliot to have written:

> Once near your heart, I was removed from it
> To lose what's fair in fear, lose fear in doubt.

The lines as Eliot has written them are undoubtedly more distinctive in diction. But they are also prosodically "off," and this is as important a factor as any in creating their effect. We are supposed to divine the latent possibility of iambic pentameter even as it fails to materialize.

Eliot invokes a revealing metaphor in his essay on *vers libre* to describe this phenomenon. He proposes that "the ghost of some simple metre should lurk behind the arras in even the 'freest' verse; to advance menacingly as we doze, and withdraw as we rouse. Or, freedom is only truly freedom when it appears against the background of an artificial limitation."[38] The implications of Eliot's trope are striking. First, the notion of a ghost portrays traditional meter as something dead. It cannot be directly engaged by the modern poet; it can only haunt his writing like an apparition or nightmare. Second, meter (or, at least, the "simple" meter Eliot has in mind) is something that is on the outer fringe of rational consciousness, something mindlessly automatic. Its presence diminishes as the mind of the poet or of the reader becomes fully awake, rationally active. Finally, the posture of meter toward the poet is threatening. It lies in ambush, advancing "menacingly" when his conscious management of rhythm relaxes. This whole passage can be read as a skewed allusion to *Hamlet*, about which Eliot was soon to write a provocative essay. Meter, in this personification, is the ghost of Hamlet's father, haunting the son with a quickened awareness of his lack of resolve. This is the imposing, even stifling weight of tradition impeding the poet's search for the new. But meter to Eliot is simultaneously the less august figure of Polonius, an old busybody hiding "behind the arras" to spy on the poet, bedeviling him with worn-out stylistic gestures, stale platitudes. Whether meter inspires dread or derision, it is something to be kept at arm's length, more to be struggled against than to be contentedly employed.

An adversarial stance toward blank verse became habitual for Eliot as for Pound. Eliot recommends that poets experiment in various forms of rhyme-less verse, and we discern irritability when he comments, "'Blank Verse' is the only accepted rhymeless verse in English—the inevitable iambic pentameter."[39] The adversarial attitude surfaces in an offhanded way in Pound's annotations to the manuscript of *The Waste Land*. The most conspicuous passage of blank verse in the poem is the opening of part 2, "A Game of Chess." Eliot's first lines in the draft read:

> The Chair she sat in, like a burnished throne
> Glowed on the marble, where the swinging glass
> Held up by standards wrought with golden vines
>
>   (2.1–3)

Next to this Pound writes "3 lines Too tum-pum at a stretch." Eliot defused the "tum-pum" by shortening the second line of the passage:

> The Chair she sat in, like a burnished throne
> Glowed on the marble, where the glass
> Held up by standards wrought with fruited vines

It is remarkable that three lines of regular verse in succession should have seemed three lines too many to these poets. Further on, there is a description of a mythological painting; in the manuscript version:

> The change of Philomel, by the barbarous king
> So rudely forced, yet ~~still~~ there the nightingale
> Filled all the desert with inviolable voice,
> And still she cried (and still the world pursued)
> Jug, Jug, into ~~the~~ dirty ear ~~of death;~~ ~~lust;~~
>
>   (2.24–28)

Here Pound writes in the margin, "too penty." He circles "inviolable" and in the last line crosses out "the" and both of Eliot's alternatives "of death" and "lust." "Lust" is not only crossed out but circled in the manuscript. The passage as printed is not much less "penty," but Eliot, while keeping "inviolable, " makes the last line more abrupt:

> And still she cried, and still the world pursues,
> 'Jug Jug' to dirty ears.
>
> (102–3)

In other lines in this section we see the sorts of Websterian warping that Eliot pioneered in "Gerontion." "In fattening the prolonged candle-flames" (91) and "Huge sea-wood fed with copper" (94) are revisions of earlier, much more "penty" versions: in the first case, "Fattening the candle flames, which were prolonged" (2.15), and in the second, "Upon the hearth, huge sea-wood fed with copper" (2.18). In compressing both lines Eliot took Pound's recommendations. The manuscript of *The Waste Land* offers notable opportunities to watch these two poets in the very act of "breaking the pentameter."

Eliot's later poetry continues his pursuit of a "contrast of fixity and flux." We can find blank-verse lines in *Four Quartets,* but they tend to be isolated amid longer passages of lines that do not hew to the pattern. In part 5 of "The Dry Salvages" Eliot describes "an occupation for the saint" as being "to apprehend / The point of intersection of the timeless / With time," and elaborates:

> x / x / x / x x / x / (x)
> No occupation either, but something given
> And taken, in a lifetime's death in love,
> Ardour and selflessness and self-surrender.
>
> (5.20–22)

The first of these lines is long, and the anapest placed where it is (straddling a comma) has the effect of a stumble into prose. For Eliot, though, this is moving toward regularity. The next two lines, more regular still, would raise no eyebrows in a traditional blank-verse poem. But this moment of fixity soon gives way to flux; over the course of the next several lines Eliot veers between conventionally scannable blank verse and lines that are longer or metrically deviant. The verse eventually expands to a line of fifteen syllables: "The hint half guessed, the gift half understood, is Incarnation" (5.32). Immediately after this, the line contracts in length, and becomes accentual rather than either "free" or accentual-syllabic; the last eighteen lines of the poem have three beats. (When Eliot is writing accentual verse he tends to favor lines shorter than five beats; his later plays are for the most part in three- or four-beat lines.)

Eliot's aversion to writing anything "too penty" was never significantly modified. (What did change, of course, was his verbal style, which moved from the
high theatrical pitch of "Gerontion" to the drier conversationalism of *Four
Quartets* in its discursive passages.) An extended passage in "Little Gidding"
(2.25–72) that stays closer to iambic pentameter than the rest of *Four Quartets*
is a special case. The poet's purpose there is to approximate in English the
movement of Dante's *terza rima,* and the higher percentage of scannable pentameters is incidental and subordinate to the movement of the rhymeless tercets in which they are embedded.

In a trenchant essay, "How Shall the Poem Be Written," the formalist poet
J. V. Cunningham expresses a dim view of Eliot's innovations. Citing Eliot's
advocacy of "taking a very simple form, like the iambic pentameter, and constantly withdrawing from it, or taking no form at all, and constantly approximating to a very simple one," Cunningham gives the result of such a practice
a name: "parasitic meter." He elaborates:

> The term is descriptive and pejorative. Such meter presupposes a meter by
> law which it uses, alludes to, traduces, returns to. To perceive it one must have
> firmly in mind the prior tradition from which it departs and to which it re-
> turns. . . . If it seems from this account that meter can be parasitic in many
> and devious ways, this is true, for the only consistent principle is that it depart
> from and return to a norm. It is the nature of parasitism that it may feed in
> different ways, that it may be irresponsible since it always has the responsible
> thing it feeds on to sustain it and keep it alive.[40]

Of course, Eliot's verse and his process of composition can be described
in less polemical terms. His metrical practice can be seen as enacting the writer's
negotiations with the past which he describes in "Tradition and the Individual
Talent":

> The existing order is complete before the new work arrives; for order to per-
> sist after the supervention of novelty, the *whole* existing order must be, if ever
> so slightly, altered; and so the relations, proportions, values of each work of
> art toward the whole are readjusted; and this is conformity between the old
> and the new.[41]

Eliot wrote this two years after "Reflections on *Vers Libre,*" and it is intriguing
to see how the rhetoric of antagonism has been banished. Here we have not a

baleful struggle between old and new but a complex give-and-take in which both are transformed as they are united. If one applied this more general conceptual scheme to the issue of verse form, one might answer Cunningham's critique by saying that Eliot's poems relate to earlier verse not through parasitism but through a form of symbiosis. Perhaps, rather than either "symbiotic" or "parasitic," a nonfigurative adjective such as "intermittent" would be preferable. Eliot's handling of blank verse can be accurately described without being tendentious in either direction. Cunningham's analysis of the way much early twentieth-century free verse operates is brilliant as description, but might seem unpersuasive to some because of its mingling of ethical with esthetic standards. Are "responsible" and "irresponsible" apposite adjectives in regard to verse forms? The animus evident in Cunningham's vocabulary is understandable as a reaction not only to the writings of Eliot and Pound but to their immense influence over several decades, which created a hostile climate for the traditional versification that Cunningham favored. Not only a hostile climate, but an uncomprehending one. Cunningham and later formalists have felt with some justice that the free-verse revolution, at least after its early years, entrenched itself as a new orthodoxy, so that apprentice poets could quite easily advance in their careers without ever learning the rudiments of traditional prosody. In such a climate, "the inevitable iambic pentameter" was no longer inevitable by any means, and much of the blank verse that was written showed the pressure of the prosodic upheaval fostered by Eliot and Pound.[42]

V

The modernist challenge to blank verse played out in several ways in the years between the two world wars. It had an effect on both the blank verse that was written and the blank verse that was not written. The latter point is, of course, not capable of proof, but common sense suggests that younger poets in these years would have been more frequently drawn to the form were it not for the discouragement spread by literary arbiters like Pound and Eliot. It is striking, for example, to note the scarcity of blank verse in the repertoire of W. H. Auden, probably the most formally versatile poet to emerge in this period. We know that as an apprentice poet Auden was influenced by Hardy, Frost, Robinson, and others discussed in the early sections of this chapter. Furthermore, we know that his discovery of Eliot's poetry was a major impetus in his superseding the earlier styles he worked in.[43] It does not seem too fanciful to suppose that Eliot's disesteem for "the inevitable iambic pentameter" would communicate itself to his disciples.

Of course, there were also poets decidedly outside Eliot's orbit who gave blank verse a wide berth. One of the more puzzling examples is Yvor Winters. It might have been expected, given his espousal of traditional versification and his frequent willingness as a critic to comment disapprovingly on the blank verse of others, that he would have employed the meter with some frequency. But his *Collected Poems* includes only one poem in blank verse, a brief narrative drawn from mythology, entitled "Theseus: A Trilogy." The writing is marmoreally impressive. These lines describe the capture of the queen of the Amazons by Heracles, comrade-in-arms to Theseus:

> Remote and thin as a bird-call over ice
> From deep in the forest came the cry of her warriors,
> Defiance from Artemis, the evasive daemon:
> Hyppolyta smiled, but Heracles moved softly
> And seized her suddenly, bore her to the ship,
> Bound her and left her vibrating like a deer
> Astounded beyond terror.
>
>   (9–15)

As a narrative of three and a half pages, the trilogy is fatally overcompressed: it reads as if it had been cut down from something much longer. It is intriguing enough, however, to leave one speculating about the poems in blank verse that Yvor Winters did not write, or at least did not publish.

Our principal concern, however, should be with the published record. In this section we shall consider a number of poets active in the twenties and thirties—some near contemporaries of Eliot, others younger, but all born before 1910. If the discussion here seems somewhat miscellaneous, it could hardly be otherwise, given the lack of consensus regarding blank verse in this period. (In the case of poets with extended careers, some of the poems to be discussed were published during or after World War II, once again requiring a jump ahead into the period covered by the next chapter. In a survey like this, chronologies are bound to overlap.) For poets of this period who might try their hands at blank verse, it was one of a widening array of formal options. They could, of course, avoid it altogether by writing certain types of free verse, such as the short-lined imagist verse of poets like H.D. or William Carlos Williams, or the longer-lined verse derived from Whitman. If they did decide to give iambic pentameter a try, the stylistic developments of the early twentieth century gave them disparate models. They could pursue experiments with rhythm similar to Frost's, applying pressure on the metrical frame from within as they explored the dramatic possibilities of conversational speech. Or they could pursue a more conventional sort of verse line in which rhythm and meter were not so obtrusively in tension with one another—a more Wordsworthian style, this might be called. Or they could opt for Websterian or Eliotic effects, if they were avant-garde in their tastes, writing poems for which the label "blank verse" would be problematic because so many of their lines did not merely strain the meter through rhythmic variations but broke it in unpredictable ways. In all three of these approaches there was ample room for individual nuances of style: twentieth-century blank-verse poets do not "sound like" each other in the way that earlier poets influenced by Milton did. In such an active and experimental literary scene, attention to terminological exactness flagged; and as we have seen, it was possible for many of the first readers of modern poetry to mistake Frost's iambic pentameters for free verse, or to fail to recognize the extent to which many passages of Eliot relied on regular blank-verse lines for a kind of prosodic underpinning.

Eliot's influence is conspicuous in the writing of his younger contemporaries Hart Crane and Allen Tate, both born in 1899. In brief lyrics such as "Garden Abstract" and "The Fernery," Crane wrote iambic pentameter with only minor anomalies. In his longer poems, however, blank verse shares the stage with numerous lines (and sometimes extended passages) that notably depart from the meter. "For the Marriage of Faustus and Helen" offers a number of regular lines: "Across the memoranda, baseball scores" (5), "The earth may glide diaphanous to death" (41), "Beyond their million, brittle bloodshot eyes" (48), "The hands Erasmus dipped in gleaming tides" (127), and others. But quoting such lines in isolation gives a misleading impression of Crane's prosody in the poem. Like Eliot, Crane does not write enough pentameters *in sequence* for them to be established as a norm. A longer passage gives a more representative sampling of his practice:

O, I have known metallic paradises
Where cuckoos clucked to finches
Above the deft catastrophes of drums.
While titters hailed the groans of death
Beneath gyrating awnings I have seen
The incunabula of the divine grotesque.
This music has a reassuring way.

(78–84)

In this passage (actually one of the more conservative ones) Crane alternates between pentameter and tetrameter in his first five lines. This might lead us to expect that line 83 would be a tetrameter, in keeping with the odd, individualized pattern that appears to be forming. But no, rather than being shorter than a regular blank-verse line, this one is longer, and is the least iambic line of the set:

```
x  /  x  /  x x  /  x  x  /    x   /
```
The incunabula of the divine grotesque. .

Crane drops two anapests in a row into the middle of the line, drawing it out to twelve syllables. The content of the following line, "This music has a reassuring way," seems ironic in ways Crane may or may not have intended. "Reassuring" is not the word that would tend to occur to one attempting to analyze the fitful movement of Crane's verse.

Allen Tate's blank verse exhibits many of the same features. In the course of his discussion of "parasitic meter," J. V. Cunningham tartly comments on how "in many of Tate's poems most of the lines are fugitives from the iambic pentameter. It is, as he says, 'a little like the man who either avoids or steps upon all the cracks in the sidewalk.' In *The Wolves* he stepped upon five cracks out of twenty-seven."[44] It is true that the poem often shuns iambic pentameter: the first lines read, "There are wolves in the next room waiting / With heads bent low, thrust out, breathing" (1–2). The conclusion settles into a somewhat less distorted movement, perhaps as an effect of closure:

Now remember courage, go to the door,
Open it and see whether coiled on the bed
Or cringing by the wall, a savage beast

Maybe with golden hair, with deep eyes
Like a bearded spider on a sunlit floor
Will snarl—and man can never be alone.

(22–27)

If Tate's veerings from the pattern here seem less extreme than Crane's, it is probably because there are not here the drastic shifts in line length. Still, the warping is apparent: only lines 24 and 27 are strictly regular. Other striking pieces in this Websterian vein by Tate include "Aeneas at Washington" and "The Meaning of Life."

Breaking the pentameter became more and more an accepted practice in the 1920s and 1930s. Readers in later decades, accustomed to a broad range of techniques in modern verse, could easily fail to notice the deliberate subversion of meter in the sorts of poems here called Websterian because the meter was no longer "inevitable" in unrhymed verse. The boundary between blank verse and free verse, for many readers and even for some poets, became blurred. The excitement and confusion of these decades can be sensed in many poets whose achievements fall somewhat short of their ambitions. Archibald MacLeish is a useful figure to ponder, because he seems always to have had his antennae out for whatever stylistic effects were in the air. He wrote numerous rhyming poems, often experimenting with off-rhyme. His unrhymed poetry is derivative of many disparate types of free verse. He also wrote his share of Eliotic blank verse, but some of his poems are in traditional blank verse whose only "modern" effects are descriptive or syntactical—a lot of sharp sensory imagery and fractured or suspended sentences. At the more traditional end of his blank-verse spectrum are pieces like "Sketch for a Portrait of Mme. G——M——" and "Eleven," both published in a collection in 1926. "Ancestral," in the same volume, shows the poet attempting to add a visual dimension to what is in almost every full line iambic pentameter with standard variations:

The star dissolved in evening—the one star
The silently
                    and night O soon, now, soon
And still the light now
                    and still now the large
Relinquishing

<blockquote>
and through the pools of blue

Still, still the swallows

and a wind now

and the tree [. . .]

(1–10)
</blockquote>

If we relineate the poem according to the marginal capitals, ten lines compress to four recognizable pentameters and at last a sort of limp hexameter. The rest of the poem follows the metrical pattern as well. This is not "breaking the pentameter" in Pound's sense, but playing around with the typewriter. MacLeish seems to be looking nervously over his shoulder in writing poems like this, pursuing his modernist credentials in a facile way. The same calculating approach is evident in "Immortal Helix" and the fine childhood memory piece "Eleven"; in these, the only conspicuous break with the meter is that the final line of each is notably short—a little modernist jolt to remind us that it is the 1920s.

The perennially overlooked Conrad Aiken displays something of the same eclecticism. Aiken wrote traditional blank verse early in his career, often employing a high lyric style that seems fusty today. He becomes more readable as he allows himself to become sardonic. "The Wedding" recounts the fatal tryst of Tithonus the grasshopper with Arachne the spider. Arachne enjoys Tithonus's song, but not enough to forgo killing him:

> Arachne heard the song grow weaker, dwindle
> To first a rustle, and then half a rustle,
> And last a tick, so small no ear could hear it
> Save hers, a spider's ear. And her small heart,
> (Rusted away, like his, to a pinch of dust,)
> Gleamed once, like his, and died. She clasped him tightly
> And sunk her fangs in him. Tithonus dead,
> She slept awhile, her last sensation gone;
> Woke from the nap, forgetting him; and ate him.
>
> (38–46)

Most critics view the two meditative sequences *Preludes for Memnon* and *Time in the Rock* as Aiken's most significant work; these were begun in the late

twenties and completed by the midthirties. Aiken's formal choices vary unpre-
dictably from section to section in these sequences. Sometimes he uses rhyme,
sometimes free verse. The works contain many blank-verse passages, but they
are more likely than the earlier poetry to employ sporadic Eliotic effects. In his
more traditional vein, Aiken's iambic pentameter is graceful and flexible, as in
his deft handling of pauses, pointed up by punctuation, in these lines:

> And, on the bough that arches the deep pool,
> Lapped in a sound of water, the brown thrush
> Waits, too, and listens, till his silence makes
> Silence as deep as song. And time becomes
> A timeless crystal, an eternity,
> In which the gone and coming are at peace.
>
> (*Preludes for Memnon*, XX, 28–33)

In his more Eliotic or Poundian vein, the lines can veer noticeably from the
pattern:

> The world is everlasting—
>
> But for a moment only,
> The sunrise sunset moment at the pit's edge,
> The night in day, timeless for a time:
> Childhood is old age, youth is maturity,
> Simplicity is power, the single heart
> Cries like Memnon for the sun, his giant hand
> Lifting the sun from the eastern hill, and then
> Handing it to the west—
>
> (*Preludes for Memnon*, XLIV, 17–24)

Aiken's variations are sometimes modest: the slight lengthening and added
stress in

> x / x / x / x \ x / /
> The sunrise sunset moment at the pit's edge

do not greatly jar the iambic movement. More noticeable warping of the line
occurs in

```
     x  /   x  /   /   x  \ x  /
```
The night in day, timeless for a time"

—compressed through loss of a syllable—and

```
     /  x    /   x  \   x  /   x  / x    /
```
Cries like Memnon for the sun, his giant hand

—expanded by a syllable and disrupted by a trochaic movement in its opening phrase. It is unlikely that Aiken would have written this way without Eliot's example; however, as with MacLeish, his metrical experimentation seems tempered by an innate conservatism. There is much pleasurable reading to be found in Aiken's meditative sequences, but they fail to create a whole that is more than the sum of their parts. Aiken's stated ambition for the works, "planned to be an all-out effort at a probing of the self-in-relation-to-the-world, the formulation of a new *Weltanshauung*," outpaced the resources of his talent.[45] The sequence structure encourages discursiveness and repetitiveness. Aiken wrote of his attempt to "approximate some sort of spiral approach to what I thought."[46] As anyone knows who has climbed a spiral staircase in a windowed tower, the same landscape presents itself each time round, but any particular feature in it will each time appear smaller. Aiken's analysis of the modern consciousness seems in fact to spiral away from any central point as it proceeds in its exceedingly refined study of nuances.

Another near contemporary of Eliot, the Scottish poet Edwin Muir, wrote many durable poems that addressed modern concerns in a traditional style. Muir's archetypal symbolism and interest in myth have affinities with modernist monuments such as *The Waste Land* and *The Cantos*, but he does not indulge in the dramatic distortion and fragmentation of the verbal surface found in such works. In the plain, understated eloquence of his style he seems more akin to Robert Graves, although the particular mythic *topoi* favored by each poet are different. Like that of Graves, Muir's blank verse is solidly crafted and for the most part unflamboyant. He allows himself the occasional lengthening or shortening of a line for dramatic emphasis or for signaling a narrative or thematic turn. Although his conversational style does not usually entail such emphatic rhythmic straining as Frost's does, Muir resembles Frost in his free use of anapestic substitutions. This has mixed results. Used judiciously, the anapests seem to aid in the representation of easily flowing speech; but when used to excess, they lessen the energy of Muir's utterance as lines meander and syntax rambles.

Muir's personal circumstances—a poverty-stricken youth and a truncated education—isolated him from modernist influences when he was forming his style; moreover, he began to write poetry only in his midthirties. In *An Autobiography* he writes with characteristic modesty:

> I had no training; I was too old to submit myself to contemporary influences; and I had acquired in Scotland a deference towards ideas which made my entrance into poetry difficult. Though my imagination had begun to work I had no technique by which I could give expression to it. There were the rhythms of English poetry on the one hand, the images in my mind on the other. All I could do at the start was to force the one, creaking and complaining, into the mould of the other.[47]

As this suggests, Muir for the most part was satisfied with received forms as vehicles of perception and experience, both of which, in his best work, are conveyed with visionary power. His many fine poems in rhyme aside, he wrote some of the most memorable blank verse in Britain from the 1930s until his death in 1959. In most of these works the verse technique is unobtrusive while fully adequate to the purpose. In the brief, harrowing allegory of the Fall called "The Gate," the speaker recalls how "We sat, two children, warm against the wall / Outside the towering stronghold of our fathers" (1–2). The end of the poem is memorable in its quiet menace, which is communicated through rhythm as well as imagery. Sitting against "that fortress life," the children observe "the well-worn scene" of hillock and pond and finally

> A little stream that tinkled down the slope.
> But suddenly all seemed old
> And dull and shrunken, | shut within itself |
> In a sullen dream. | We were outside, alone. |
> And then behind us the huge gate swung open.

> (20–24)

Of course, the shortening of line 21 enacts the withering into "shrunken" adult reality for the children whose innocence is here meeting its end. The short line inaugurates a sequence of closely placed pauses that cut into short segments the phrasing, which earlier in the poem had been dreamily flowing. The last line, with horrible irony, swings open with an effect of pitiless closure:

```
        x    /   x  /    x   x   /    /    x    / (x)
      And then behind us the huge gate swung open.
```

This scansion actually downplays the terrific weight implied by the stressing, since a performer might well give a full stress to "swung." After all the loading of stresses toward the end of the line, the feminine ending offers a last, unsettling note, a touch of queasy cliffhanging. This is one of the most perfectly paradoxical conclusions ever given a poem, since in one sense all is "open" for these neophytes and in another sense nothing is. With beautiful simplicity, the rhythm shaping the last line mimes the paradox by setting heavy and light stresses in a skewed balance.

Muir usually employed blank verse for traditional modes—narratives and dramatic monologues, often mythical or visionary. His technical devices often hark back to poets before his own century. One bravura example is in "The Labyrinth," a monologue based on the myth of Theseus and the Minotaur.[48] The first thirty-four and a half lines of the poem are a single sentence, an ongoing maze of syntax whose convolutions and doublings-back reflect the labyrinth of the hero's ordeal. This is reminiscent (unusually for modern poetry) of some of Milton's extraordinarily intricate and sustained syntactic spans. The prodigious sentence takes up nearly half the poem.

This is not a typical device of Muir's. Normally his conversational style encourages shorter, simpler sentences. In his better poems, style often seems to attain a kind of transparency, so that the reader is impressed by the immediacy of what is conveyed. One of the finest religious poems of the twentieth century, "The Transfiguration," is also an outstanding example of Muir's blank verse. The poem narrates the Gospel story in the voice of one of the witnessing Apostles; in Muir's account not only Christ but the world surrounding him is transfigured:

> The source of all our seeing rinsed and cleansed
> Till earth and light and water entering there
> Gave back to us the clear unfallen world.

> (5–7)

With the fading of the vision, it comes to be for the speaker a portent of the Second Coming:

> Then he will come, Christ the uncrucified,
> Christ the discrucified, his death undone,
> His agony unmade, his cross dismantled—
> Glad to be so—and the tormented wood
> Will cure its hurt and grow into a tree
> In a green springing corner of young Eden,
> And Judas damned take his long journey backward
> From darkness into light and be a child
> Beside his mother's knee, and the betrayal
> Be quite undone and never more be done.

                                                (56–65)

This ten-line sentence, the conclusion of the poem, has nothing like the length and intricacy of the first sentence of "The Labyrinth." But this simpler phrasing nonetheless sustains a commanding eloquence. Any reader surveying Muir's blank verse should devote time to this piece, as well as others. Besides those already mentioned, some interesting ones are "Troy," "The Dreamt-of Place," "The River," "Moses," "The Killing," "Double Absence," "Antichrist," and "Prometheus."

It is not hard to find other poets who began writing between the two world wars and who resisted the blandishments of Eliot in favor of a stricter prosody. Robert Francis, who, as earlier noted, was critical of some of his mentor Frost's blank-verse effects, wrote numerous poems in the meter himself. These tend to be metrically conservative, with no Eliotic effects, although a reader may be amused to note how frequently they stray into what Frost called "loose iambic" through a free use of anapests. Especially in his earlier work, Francis recalls Frost in his subjects as well as his style, focusing on the New England countryside. Francis wrote one book-length poem in blank verse, *Valhalla*, which is more Robinsonian than Frostian in design, and which in any case is not a success. His better poems in the meter are shorter—usually much shorter than Frost's—and in their compression they operate within a lyric sphere rather than a narrative or a dramatic one. Clarity of description, conveyed through the voice of an unobtrusive observer, is the leading characteristic of such pieces, as the following excerpt will suggest:

Far inland from the sea the onion fields
Flow as the sea flows level to the sky.
Something blue of the sea is in their green.
Something bright of the sun on little waves
Of water is in the ripple of their leaves.

("Onion Fields," 1–5)

Francis's experiments with blank verse are not typically with the metrical line but with the forms within which his lines are contained. He is one of many twentieth-century blank-verse writers who try to give the meter a new look, as it were, by arranging it in stanzas. This practice, together with Francis's customary brevity, runs counter to traditional expectations of blank verse, which readers tend to associate with amplitude and with divisions into verse paragraphs of varying lengths. As the twentieth century wore on, it became clear that such assumptions were less firmly founded in regard to emerging work. Some of Francis's poems in unrhymed stanzas, like "Old Man Feeding Hens" and "Seagulls," are shaped with such lapidary precision that one feels in them something like the ghost of rhyme, governed as they are by structural balance, symmetry, and closure. When the poems on rare occasions extend to more than a page, as in "Juniper" and "As Near to Eden," both nonstanzaic, the verse is supple and as well suited to narrative and meditative purposes as to descriptive ones. Perhaps a need to stay clear of Frost's shadow kept Francis from writing more such pieces. As it is, much of his best work in the meter has an almost epigrammatic terseness. Other exemplary poems by him include "Meeting," "Hay Heaviness," "Waif," "Encounter," "The Dandelion Gatherer," and "Legend of Orient Point." The use of blank verse in the last named is somewhat paradoxical, since it is a tribute to Walt Whitman.

The long poem still had its devotees among conservative stylists. One such poet, regrettably little known in the United States, is the Canadian E. J. Pratt. Pratt, who lived from 1882 to 1964, was born and reared on the coast of Newfoundland and wrote many poems about life and death at sea. Many of these energetic narratives are rhymed and in this, as well as in their topics, they recall the work of John Masefield. The two extended poems in blank verse that fall within our survey are *Brébeuf and His Brethren* and *Toward the Last Spike*. *Brébeuf and His Brethren*, a work of 2,136 lines, tells of the mission and martyrdom of French Jesuits seeking to convert the Huron tribes in the early seventeenth century. *Toward the Last Spike* recounts in 1,626 lines the history of the building of Canada's transcontinental railroad in the late nineteenth century. Both poems are highly readable; in both cases, Pratt's dexterity in arranging an imposing quantity of historical data without esthetic compromise is impressive. Few modern works have been as successful in merging history and poetry.

Admittedly, some passages in these works present a challenge to the non-Canadian reader, for whom an annotated edition is advisable.[49] Even with annotation, some of the ins and outs of political and economic policy disputes narrated in *Toward the Last Spike* remain hermetic. The poem comes fully to life in depicting the epic struggle of man and his machines against a recalcitrant, sometimes deadly climate and terrain. Pratt's evocation of the wilderness slips without strain into the sublime when he expands on one politician's metaphor of the "seas of mountains" the railway line would have to cross:

> The big one was the mountains—seas indeed!
> With crests whiter than foam: they poured like seas,
> Fluting the green banks of the pines and spruces.
> An eagle-flight above they hid themselves
> In clouds. They carried space upon their ledges.
> Could these be overridden frontally,
> Or like typhoons outsmarted on the flanks?
>
> (953–59)

The same awareness of nature's peril and allure is just as strongly present in *Brébeuf and His Brethren*. Here, too, historical materials are absorbed with intelligent tact, and the greater challenge to the imagination of going so much farther back in time is effectively met. Pratt was an ordained Methodist minister who spent most of his career teaching English at Victoria College in the University of Toronto. This may seem an unlikely background to bring to bear upon this historical episode; nevertheless, the poet evokes the experiences of the Jesuit martyrs, including their devotional and mystical ones, with sympathetic understanding. One of the more remarkable features of the poem is its treatment of the tortures inflicted by the Huron and Iroquois upon the Jesuits and other victims. This is something that a lesser writer could easily sentimentalize or sensationalize. Pratt does neither. Without prettifying the events, he

keeps the martyrs' sometimes grotesque sufferings within the spiritual perspective that supplied their fortitude. The result is a somber, memorable drama
played out against a backdrop that is just as memorable, the wilderness

> Where in the winter the white pines could brush
> The Pleiades, and at the equinoxes
> Under the gold and green of the auroras
> Wild geese drove wedges through the zodiac.

> (77–80)

Pratt shows consistent skill in governing the strands of a complex narrative
and keeping the story moving; at the same time, as the lines above indicate, he
is able to glide effortlessly into a high lyric style at appropriate moments.
American readers will do themselves a favor by seeking out his work.

Another traditional stylist who may be mentioned here is John Betjeman.
His sort of career has no American equivalent: he parlayed his fascination
with Victoriana and British folkways into long-running success as a cultural
journalist and media personality. He even managed to engage an audience with
his passion for church architecture. Betjeman's poems are so self-consciously
English that they have deterred many American readers unfamiliar with the
locales and social nuances on which they focus. There is also a determinedly
antiquarian air to some of them, in which Betjeman writes as if he were a reincarnation of some minor Victorian poet. This act, or pose, is thoroughgoing:
Betjeman's early collections were set in typefaces and with page layouts that
deliberately recalled the formats of nineteenth-century books of verse. Betjeman
has a stong comic sense and obviously gets a lot of fun out of his Victorian im-
personations. He has been too easily pigeonholed as a nostalgic eccentric and
as a writer of light verse; neither characterization appreciates the subtlety of
his best writing. Some of his reanimations of outmoded verse forms demonstrate their viability for both poets and readers of the present day; and often
enough his apparently "light" poems gradually reveal a serious undercurrent,
fully disclosing it only near the end. His shorter blank-verse poems are not
numerous, but they illustrate well his strengths as a social observer and satirist.
Often the satire is intermittent and affectionate, as in the idyll "Beside the Sea-
side," a compact yet panoramic view of the typical middle-class family's summer holiday, and the similar "North Coast Recollections." Whether he is

describing people or their surroundings, Betjeman's ability to bring scenes to life has something of the art of the novelist. Side by side are passages of sensory immediacy and of social awareness; in the following lines we see one mode merge into the other:

> One child still zig-zags homewards up the lane,
> Cold on bare feet he feels the dew-wet sand.
> Behind him, from a walk along the cliff,
> Come pater and the mater and the dogs.
>
> Four macrocarpa hide the tennis club.
> The children of a chartered actuary
> (Beaworthy, Trouncer, Heppelwhite and Co.),
> Harold and Bonzo Trouncer are engaged
> In semi-finals for the tournament.
> "Love thirty!" Pang! across the evening air
> Twangs Harold's racquet. Plung! the ball returns.
>
> ("North Coast Recollections," 56–66)

The satiric blade is sometimes sharpened, as in "Bristol and Clifton," a dialogue poem in which an odiously smug churchwarden reveals with complete unselfconsciousness his littleness of soul.

Betjeman's longest poem in blank verse is the book-length *Summoned by Bells*, which tells the story of his early life until his departure from Oxford. The model here is clearly *The Prelude*, and Betjeman certainly recalls Wordsworth's theme of "the growth of a poet's mind" in amassing the enduring memories of childhood and youth that have nurtured his poetry. The work is nowhere nearly as profound as Wordsworth's, but it is well-written and by turns shrewd, funny, and touching. In one startling scene the schoolboy Betjeman gives copies of his poems

> To one who, I was told, liked poetry—
> The American master, Mr. Eliot.
> That dear good man, with Prufrock in his head
> And Sweeny waiting to be agonized,
> I wonder what he thought? He never says
> When now we meet, across the port and cheese.

He looks the same as then, long, lean and pale,
Still with the slow deliberating speech
And enigmatic answers. At the time
A boy called Jelly said "He thinks they're bad"—
But he himself is still too kind to say.

(Chapter 3, "Highgate," 128–38)

This work was published in 1960, just as the vogue for "confessional" poetry was emerging. It makes an interesting contrast, showing how a less sensationalized kind of autobiography, cast in a traditional meter rather than in the jaggeder verse of Robert Lowell's *Life Studies*, might in its quieter way find a niche.

Of the poets in this age-cohort there were many who made only sporadic forays into the meter. For example, Robert Penn Warren in his lengthy "Tale in Verse and Voices," *Brother to Dragons*, writes numerous lines of conventional blank verse but often veers fitfully into blank verse of a more Eliotic sort or into free verse. The poem's lurid plot, concerning the murder of a slave by two of Thomas Jefferson's nephews, tends to draw more attention than its unpredictable prosodic shifts. Born the same year as Warren, Stanley Kunitz, in the first, more formalist portion of his career, writes a number of blank-verse poems in an energetic but florid style. The simpler rhetoric of a later poem like "Indian Summer at Land's End" is more pleasing, and the meter of the piece is trim:

The season stalls, unseasonably fair,
blue-fair, serene, a stack of golden discs,
each disc a day, and the addition slow.

(1–3)

Kunitz is one of many poets of his generation—among them Auden—who use the meter sparingly. For some, the pressure of modernism may have been a discouraging factor, as we may suspect of the young Auden. But for others like Kunitz, it may have been simply an acceptance of the traditional association of the form with longer poems that held them back. With rare exceptions, the younger Kunitz concentrated on brief, rhyming lyrics, and might well have seen blank verse as peripheral to the scope of his talent. A similar set of conjectures might apply to Kunitz's close friend Theodore Roethke, who used the form even less frequently than Kunitz did.

It is likely that this traditionalistic view of genre, which tended to segregate blank verse from lyric, was shared by many women poets of this age group. Nowadays, critics are less likely than they once were to group together women poets of this or of any period. Doing so here may be useful in pointing up the surprising paucity of the form in the writing of several accomplished formalists of the time who were frequently linked in the mind of the reading public. It is clear that in the first half of the twentieth century most women poets were exploring different poetic terrains. Some unconventional stylists, such as Marianne Moore, Mina Loy, and H.D., wrote in free verse or in syllabics for the most part. At the other end of the stylistic spectrum, traditionalists like Elinor Wylie and Edna St. Vincent Millay were devoted to rhyme and showed little interest in prosodic experimentation. A small number of women poets, formalists of various kinds who specialized in lyric, wrote blank verse on occasion. It seems very much in order to give some attention to this slender but intriguing body of work before concluding this section.

Adelaide Crapsey intended to make the study of versification the center of her academic career; before her early death from tuberculosis she wrote a number of highly disciplined poems in old and new forms. She is best known for having invented the short syllabic poem called the cinquain, and produced many examples of it herself. Her principal piece in blank verse is "To the Dead in the Graveyard Underneath My Window," which she wrote while receiving unavailing treatment in Dr. Trudeau's famous sanitarium at Saranac Lake. It begins:

> How can you lie so still? All day I watch
> And never a blade of all the green sod moves
> To show where restlessly you turn and toss,
> Or fling a desperate arm or draw up knees
> Stiffened and aching from their long disuse;
> I watch all night and not one ghost comes forth
> To take its freedom in the midnight hour.
> Oh, have you no rebellion in your bones?
>
> (1–8)

The poem is marred toward the end by sprinklings of antiquated diction, but the poignancy of the speaker's protest, of her own rebellion against the fate to which so many of her fellow patients have succumbed, remains memorable.

Louise Bogan, like many women poets of her generation, was strongest as a writer of rhymed lyrics. Her excursions into blank verse were rare, and she seems to have been dissatisfied with the results: both "The Flume" and "A Letter," one narrative, the other epistolary, are left out of her definitive selection of her poems.[50] Both poems are certainly problematic, but they are well worth reading. Bogan had a subtler command of rhythm than other poets more widely acclaimed at the time, such as Wylie and Millay. She had some success as a writer of short stories. It would seem that she of all poets might find blank verse a congenial medium. One suspects that the inhibiting factors were psychological rather than technical. Some of the traumatic experiences that Bogan dealt with in an ellipitical and symbolic way in her memorable lyrics may have seemed overwhelming when approached within the more open framework of narrative. This supposition is supported by the fact that she was unable, despite many attempts, to write a prose book about her early life, either as a memoir or recast as fiction.

Of the two poems, "A Letter" is less metrically orthodox. The implied background is one of convalescence: the speaker, recovering from a nervous breakdown in the country, addresses a former lover who may or may not have precipitated her crisis. As an isolated observer, she registers the details of her surroundings with a sort of entranced particularity: "The thickets not yet stark, but quivering / With tiny colors, like some brush strokes in / The manner of the pointillists" (4–6). The avid concentration on minutiae comes to seem morbid and overwrought, and the rhythms reinforce this by giving to many lines an uneasy, rocking motion. Many of these lines are also long, sometimes by several syllables:

> Here I could well devise the journey to nothing,
> At night getting down from the wagon by the black barns,
> The zenith a point of darkness, breaking to bits,
> Showering motionless stars over the houses.
> Scenes relentless—the black and white grooves of a woodcut.
>
> (15–19)

Statistically, the majority of lines in the poem are given to breaking into this sort of anapestic or dactylic canter. It is as though the speaker's raw nerves resist the tranquility of iambic movement.

"The Flume," a narrative similar in length to one of Frost's, has a larger share of standard pentameters but allows itself a good many longer lines. It, too, deals with fraught emotions, using the imagery of the eponymous water-course to represent a woman's troubled marriage and the turbulence of her jealousy. Bogan describes her protagonist crouching in fright during a thunderstorm while struggling with her other tumultuous feelings:

> One woman frightened in a dusty corner
> Who bit her fist and wished to pluck the thunder
> From its swinging tree, to throw it down forever
> Against the pastures it could not destroy,
> And after the thunder, run and stop the dam,
> The endless fountainous roar of falling water,
> And scratch her heart free from the itching love
> So much like sound, never spending itself,
> Never still, in any quietest room.
>
> (88–96)

Here there is not as much lengthening of the lines; the last line is in fact what metrists call a "clipped" or "headless" pentameter, missing its first unstressed syllable. (An anapestic substitution in the last foot evens out the syllable count in this particular case.) Overflowing their bounds or clenched tight within them, Bogan's blank-verse lines are imbued with energies of an unhappy kind. "The Flume" ultimately founders from an unconvincing narrative resolution, but like "A Letter" it offers vivid evocations of place viewed from a disturbed perspective.

Two of Bogan's American contemporaries, Babette Deutsch and Marya Zaturenska, used blank verse for markedly different purposes; like Bogan, they used it infrequently. Deutsch wrote both in free verse and in fixed forms, in which she usually rhymed. Her few blank-verse poems engage the meter tentatively. "Need" raises questions of definition, since its twelve lines include five with end-rhyme, and there are a few internal rhymes as well. The rhymes are so widely spaced, however, that they do not greatly impress themselves, at least at first, upon the reader. Another piece, "Departure," which is one line longer than a sonnet, also includes occasional rhyme and assonance. When Deutsch dispenses with rhyme in a third piece, "Urban Pastoral," the prosody becomes far more restless than in the other two pieces. Iambic pentameter provides the underpinning which can be heard in lines like "Here the afternoon city plays at being / A dream of summer's: gaiety in repose" (9–10). In other cases Deutsch seems to aim for a kind of balance by playing off a shorter line against an expanded one; as in the first two lines in the following passage:

> The walks are for pigeons and ladies
> Like parched pigeons, avoiding the bench where a tramp
> Rustily sleeps. The carriages in the park
> Are babies' now; children make all the traffic.
>
> (4–7)

A little lurch, and then the pentameter returns. Deutsch's modifications here are hardly drastic, but perhaps for that very reason one wonders why they seemed desirable to her. They may bespeak a slight discomfort with the received form, which perhaps did not entirely accord with her conceptions of lyric.

We find a similar caution and individualistic tweaking in Marya Zaturenska's blank verse. Again, it is a slender corpus. In one early poem, "The Dream," the speaker recounts her dream of visiting a flower-bedecked cemetery (at the end of the piece she finds herself looking at her own tombstone). The mild distortion of some lines is reminiscent of Deutsch's (and for that matter, of numerous other modern poets').

> The cemetery reached, I saw the flowers,
> Live roots among the dead, blazing in dark
> Red bloom on marble, purple on the tombs,
> Flushed in the light, like an expiring passion—
> No ghost, no shadow stirred.
> The reassuring blood raced through my veins,
> x / x / x \ x /   / x
> Aware and deathless in the dead meadow.
>
> (5–11)

Line 9, marking a notable pause, is conspicuously short (missing its last two feet), but it is regularly iambic. Line 11 is more subtly expressive. The relative weakness of "in" as an accented syllable and the unusual trochee in place of a final iamb give the line a crumbling or curdling quality which ironically undercuts the "reassuring" note of the line preceding it. Zaturenska's most imposing work in the meter is a dramatic monologue, "Daydream and Testament of Elizabeth Eleanor Siddall," giving voice to D. G. Rossetti's ill-fated wife, model, and muse, who speaks on the verge of committing suicide. Here the handling of meter is freer than in "The Dream." In this intense piece Zaturenska gravitates between iambic pentameter and fairly numerous longer lines:

> The dark horizon narrowed, shrunken, closing
> Until it crushed the heart, and the deep heavenly music
> Floated unheard into a netherworld.
>
> (34–36)

Zaturenska manages this ebb and flow in line length gracefully enough, but as with Bogan and Deutsch, one wonders if many of the same effects might not have been achievable through a less fitful array of variations.

The English poet Ruth Pitter, a contemporary of the Americans just discussed, seems more at ease than any of them in her blank verse, although it was not for her a frequently chosen form. Her finest poems are rhymed, many of them mystical in theme, such as "The Eternal Image" and "The Task." Pitter's blank-verse poems are too singular to seem derivative, but they are happily at home in the English poetic tradition. "Storm" describes an actual thunderstorm and meditatively develops it as a metaphor for the mind's internal tempests. Pitter is not afraid of a higher level of diction, as when she describes

> the hideous face of storm,
> All in a moment changing balefully
> Wholesome to fell, and homeliest to strange:
> A yellow awe and a swift pestilence
> Precipitating natural decays.
>
> (6–10)

The somewhat "literary" vocabulary is anchored firmly to exact sense impressions, here registering the startling change in light that precedes a storm, which the first line of the poem describes even more succinctly: "I have seen daylight turn cadaverous." In the briefer "The Strawberry Plant" Pitter renders her subject with Pre-Raphaelite exactitude:

One greenish berry spangling into yellow
Where the light touched the seed: one fruit achieved
And ripe, an odorous vermilion ball
Tight with completion, lovingly enclasped
By the close cup whose green chimed with the red [. . .]

                                                    (5–9)

Her most technically remarkable poem in blank verse is "The Swan Bathing."
This has the sort of descriptive finesse found in one of Marianne Moore's or
Elizabeth Bishop's animal poems, but it has a more elaborate lyric quality than
is typical of those poets. This is achieved through the slow, fluent rhythmic
handling and suspended syntax, with shifts in stress to accord with described
motions, but even more through the brilliant proliferation of feminine endings in the piece. Of the twenty-six lines, all but three have feminine endings.
The poem draws the reader into its current, tracing the choreography of the
swan's movements:

        then as if fainting he falls sidelong,
    Prone, without shame, reveals the shiplike belly
    Tumbling reversed, with limp black paddles waving,
    And down, gliding abandoned, helplessly wallows,
    The head and neck, wrecked mast and pennon, trailing.

                                                    (7–11)

Pitter also wrote many humorous animal poems, some of which are in blank
verse with tongue-in-cheek antique touches.

A word should be added about Kathleen Raine, another British poet inclined toward expressing visionary experience in verse. As with Pitter, her best
poems of this kind are in other forms—in Raine's case sometimes rhyme,
sometimes open form and shorter lines (see, for instance, the fine lyric "The
Moment").[51] Two poems in blank verse, both of nearly epigrammatic brevity,
are the untitled piece beginning "Happy the captive and enchanted souls" and
"Whitsuntide, 1942." Both poems affirm the divine presence in nature and, in
the case of the second, yearn for more continuous awareness of it. Raine's attraction to spiritual themes and to an incantatory style seems to have led her
away from blank verse—perhaps, even at such a late date, the shadow of Milton
was an inhibiting factor.

Here must end what threatens to become an endless catalogue. Populous as it has become, this account of blank-verse writers in the first half of the twentieth century has one conspicuous gap. The next (and final) section of this chapter will undertake to fill it.

VI

Wallace Stevens requires a section to himself for several reasons. First, there is the level and breadth of his achievement. Stevens was one of the most prolific writers of blank verse among the modernists of his generation, and some of his poetry in the form is superb. "Sunday Morning," of course, is one of the great blank-verse poems not just of the twentieth century but of all time. Harvey Gross speaks for many critics in writing, "It would require a small book to assay the prosodic gold which shows in Stevens' blank verse. He is the superlative modern master of the form."[52] Gross's last sentence prompts the second reason for some extended discussion, which may begin with a cluster of questions. How accurate is this judgment, and what did Stevens's mastery consist of? What are the distinctive traits of Stevens's blank verse that made it memorable in so many poems? Furthermore, is Stevens's blank verse all of a piece, or did it metamorphose from the early to the later phases of his career? The answer to this last will be obvious to most knowledgeable readers: "Sunday Morning" and "An Ordinary Evening in New Haven" do not sound very much alike. Why so great a difference, if the same meter remains a central resource to Stevens over the course of several decades? Looking at these and related matters, we will find ourselves focusing on issues of general significance to the study of blank verse in the modern period. Stevens was as idiosyncratic a poet as ever lived, and yet his experiments with prosody shed light on the practice of other poets—not only his contemporaries, but poets who were born after his death.

If we begin by looking at the blank verse of poems in Stevens's first collection, we must remind ourselves that these are early poems, but not youthful ones. *Harmonium* was not published until Stevens was well over forty. The poised and fluent blank verse of "Sunday Morning" and its companions in the volume demonstrates a full awareness of the ins and outs of traditional iambic pentameter as well as occasional indulgence in modernist embellishments. "Sunday Morning" very quickly settles into a blank verse which has for many critics recalled Keats and Tennyson, although its first sentence reveals hints of the modernist challenge to tradition:

> x   / x \ x   x   /   x   x   /
> Complacencies of the peignoir, and late
>
> / x   x   / x   x   / x / x   /
> Coffee and oranges in a sunny chair,
>
> x   x   /   / x / x / x /
> And the green freedom of a cockatoo
>
> x / x /   / x x / x /
> Upon a rug mingle to dissipate
>
> x / x /   x /   x   / x /
> The holy hush of ancient sacrifice.

(1–5)

Line by line the verse becomes less eccentric, more identifiable as blank verse until it reaches absolute regularity in line 5. Beginning with the odd bumpiness of two successive anapests in line 1, which on top of that is a foot short, each departure from the pattern is progressively less peculiar; line 5 as the conclusion of this sequence comes to seem something of a goal, an achieved destination, a perfected design.[53] And from here on the poem generally observes the requisites of the meter with standard variations, gracefully applied. It is not altogether fanciful to associate the complacencies of the lady and the freedom of the cockatoo with the laxity of metrical norms; the more regular meter that follows could be said to be attuned to the disciplined meditation on the decline of religious belief in modern Western civilization that occupies the remainder of the poem. This tightening of the verse does not prevent Stevens from embodying his argument in images as sensuously appealing as those of lines 1–3:

> Their chant shall be a chant of paradise,
> Out of their blood, returning to the sky;
> And in their chant shall enter, voice by voice,
> The windy lake wherein their lord delights,
> The trees, like serafin, and echoing hills,
> That choir among themselves long afterward.

(96–101)

Other poems in *Harmonium* demonstrate equally well Stevens's gift for joining iambic pentameter to his characteristic idiom. Two fifteen-line pieces that appear side by side, "On the Manner of Addressing Clouds" and "Of Heaven Considered as a Tomb," are models of Stevens's use of regular meter in the short form. Both poems tackle a serious theme in a playful style; though their central images differ, both are about the human weakness for anthropomorphizing natural phenomena. The second piece is especially memorable, toying with the image of the stars as lanterns carried by wandering ghosts, inviting from them a response to human curiosity that the speaker's ironic tone suggests is not likely to materialize: "Make hue among the dark comedians, / Halloo them in the topmost distances / For answer from their icy Élysée" (13–15). We also find regular meter, for the most part, in poems ranging from the brief "The Worms at Heaven's Gate" to the expansive picaresque narrative, "The Comedian as the Letter C," the longest poem in *Harmonium*.

Of course, even in this early phase Stevens tries out some idiosyncratic tactics in certain pieces. Some poems often classed as blank verse use rhyme more than incidentally: "Le Monocle de Mon Oncle" is an example, as is "Sea Surface Full of Clouds," which not only rhymes at key junctures but rhymes bilingually on an altering French refrain. While the fifteen-line sections of "Sunday Morning" are large enough to seem equivalent to the verse paragraphs of longer blank-verse poems, "Le Monocle de Mon Oncle" is in eleven-line sections; that does not sound like a great difference but nonetheless serves to give the work a choppier, stanzaic feel. And many pieces exhibit the sort of bending of versification found in the opening lines of "Sunday Morning." Sometimes, as it did there, the irregularity supports a mood or a turn of argument with its small injection of disorder. For instance, "A High-Toned Old Christian Woman" contrasts the conventional worldview of its title character with the agnostic estheticism that declares in the wrenched opening line,

> /x x / x x /   / x   x /
> Poetry is the supreme fiction, madame.[54]

The contrast depends in part on images of music: for the devout old woman "The conscience is converted into palms, / Like windy citherns hankering for hymns" (4–5). The speaker, though, allies himself with the procession of "disaffected flagellants" (i.e., those who have lost their faith), who, while they are

Proud of such novelties of the sublime,

    x   /   x   /   x   /   x   /   /

Such tink and tank and tunk-a-tunk-tunk,

May, merely may, madame, whip from themselves

A jovial hullabaloo among the spheres.

(17–20)

Stevens could easily enough have written "Such tink and tank and tunk-a-tunk-a-tunk," satisfying the meter as well as his yen for xylophone effects. But he wrote "tunk-a-tunk-tunk," omitting the unstressed syllable from the last foot to give the end of the line a ragtime movement, pointing up the difference between these earthier tunes and the sort of decorous, anemic hymns one can imagine issuing from the old woman's windy citherns. This is not the same as a rhetorical shift in stress creating what Frost called "strained relation" between rhythm and meter in a line, but it seems an analogous device in that it is localized and used for tonal emphasis. If tactics such as this defined the scope of Stevens's prosodic experiments, his record as a writer of blank verse would be far less problematic than it is.

Stevens's practice in wielding the iambic pentameter line becomes more aberrant after *Harmonium:* not all at once, and not according to some graphable progression, but increasingly though spasmodically. Certainly some poems later than *Harmonium* exhibit considerable regularity: "Academic Discourse at Havana," for instance, or "Lions from Sweden," or the deservedly famous "The Idea of Order at Key West," although this last makes significant use of rhyme and includes some lines that overrun the pentameter or are only dubiously iambic. What happens in Stevens's work as his career unfolds is that such anomalous lines become far more frequent. One wonders if his strange midcareer hiatus, the several years in the late twenties and early thirties during which he wrote little poetry, had a fundamental if mysterious effect on his later writing. (Stevens himself touches on this idea, writing to Morton Zabel in 1933: "I do not much like the new things that I write. Writing again after a discontinuance seems to take one back to the beginning rather than to the point of discontinuance."[55]) Critics typically take refuge in generalities in discussing this development (or deterioration). We find "prose" or "conversation" invoked to explain the loosening of meter, as in some comments by Harvey Gross, who is far more particular in his analyses than most. Writing about some lines from "To an Old Philosopher in Rome," Gross describes them as having "a blank verse base and prose rhythm."[56] About the later Stevens in general, he remarks, "Stevens never wrenches his tone to accommodate the meter. He never omits syllables to achieve a more precise beat, but allows the movement of conversation to take over whenever the argument of the poem demands it."[57] This last comment, of course, comes perilously close to inviting the question, "Why have meter at all?" If the "argument" is what is of paramount importance, and if regular meter is seen as an obstacle to its development, then it is difficult to see why Stevens should dally at all with what is to be so frequently distorted or abandoned.

One of the most helpfully exact discussions of Stevens's versification, compact but nicely detailed, comes in an essay by Donald Justice, "The Free-Verse Line in Stevens." Justice sees Stevens as following Eliot's suggestion of withdrawing from a simple metrical form, in this case iambic pentameter, and he points out that the most frequent means by which Stevens does this is through anapestic substitutions. He asserts that

> what is remarkable and unexpected about Stevens's practice is that, within the generally loosening line, the foot itself is loosened almost exclusively in one way only: an anapest takes the place of the basic iamb. In the history of versification this is probably unprecedented. In Stevens the traditionally reversed foot, a trochee for an iamb, does occasionally appear, but far more common is his addition of a third syllable to the two syllables of the basic iamb—"anapestic stretching." Conventionally, extra syllables of this type are thought to lighten the movement of the line, but the effect of lightness is intermittent in Stevens's handling and surely no significant part of the metrical intention.[58]

The description of Stevens's recourse to anapests as "unprecedented" may be overstated, but Justice has identified an undeniably prevalent feature in Stevens's later approach to (or we might rather say his departure from) blank verse. From his middle period on, numerous lines are provided with an anapestic bounce, or more than one. Here are some examples:

> The meaningless plungings of water and the wind
>
> ("The Idea of Order at Key West," 30)

> Without the inventions of sorrow or the sob
>
> ("Esthétique du Mal," V, 2)

> The quiet was part of the meaning, part of the mind
>> ("The House Was Quiet and the World Was Calm," 11)

> The major abstraction is the idea of man
>> (*Notes Toward a Supreme Fiction*, "It Must Be Abstract," X, 1)

As Justice notes, in some of Stevens's very late poems, the distending of the line becomes extreme. Here is an example from one of the best known:

> x   / x   /   x   / x   / x x   /
> The threshold, Rome, and that more merciful Rome
>
> x /   x / x / x x /   x x   /
> Beyond, the two alike in the make of the mind.
>
> / x x / x x / x   / x /
> It is as if in a human dignity
>
> x / x / x x   / x x   / x x   /
> Two parallels become one, a perspective, of which
>
> /   x   x   / x x / x   / x /
> Men are part both in the inch and in the mile.
>> ("To an Old Philosopher in Rome," 6–10)

If line 9, with its substitution of three anapests for the last three iambs, illustrates Justice's description obviously, the following line shows how the penchant for anapests combines with other tactics to complicate the sound. The enjambment and the lack of a definite article throws a strong stress onto "Men." There follows the pair of anapests and the return to iambs. If the line is scanned this way it can be rationalized by viewing "Men" as the stressed half of a clipped iamb. The manipulation seems to underscore the waltz-like rhythm of the first part of the line. This is a small detail, but it serves to point out that the proliferation of anapests is not the only sort of prosodic phenomenon to be observed in such poems. And this passage, like many another in Stevens's middle and later work, suggests that his aim more and more became one of evading the metrical norms he began with, in an adaptation keyed to his own style of Eliot's program of pentameter-breaking.

Stevens's loosening of the iambic pentameter line is concurrent with his increasing use—especially in longer poems—of the unrhymed tercet. It would be difficult to establish a cause-and-effect relationship, but it seems likely that the two things are linked at some level. As we have noted before, any type of stanza is somewhat at odds with the traditional uses of blank verse, transferring attention as it does from the line to the recurring segment that contains it. Stevens showed an interest in the tercet early, in "Sea Surface Full of Clouds" and other poems, and one can find examples among these in which regular meter is maintained. "Tea at the Palaz of Hoon," save for admitting two hexameters in its final stanza, is regular, as is "Sea Surface Full of Clouds." But this settled state of things was not to last, as we see from these stanzas from *Notes Toward a Supreme Fiction:*

> To sing jubilas at exact, accustomed times,
> To be crested and wear the mane of a multitude
> And so, as part, to exult with its great throat,
>
> To speak of joy and to sing of it, borne on
> The shoulders of joyous men, to feel the heart
> That is the common, the bravest fundament [...]

("It Must Give Pleasure," I, 1–6)

Here most of the lines find room for an anapest. This, however, is conservative in stretching compared with the final three stanzas of "An Ordinary Evening in New Haven":

> These are the edgings and inchings of final form,
> The swarming activities of the formulae
> Of statement, directly and indirectly getting at,
>
> Like an evening evoking the spectrum of violet,
> A philosopher practicing scales on his piano,
> A woman writing a note and tearing it up.
>
> It is not in the premise that reality
> Is a solid. It may be a shade that traverses
> A dust, a force that traverses a shade.

(XXXI, 10–18)

It is speculative but not unreasonable to think that Stevens's concentration on the larger unit of the tercet encouraged his increasing laxity in regard to the integrity of the individual line. Sometimes it seems that the tercet provides an arena in which regular lines can be played off against those less regular:

> Here, being visible is being white,
> Is being of the solid of white, the accomplishment
> Of an extremist in an exercise . . .
>
> ("The Auroras of Autumn," II, 13–15)

It may seem surprising that such leaps in and out of regular meter do not disrupt the reader's attention more than they do. Probably much of the credit for this is owing to Stevens's imposingly extended sentences, often overriding the bounds not merely of a few lines but of several tercets. A nagging feeling may eventually accost some readers, a suspicion that the later Stevens is more interested in writing sentences than in shaping lines of verse. This brings us back to the applauding views of Stevens's prosody that we quoted earlier, perhaps with an additional skepticism both in regard to them and to Stevens. To Harvey Gross, Stevens's adventures with meter chart a course of esthetic progress, as we see from his discussion of the tercet form: "The three-line stanza, the open rhythms approaching blank verse, and a new clarity of texture mark the final evolution of Stevens's prosody."[59] Writing about the late poem "The World as Meditation," the same critic drifts into metaphor: "Specific phonetic values, the densities of consonant and vowel hardly exist as 'prosody'— though we may hear, something like a string quartet playing in some distant room, the music of blank verse."[60] Although he is more down-to-earth in his appreciation than Gross is, Donald Justice also writes out of an assumption that Stevens's changes were positive in their results. He summarizes Stevens's handling of the blank-verse line as a history of "treating it with ever increasing casualness—the easy condescension of the master—until in the general loosening process both the iambic and the pentameter were to become nearly inaudible. Only the pattern, or in some lines the mere outline of a pattern, was left."[61] Like Gross's distant string quartet, Justice's "nearly inaudible" pattern is presented as the summit of achievement. We notice here Justice's phrase, "the easy condescension of the master," and we recall Gross's hailing of Stevens as "the superlative modern master" of blank verse. Leaving aside the question of whether it is a poet's place to condescend to this or to any meter, we may feel puzzled by this conception of mastery. Usually mastering a technique means making creative use of it, but in this case it seems to mean getting as far away from it as possible. Stevens himself was both cavalier and candid in a statement contributed to an anthology in 1938: "There is such a complete freedom now-a-days in respect to technique that I am rather inclined to disregard form so long as I am free and can express myself freely. I don't know of anything, respecting form, that makes much difference."[62] In fact, this is only a slightly more extreme version of the attitude expressed by Eliot in a sentence quoted earlier: "Swinburne mastered his technique, which is a great deal, but he did not master it to the extent of being able to take liberties with it, which is everything."

We are venturing, together with these critics, onto some slippery, paradoxical ground. Justice's essay is entitled "The Free-Verse Line in Stevens," though, as we have seen, his analysis of this particular type of free verse line treats it as an adaptation of iambic pentameter. At what point does blank verse become free verse under the pressure of experimentation? This is a time-honored question. As J. A. Symonds noted in the 1890s, "Indeed, so variable is its structure that it is by no means easy to define the minimum of metrical form below which a Blank Verse ceases to be a recognizable line."[63] Stevens in his later work illustrates the truth of this with a vengeance. He operates on the treacherous border between metrical and free verse, and his most admiring critics do not always seem sure when the border has been crossed.

If we think of "Sunday Morning" as one end of a spectrum and "To an Old Philosopher in Rome" as the other, we can see Stevens's writing as epitomizing the early twentieth-century poet's experience of blank verse—first as something to be mastered, then, more dubiously, as something to be modified. Both poems have their excellences, but it is the first, not the second, that is held up to students as a model of the form. Stevens undoubtedly was a master of blank verse when he chose to be; frequently, though, he indulged in metrical manipulations that severely distorted the character of the line. His practice, including some of his quirks and what can be viewed as confusions, has left its mark on later poetry.[64] Stevens's late poems in this form (if they *are* in this form) are sometimes masterly, but they may be thought by certain readers to succeed despite rather than because of their idiosyncratic prosody.

AFTER MODERNISM

|

THE LAST chapter ended on a cautionary note regarding the later blank verse of Stevens. This chapter needs to begin by posting a warning sign yet more emphatic and more generalized. In the period we are about to explore (roughly, the late 1930s to the present), many poets have treated iambic pentameter more as a point of departure than as a form consistently sustained. The great volume and variety of their modernist-influenced experiments make this period a perplexing one for the young poet in search of models. Suppose such a serious novice has in his head the sound of the traditional pentameter, something on the order of Tennyson's "The woods decay, the woods decay and fall." What then will he make of the opening of a poem like this one, by Delmore Schwartz?

>   /   x / x / x / x /
> In the naked bed, in Plato's cave,
>
>   x / x / x / x / x /
> Reflected headlights slowly slid the wall,
>
>   / x x / x / x x / x / x
> Carpenters hammered under the shaded window,
>
>   /   / x x / x / x / \ /
> Wind troubled the window curtains all night long,

```
x   /  x   /      /    x   /    /   x
A fleet of trucks strained uphill, grinding,

     x    /      /  x   x   / x /
Their freights covered, as usual.

   x   / x   /   x    x  /    x   /   x   /x   /
The ceiling lightened again, the slanting diagram

    /   /  x   /
Slid slowly forth.
```

("In the Naked Bed, in Plato's Cave," 1–8)

The first line is docked of its first syllable but is otherwise, like line 2, perfectly regular. But after this, Schwartz sacrifices meter to expressive sound effects: the tap-tap-tap of hammers in line 3, the rumpling flap of curtains in line 4, the uphill grind of the trucks in lines 5 and 6. There is no such obvious expressive purpose for the long, ungainly line 7, but by this time the poem has moved so definitely away from an iambic pattern that its awkwardness is less jarring than it would be in a more regular verse passage. Schwartz returns intermittently to regular meter in the rest of the piece: of its twenty-eight lines, nine are regular or exhibit only minor variations. All these rhythmic gymnastics make it an interesting poem to read, but *as a model of blank verse* it is decidedly wanting.

We will meet with such phenomena recurrently throughout this chapter. To the apprentice poet wishing to master the form, it is only fair to urge great selectivity in the search for archetypes. Robert Lowell, Mona Van Duyn, Dylan Thomas, and a good many others we shall be looking at are well worth reading, but it appears that in shaping the blank-verse line, maintaining traditional versification was not their highest priority. On the other hand, we can confidently recommend as models poets who write according to exacting prosodic standards while employing a contemporary idiom: Richard Wilbur, Edgar Bowers, Charles Gullans, Helen Pinkerton, Turner Cassity, Philip Stephens, and Joshua Mehigan, among others. Anyone who reads the blank verse of the twentieth century widely and carefully will find it an interesting game to arrange poets along a scale of prosodic practice: some have stayed comfortably within bounds while others operate on the fringe of meter. And some have gravitated back and forth, as we shall see.

II

Looking at the poets born in the decade preceding 1920, we may feel less compelled than at other points to apologize for the artificiality of period categories. These, after all, were poets who spent their youth living through the back-to-back traumas of the Great Depression and the Second World War, in which several of them saw combat. These were defining experiences of a kind that puts a lasting stamp on a generation and its literature. As to literature, much of the discussion in the last chapter about poets in the wake of modernism applies to these younger ones as well: that gigantic influence was still being absorbed, assimilated, or resisted by this group, as by its elders, in the 1930s and beyond. The prevalence of Eliotic or other looser forms of blank verse during this epoch demonstrates as much.

If we make allowance for this trend toward a looser line, blank verse is by no means hard to find in the writing of numerous poets who came of age in the thirties. One who made copious use of it was Randall Jarrell. Jarrell first became widely known for his many poems on military life and death—often with a focus on the air force—during the war. In "Second Air Force," a woman visiting her airman son views the activities of the base as they say good-bye at the gate:

> The armorers in their patched faded green,
> Sweat-stiffened, banded with brass cartridges,
> Walk to the line; their Fortresses, all tail,
> Stand wrong and flimsy on their skinny legs,
> And the crews climb to them clumsily as bears.

> (11–15)

Later in the poem she fantasizes a battle scene:

> She hears the bomber calling, *Little Friend!*
> To the fighter hanging in the hostile sky,
> And sees the ragged flame eat, rib by rib,
> x /   x   / x \   x   /   / x x   /
> Along the metal of the wing into her heart:

> The lives stream out, blossom, and fall steadily
> x x /   x x /   x   /
> To the flames of the earth, the flames
> That burn like stars above the lands of men.

(37–43)

By the time Jarrell wrote this, departures from standard meter (slight in the first passage, greater in the second) were unsurprising to readers of blank verse. Jarrell juxtaposes perfectly regular lines with wrenched ones. In this piece, and often in others, the prosodic disturbances are linked to moments of emotional intensity or emphasize elements of description. As stresses are shifted and syllables added or subtracted, one senses improvisation more than technical assurance. Jarrell's poems hold attention more through sharpness of observation and (in some pieces) the wit or pathos of their phrasing than through their prosody. For Jarrell as for many others, Eliot's method proved difficult to apply with sensitivity. What we discern in the passage above is not the continued presence of the ghost of meter, but an almost mechanical pattern of lurches back and forth between a workaday sort of pentameter and whatever weird assault on its contour strikes the poet's fancy.

Jarrell used his version of blank verse extensively (without mercy, one might say) throughout his several collections. For the reader willing to overlook patches of rhythmic monotony and the punctuating jolts that interrupt them, a good many of these poems retain interest. Some other pieces on the war that are strong in whole or in part are "A Pilot from the Carrier," "A Front," "Losses," and "1945: The Death of the Gods." Among his nonmilitary pieces, there are attractive examples in a variety of modes. "The Place of Death" is a meditation on mortality by means of a near-photographic depiction of a cemetery with interwoven references to the philosophy of Spinoza. "The Knight, Death, and the Devil," with its punctilious rendering of Dürer's famous engraving, is one of the best modern ecphrastic poems. The late poem "Well Water," almost brief enough to be an epigram, is agile and graceful in encapsulating wisdom. Some pieces, once widely admired, like "A Girl in a Library," now seem dated as well as arch and condescending. In general, Jarrell's hand is less sure in the nondescriptive parts of his narratives and in most of his dramatic poems. He admired poems like Frost's "A Servant to Servants" extravagantly, but he had nothing like Frost's ability to create character through a voice. His disturbed women in "*Seele im Raum*," "The Woman at the Washington Zoo," and others remain two-dimensional case studies. (The one exception to this is the female speaker in the fine late poem "Next Day," but that is done in elaborate rhymed stanzas.) If he faltered in portraying others, he fared better at self-portraiture. Among his late autobiographical works, his meditation on memory and childhood, "Thinking of the Lost World," stands high as a touching and unsolemn approach to a Wordsworthian theme. This is a particularly good example of a poem whose charm transcends its meter, which is loose indeed. One's skeptical reactions to Jarrell's versification should no doubt be balanced by acknowledging that his frequent use of iambic pentameter helped keep the meter in view—albeit in a problematic form—in the middle years of the twentieth century. Like so many of his circle, Jarrell died prematurely, but not before leaving a sizable body of work that grounds itself in the meter even as it pursues sometimes questionable variations on it.

Delmore Schwartz was another who found blank verse an inviting and flexible option. We have already glanced at one of his poems. Schwartz wrote in both tighter and looser pentameters and used the meter for lyric, narrative, and dramatic purposes. His lyrics feature ostentatious distortion of the iambic movement. The last lines of "Cambridge, Spring 1937" aim for deliberate awkwardness to suggest the balkiness of spring's arrival in New England:

> Winter passes as the lighted streetcar
> Moves at midnight, one scene of the past,
> Droll and unreal, stiff, stilted and hooded.

> (10–12)

Line 10 is trochaic, with all its feet reversed; the shifting of stresses and the chopping by commas in the last two lines complete a subordination of prosody to metaphor, as Schwartz gives his lines the jouncing, start-and-stop movement of a streetcar. Such is not Schwartz's invariable practice: the thirty-four-line piece "I Am to My Own Heart Merely a Serf," for example, is largely regular except for a few added or docked syllables in some lines. Clearly, though, Schwartz was not afraid to experiment, especially in short poems. Donald Justice in his essay on Wallace Stevens cites the opening of one poem, whose title is its first line, as an example of the sort of loosened pentameter he finds in Stevens and others:

> Tired and unhappy, you think of houses
> Soft-carpeted and warm in the December evening,
> While snow's white pieces fall past the window,
> And the orange firelight leaps.
>
> (1–4)

Here the bendings of iambic movement are not obviously emphasizing figurative or descriptive language, though one can imagine an impressionistic reader claiming a link between Schwartz's rhythms and the moody atmosphere of this Depression lyric. (The rhythms do seem, if not "tired," at least drowsy.) What is certainly demonstrable is that Schwartz, like many of his contemporaries, was affected by modernism's aura when he made prosodic decisions.

His longer works are spirited but quixotic; none of them succeeds in embodying the vivid ambition in which it was conceived. Schwartz had theatrical leanings early on, but even the works that received favorable comment at the time cannot be said to have survived, either in the repertory or for readers of poetry. The difficulties attendant upon modern verse drama, as discussed in the last chapter, apply in this case as in so many others. His one-act play *Shenandoah* is included in Alfred Kreymborg's more-than-800-page anthology *Poetic Drama* (1941) as the final piece in a volume that begins with Aeschylus. The play alternates a narrator's soliloquies in blank verse with the dialogue in prose spoken by the other characters. Schwartz is more observant of the meter in this (and in his other longer works) than in his lyrics. Here are some sample lines:

> O to what difficult and painful feat
> Shall I compare the birth of any child
> And all related problems? To the descent
> Of a small grand piano from a window
> On the fifth-floor: O what a *tour-de-force*,
> Clumsy as hippos or rich men *en route*
> To heaven through the famous needle's eye!
>
> (p. 844)[1]

This play is not likely to emerge from the stacks, but it has some genuine charm. In it Schwartz deals with his obsessions (the immigrant experience, assimilation, Freudian ideas on parents and children) with a lighter touch than he brought to his other longer efforts.

Two other long works that use blank verse extensively are *Coriolanus and His Mother* and *Genesis: Book I.* Buried in each are interesting, well-written passages, but the works are obdurately misconceived. *Coriolanus and His Mother* is a running commentary on Shakespeare's tragedy that is liberally laced with Marx and Freud and glacial in its pace. *Genesis: Book I* is a narrative in prose and verse based on the poet's family history, beginning with lightly fictionalized portraits of his immigrant forebears and including his own childhood memories. Again, pace is a problem. Schwartz's alter ego in the book is only seven years old when it peters out at 208 pages. But the formal design is more off-putting still. Schwartz tells the story in extended prose passages, which are then commented on by a chorus of ghosts inhabiting (it seems) the sleeping mind of the protagonist as he relives his life. The effect is not only one of slowness but of redundancy, as the verse passages rehash what the prose has unhurriedly conveyed. Schwartz thought of his choruses as similar to Hardy's spirit choruses in *The Dynasts.* In his preface, besides mentioning this structural model, he comments on his verse:

> I have no wish to emulate Swinburne, but rather the "morbid pedestrianism" of such poets as Donne and Hardy, Webster and Wordsworth. The diction of this deliberate flatness—and the heavy accent and the slowness—is an effort to declare the miraculous character of daily life and ordinary speech. I should also like to think that I am one more of the poets who seek to regain for Poetry the width of reference of prose without losing what the Symbolists discovered.[2]

There is certainly a good amount of pedestrianism, morbid or otherwise, in the work, but here and there Schwartz's querulous ghosts strike a nerve in their ruminations:

> What have we now
> But this eternal knowledge and regret,
> Not an oblivion . . . at best, a sweet drugged sleep
> When we are lucky! the sleep of hospitals—
> True, one gets *used* to pain as one gets used
> To living near a waterfall or trains,
> But I cannot believe I will become

>   *Used* to regret, return, the infinite
>   Apocalypse of all that might have been [. . .]
>
>   (p. 105)[3]

If Schwartz had found a more accessible means of framing his longer works, his record as a writer of blank verse would be better known. As it is, much of it remains in obscurity, and the poet is best remembered for lyrics in different forms: "The Heavy Bear Who Goes With Me" and others.

Schwartz's somewhat defensive rationale for "the heavy accent, the slowness" of his verse in *Genesis: Book I* hints at a tendency observable not only there but in the work of many poets of his generation. By this time, modernism and its exaltation of free verse was fully established. Schwartz, who greatly admired Eliot, nevertheless used the phrase "literary dictatorship" to refer to the older poet's influence.[4] For poets born in the second decade of the century, blank verse in its Eliotic form was hardly a revolutionary medium. Schwartz and his confreres understood, perhaps intuitively, that writing Eliot's sort of blank verse could be ultimately unsatisfying if one were not Eliot. In literature the way to move forward often entails some doubling back. Just as Eliot rediscovered and adapted Webster to his purpose, so the young poets of the thirties found themselves ready to flirt with regularity once they had explored Websterian byways. There is more of Wordsworth than of Webster in *Genesis: Book I*. In the context of the late thirties and early forties, Schwartz's embrace of "morbid pedestrianism" assumes the overtone of irony suggested by his quotation marks. His preface is not simply an apology; to a significant degree it is a challenge to Pound's and Eliot's ascendancy. The failure of *Genesis: Book I* to live up to the poet's ambition for it should not be allowed to obscure the intriguing stylistic development it heralds: a withdrawal and retrenchment by many younger poets from the outer reaches of free verse, and a rekindled interest in the possibilities of older forms. The prosodic spectrum covered by poets using blank verse at this time, ranging from flamboyant rhythmic contortions of the pentameter to an almost copybook regularity, is a testimony to this reassessment, at times painfully tentative, of the entire tradition of the meter.

Before he conceived the baroque stanzas of *Homage to Mistress Bradstreet* and the bluesy ones of *The Dream Songs*, Schwartz's friend John Berryman wrote his share of blank verse, much of which found a place in his 1948 volume

The Dispossessed. "Desires of Men and Women" seems a twin of Schwartz's "Tired and Unhappy, You Think of Houses" in its opening, but develops by the end into a pointed, Audenesque probe of the psyche of the generalized "you"— "Where now you are, where now you wish for life, /Whence you project your naked fantasies" (18–19). The somewhat stilted placement of "now" in both phrases of line 18 shows us that Berryman was determinedly in quest of un- ruffled iambs here. A Frostian, more conversational approach would have fa- vored "Where you are now, where you wish now for life" as more natural. The primness of the verse movement suits Berryman's accusatory tone. He uses regularity for another purpose in "World-Telegram," which summarizes, for the most part without comment, the contents of a daily newspaper:

> Right of the centre, and three columns wide,
> A rather blurred but rather ominous
> Machine-gun being set up by militia
> This morning in Harlan County, Kentucky.
> Apparently some miners died last night.
> 'Personal brawls' is the employer's phrase.
>
> (21–26)

Deadpan rendering of current events has become such a common tactic that this poem has lost much of its original force. Nevertheless, one can see how well the rather stiff framing of the verse fits the numbed and passive tone of the piece. Other poems, some in tighter, others in looser versions of the meter, include "Ancestor," "The Ball Poem," and the much later religious piece "The Facts & Issues."

One of Berryman's best poems in blank verse is the stanzaic "Winter Landscape." The poem is a description of a painting by Breughel of hunters in the snow, but the subtext (alluded to in the phrase "the evil waste of his- tory") is civilization's fateful slide into World War II (12). Berryman contrasts the serenity and beauty of art with the turbulence and suffering of history, perhaps following the lead of Auden's poem about another Breughel painting, "Musée des Beaux Arts." His writing exhibits great coordination of syntax, rhythm, and tone. The poem is in five stanzas of five lines apiece; it is also con- structed as a single sentence (though some would say Berryman fudges a bit by having recourse to a colon in stanza 3). The tense, almost overstrained quality of the speaker's attention is highlighted by the extended syntax: grammatical suspension creates, for the reader, suspense. Berryman is skillful in his enjambments and in shrewdly placed variations in stress. At the end, the viewer of these hunters returning home is still in the spell of the picture, pondering

> What place, what time, what morning occasion
>
> Sent them into the wood, a pack of hounds
> At heel and the tall poles upon their shoulders,
> Thence to return as now we see them and
> ```
> /   x   /   x   /   x   x   /  x   /
> ```
> Ankle-deep in snow down the winter hill
> ```
> x   /   x   /   x   /   x   x   /   /
> ```
> Descend, while three birds watch and the fourth flies.
>
>   (20–25)

We notice how the falling movement of the trochees in line 24 (intensified by the preceding enjambment) mimes the descent down a slippery slope. In the final line the pyrrhic followed by a spondee at the end—a combination we find as far back as Shakespeare as well as in much modern blank verse—is used with uncommon sensitivity to focus attention sharply on the one bird flying. It becomes an emblem for all who wished desperately to escape "the evil waste of history" that was Europe in the thirties and forties.

Although he was a few years younger than Berryman, Schwartz, and Jarrell, Robert Lowell became their sometimes competitive friend and eventually eclipsed them all in celebrity. Like these elders, Lowell led an emotionally volatile life and died in middle age. Unlike them, he came to blank verse late. Most of his work in the meter is in the unrhymed sonnets that occupied him in the late sixties and early seventies. The form was not originated by Lowell—"What the Thrush Said," by Keats, is a particularly fine earlier example—but it has probably never been employed in such quantity as it was by Lowell in amassing several collections. Theoretically, the form offers much that is appealing. Less skillful sonnets in English often are weak because of the rhymes; or, more precisely, the rhymes serve to call attention to their other deficiencies. They can seem over- or understuffed, and uninspired rhyming will inevitably emphasize disproportions in the material. An unrhymed sonnet presumably might allow for a less crimped development of the poem's argument, with the possibility of an expansive range of sonorities going beyond the predictable patterns of end-rhyme offered by the traditional schemes.

In practice, at least in Lowell's hands, the form did not live up to its potential. For him it became something so habitual as to be a product as much of reflex as of thought. One is reminded of the tercets of the later Wallace Stevens; in both cases the form comes to amount to little more than a familiar box to fill, and in both the ability of the form to contribute energy to the total effect of the piece is limited. That being said, there are some acute poems—most often sketches of other writers or of historical figures—sprinkled through the overextended volume *History* (1973). When Lowell's lines are tighter, they sound like this:

> Goethe thought logical consistency
> suited the genius of hypochondriacs,
> who take life and art too seriously,
> lacking the artist's germ of reckless charm.
>
> ("Goethe," 1–4)

Quite frequently, though, lines will contract or swell without warning, gravitating around regular meter as if held by an anchor (such as line 12, below):

> Death will make melodrama of most of us,
> change her chilled, unwilling audience to actors. . . .
> These years of my dead friends, still mine—what other possession
> allows no aging or devaluation?
> Their names have kept their voice—*only in the movies,*
> *the maiden lives . . . in the madness of art.*
>
> ("Death and the Maiden," 9–14)

One notices in both passages how little the meter, regular or distorted, does for the material. The interest generated is all from Lowell's decisive phrasing and the shrewd or skewed perceptions it conveys. Lowell's devotion to his particular kind of conversational style makes meter something of an afterthought, certainly an underused expressive resource. As examples of modern blank verse, his sonnets are shadowed by idiosyncrasy. In an earlier piece like the splendid "Falling Asleep over the *Aeneid*" Lowell fielded pentameter lines in taut, energetic heroic couplets. Forgoing rhyme as he did later on seems to have left him adrift at times in his efforts with the line.

Anyone familiar with his career might have expected Robert Fitzgerald to favor a stricter approach to iambic pentameter. In the 1960s and '70s at Harvard he taught a versification course as well as a poetry writing course that had some of the same stress on technique. Several of his students went on to take part in the New Formalist movement in later decades. Fitzgerald's own poetry was overshadowed (and still is) by his reputation as a translator of Homer and Virgil. His versions of the classical epics, done in blank verse, are still widely read, and set a standard for accuracy that does not impinge on reading pleasure. (As with other translations, these are beyond the scope of this study.) Clearly, Fitzgerald was a poet steeped in the demands and opportunities of standard prosody, in more than one language. He was a poet who did not feel unduly burdened by tradition. It is all the more intriguing, then, to find in some of his blank-verse poems the fashionable warpings of the line sanctioned by Eliot. Here are some lines from a poem of the 1930s, "Manuscript with Illumination." The speaker recalls his boyhood experiences of school and foretells what is to become of himself and his classmates:

> How earth pulls us and pulls the moon
> Our bones know casually. We are diminished
> Who grow with treasure of certainty toward
> Delicate gestures, smiling in the rooms;
> Likewise our desperate shifts for
> Appeasement of the beast, the spirit,
> Walking in darkness and the check from home,
> Waste us wanderers. Several will be
> Sheeted in wards, others give autographs,
> And one perhaps will live in a cool place,
> Devoted to Greek participial loveliness.

(34–44)

If one is looking for a thoughtful and sensitive use of Websterian effects, here it is. The prosody tracks the sense of the lines, not with cartoonish emphasis, but through subtle aural reinforcement of each successive thought. Fitzgerald's usual tone is elegiac, as in this and several other blank-verse pieces: "Midsummer" and "Souls Lake" (both stanzaic), "Night Images," "Counselors," and "History." But he was fully capable of applying the verse to something as boisterous as the opening of "Cinema":

> A square of sucking brilliance in the dark.
> Over it in the depth and distance a rider
> Leaving a comet's furrow of dust. Blink:
> Down the gigantic mountain the booted daredevil
> Twists the piebald, making play with his bridle:
> The savior of the overland stage.
> > > > Why, ma'am,
> That wasn't no ride atall. Well, Miss Ginger,
> Guess I ain't ever seen a gal so purty.

> > > > > > > > > > (1–8)

Another poet who acquired an impressive knowledge of prosody and shared it with his readers was Karl Shapiro. Shapiro modeled his knowledge in his own poems, of course, but he was also the coauthor (with Robert Beum) of one of the standard reference works of the midcentury on the subject, *A Prosody Handbook* (1965). The entry on blank verse in this book is sensible and succinct. After describing it as "the easiest kind of verse to write," but "one of the hardest to master," the authors elaborate:

> The absence of rhyme and stanza form invites prolixity and diffuseness—so easy is it to wander on and on. And blank verse has to be handled in a skillful, ever-attentive way to compensate for such qualities as the musical, architectural, and emphatic properties of rhyme; for the sense of direction one feels within a well-turned stanza; and for the rests that come in stanzas. There are no helps. It is like going into a thick woods in unfamiliar acres.[5]

One can only wish that more poets had buckled this caution into their backpacks before plunging into the wilderness.

Shapiro's shorter poems in the meter display his desire, to use his word, to "compensate" for certain of the advantages blank verse typically forfeits. Given the eloquent account above of what is offered by "a well-turned stanza," it is no surprise to find Shapiro casting blank verse in stanzaic forms. The early "A Cut Flower" is one of the loveliest poems ever written in blank-verse stanzas. Shapiro gives a voice to the flower that speaks throughout; the piece begins as something fresh and charming and ends as something memorably poignant. Pondering the lady who at length will use the shears, the flower asks:

> Who softens the sweet earth about my feet,
> Touches my face so often and brings water?
> Where does she go, taller than any sunflower
> Over the grass like birds? Has she a root?

(10–13)

Shapiro seems often to calibrate the level of regularity in his verse to accord with the speaker or subject. Here the even movement of the lines fits the docile voice of the flower. Regular movement meets a different purpose in "The Synagogue," where stanzas like the following one reinforce the ritual gravity of the piece:

> The altar of the Hebrews is a house,
> No relic but a place, Sinai itself,
> Not holy ground but factual holiness
> Wherein the living god is resident.
> Our scrolls are volumes of the thundered law
> Sabbath by Sabbath wound by hand to read.

(13–18)

Shapiro varies his rhythms more in other pieces, but in general his approach to blank verse is conservative for a poet of his generation. When he wants an extreme emphasis he is more likely to cut a line short than to disrupt iambic movement markedly. There is not much of the free use of anapests that we saw in Stevens and others. Most of Shapiro's notable metrical or rhythmic variations are governed by his personal sense of decorum, of appropriateness to the matter at hand. One of his best-known poems, "Auto Wreck," features some of his more agitated prosody. Although a majority of his thirty-nine lines are pentameters, Shapiro intermingles shorter lines: tetrameters and lines of nine syllables that seem to hover between tetrameter and pentameter. Variations within the line are deployed expressively. The first sentence of the poem illustrates such tactics:

```
x   /   x   /  x   /   /  x   /  x
```
Its quick soft silver bell beating, beating,
And down the dark one ruby flare
Pulsing out red light like an artery,
The ambulance at top speed floating down
Past beacons and illuminated clocks
Wings in a heavy curve, dips down,
And brakes speed, entering the crowd.

(1–7)

Shapiro uses his shortened lines either to intensify focus on an image (the red light in line 2) or to imitate motion (the slowing of the vehicle in lines 6–7). The brilliant first line gives us an effect of speed in its first three feet with their light vowels, and adds an effect of urgency by the repetition of "beating," which also disrupts the iambic pattern with its reversal of two feet in a row at the end of the line—a very unusual substitution. Reading a poem like this, which uses the resources of traditional versification to evoke most vividly a scene of carnage, may make us wonder why so many modernists took the further step into Websterianism. As we see here, the meter is not at all robbing the scene of energy; it is actively supplying it.

Shapiro first became well known as a poet while serving in the Pacific theater in World War II. (One of his collections was awarded the Pulitzer Prize while he was overseas.) Some of his war poems in blank verse (often stanzaic with very occasional rhyming) stand up well: "Troop Train," "Melbourne," and "Homecoming" are examples. He also wrote many poems such as "The Synagogue," already mentioned, on Jewish themes, as well as a wide range of blank-verse lyrics: "A Garden in Chicago," "Crossing Lincoln Park," "The House," "Connecticut Valley," to name a few. His most prodigious piece in the meter, if not his most popular, is the book-length *Essay on Rime* (1945). In this, Shapiro uses blank verse in a prolonged expository manner virtually unknown since the eighteenth century. Unabashedly didactic, this treatise consists of three main parts, headed "The Confusion in Prosody," "The Confusion in Language," and "The Confusion in Belief." Not only these, but the "Foreword" preceding them and the "Note and Acknowledgment" following them are in blank verse: Shapiro clearly is determined to demonstrate the utilitarian possibilities of the meter.

This book is now little known; probably its very conception is hopelessly quixotic when one considers the limited audience for books on prosody written in prose, let alone one like this, done in 2,072 lines of iambic pentameter. Although Shapiro's particular points of emphasis are very much of his time, the book often exhibits his sharpness and cleverness both as a critic and as a poet. Here are some lines on Eliot's and Pound's habit of sprinkling their work with foreign phrases:

> We take the word of Eliot that *da-ta*
> And *coco-rico* have their definitions,
> And dare not smile when English is not enough.
> We must have new glossarial editions
> And variora on final variora,
> Headnotes and footnotes and appendiceal
> Behindnotes to the poem. I do not scoff,
> I merely ask; I merely quote MacLeish,
> *Señora, it is true the Greeks are dead*
> And sadly add, but jabberwocky lives.
>
> (1262–71)

Shapiro offers a charmingly candid profile of his method near the end of the "Note and Acknowledgment" section:

> The metric of this book is made upon
> The classic English decasyllable
> Adapted to the cadence of prose speech;
> Ten units to the verse by count of eye
> Is the ground rhythm, over which is set
> The rough flux and reflux of conversation.
>
> (2057–62)

It is remarkable that Shapiro wrote this poem while serving in uniform in the Dutch East Indies; it is nearly as remarkable that he found a publisher for something so uncompromising in its literary seriousness. The work has its dull spots, and sometimes Shapiro's "rough flux and reflux of conversation" loses the verve of his tauter verse. But it is an admirable achievement that deserves to be better known. Even more explicitly than Schwartz's *Genesis: Book*

I, this prolonged exercise in iambic pentameter can be seen as a counterblast to modernist attacks on the meter.

We may mention more briefly some other poets born in the second decade. John Ciardi, who, like Shapiro, first became known for poems he wrote while serving in the war, became a prominent cultural figure in the middle and later decades of the century. He translated Dante, served as poetry editor for *Saturday Review* (a high-minded middlebrow magazine), and appeared on what was then called "educational television." He wrote poetry prolifically: a posthumous *Collected Poems* includes 450 poems, less than two-thirds of those published in twenty individual volumes. Ciardi seems less disposed toward blank verse in shorter poems, but he uses it at length in an autobiographical sequence, *Lives of X* (1971). He writes, at times affectingly, of growing up as the son of a widowed mother in an Italian immigrant family in the environs of Boston. Ciardi has some good stories to tell, but the treatment is often heavy-handed. It would be wrong to say that in making the same point over and over again he runs out of energy; it is the reader who does that. Besides verbosity, Ciardi shares at times the tendency of American realism to mistake crudity for strength. When he is not being obsessively gritty, he can produce something as winning as his memories of being taken along, as a very young child, to market in Boston's North End:

> The stores were cellars and they smelled of cheese,
> salami, and olive brine. Dark rows of crates,
> stacked back to damp brick where the scurries were,
> made tunnels in whose sides the one-eyed beans
> were binned so deep I could lose all my arm
> into their sliding buttons. In a while
> I got my cookie and knew I had behaved.
>
> ("The Shaft," 23–29)

Ciardi is one of many poets who wrote (or at least published) more than was good for their later reputations. He was informed, skilled, and professional, but he too often subordinated his talent to facility, and his better work needs to be disinterred from much that is uninspired.

Given his scathing comments on the "parasitic meter" of Eliot and others, one might have looked to J. V. Cunningham to provide some orthodox examples of the form. He did; but like his fellow Stanford University formalist Yvor Winters, he tried his hand at it only infrequently. There are philosophical musings on the nature of passion and of choice ("All Choice Is Error," "Agnosco Veteris Vestigia Flammae") and on mortality ("Consolatio Nova"); and there is a satirical, slightly Stevensian elegy, "Obsequies for a Poetess." Cunningham's numerous epigrams, a form of which he was the principal master of modern times, include some in blank verse, but the great majority of them rhyme. Probably his most memorable piece in the meter is the uncharacteristic "Montana Fifty Years Ago." This is a bleak and harrowing narrative, ferociously concise (seventeen lines; it makes Frost's "The Vanishing Red," at twenty-nine, seem garrulous). Cunningham's characters—an old man on an isolated farm in the Great Plains; a woman who, with her child, boards with him in exchange for keeping house—are barely sketched. Most of the poem delineates the comfortless landscape: "a land / Of gophers, cottontails, and rattlesnakes" (7–8). The "plot" is sprung with awful suddenness in the final lines:

> So he came to her one night,
> To the front room, now bedroom, and moved in.
> Nothing was said, nothing was ever said.
> And then the child died and she disappeared.
> This was Montana fifty years ago.
>
> (13–17)

We know almost nothing about these characters; yet the poem discloses just enough to make itself indelible. A line like "Nothing was said, nothing was ever said" can be profitably studied for what it suggests by means of taciturnity. It is a prime example of what Frost meant by "the sound of sense."

There are other examples of poets in this age group who wrote blank verse infrequently but artfully. Anyone interested in the meter should enjoy seeing how Dudley Randall uses it to create his compact, bitter portrait-poem "Old Witherington." Its twenty-one powerful lines are about an old man in the habit of picking fights when drunk:

> Prune-black, with bloodshot eyes and one white tooth,
> He tottered in the night with legs spread wide
> Waving a hatchet. "Come on, come on," he piped,
> "And I'll baptize these bricks with bloody kindling.

> I may be old and drunk, but not afraid
> To die. I've died before. A million times
> I've died and gone to hell. I live in hell.
>
> (4–10)

The dignity emerging in the old man's speech, so much at odds with the degraded situation, is startling. Robert Hayden shows a similar sensitivity to character at greater length in "Witch Doctor," which focuses on the leader of a religious cult—a sort of Father Divine figure, clearly a con man:

> He dines alone surrounded by reflections
> of himself. Then after sleep and benzedrine
> descends the Cinquecento stair his magic
> wrought from hypochondria of the well-
> to-do and nagging deathwish of the poor [. . .]
>
> (1–5)

The partial pun created by enjambing "well- / to-do" is a fine sardonic touch. The poem is descriptively brilliant throughout, following the course of a charismatic service. The delicate ambiguity of the climax is particularly impressive: while making clear that every move the "witch doctor" makes is calculated in advance, Hayden hints that he is swept up beyond his own cynicism, infected by the fervor of his congregation—"a power he has counted on / and for a space allows to carry him" (63–64). Finally,

> He dances from the altar,
> robes hissing, flaring, shimmering, down aisles
> where mantled guardsmen intercept wild hands
> that arduously strain to clutch his vestments,
> he dances, dances, ensorcelled and aloof,
> the fervid juba of God as lover, healer,
> conjuror. And of himself as God.
>
> (69–75)

Both Hayden and Randall, in their sparse use of the meter, stand in contrast with African American formalist poets who preceded them; throughout the nineteenth century blank verse was a widely used form for such poets.[6]

A more encyclopedic study might well devote more than a bare mention to work such as Winfield Townley Scott's (a monologue for Christopher Columbus, "May 1506," and other pieces) and William Meredith's ("A Korean Woman Seated by a Wall," and other sensitive, civilized pieces in loosened pentameters). But we must move on, closing this section with a glance at a few British examples—and they really are few among poets of this age group, who perhaps were influenced toward favoring different forms by the slightly older Auden circle. For instance, Dylan Thomas usually preferred sonorous patterns of rhyme, off-rhyme, and assonance, cast in stanzas, or syllabics, as in the late poem "Fern Hill." Digging deep, we find regular iambic pentameter in the brief, riddling "Was There a Time." A more accessible poem, "After the Funeral," offers an iambic pentameter line that occasionally billows in response to gusts of florid phrasing:

> But I, Ann's bard on a raised hearth, call all
> The seas to service that her wood-tongued virtue
> Babble like a bellbuoy over the hymning heads,
> Bow down the walls of the ferned and foxy woods
> That her love sing and swing through a brown chapel,
> Bless her bent spirit with four, crossing birds.

(21–26)

Thomas's sound effects are so insistent that they draw attention away from the meter, which may be just as well in the case of a line like

> / x x x / / / x x / x /
> Babble like a bellbuoy over the hymning heads.

An impressionistic reader might argue that the severe disruption of the middle three feet of the line conjure the swell and fall of a wave below the (entirely figurative) bellbuoy. Perhaps. It may simply be, though, that Thomas's fondness for alliteration swept aside other considerations, including a more exact prosody.

Roy Fuller wrote more blank verse than Thomas, and he wrote it in a decidedly less ornate style. Although influenced by Auden, he was evidently more willing than many of his contemporaries to give the form a try. He served in the navy and spent some time in East Africa during the war. Some of his strongest work presents the African landscape: "The Giraffes," which uses occasional rhyme; "The Plains"; and "The Green Hills of Africa," whose pessimistic view of the impact of Europe on Africa emerges only after an exalted view of the poet's surroundings:

> The green, humped, wrinkled hills: with such a look
> Of age (or youth) as to erect the hair.
> They crouch above the ports or on the plain,
> Beneath the matchless skies; are like a strange
> Girl's shoulders suddenly against your hands.
>
> (1–5)

Other wartime poems, "Good-bye for a Long Time" and "The Photographs," deal strikingly with the separation of lovers during combat. Fuller wrote several later poems in the meter as well: the sinister travelogue "Côte des Maures," the eerily futuristic "Pleasure Drive," the autobiographical "Youth Revisited." "Expostulation and Inadequate Reply" is an unusually elegant meditation on the relation of the poet to society. Fuller's poetry is not well known in the United States, which is a pity. Its clarity of statement, sharpness of observation, and strong but understated emotion make it attractive reading.

As this section has made apparent, the fortunes of blank verse from the 1930s through World War II (and indeed, later) present a mixed picture. The dictum of modernism that condescended to "the inevitable iambic pentameter" undoubtedly continued to have its discouraging effect in many quarters. Yet, as we have seen, significant examples of traditional blank verse continued to be written even as the looser modernist approach was in vogue. And as the remainder of this chapter will show, both forms continued to appeal to poets born in 1920 and later.

III

Four poets—Howard Nemerov, Richard Wilbur, Anthony Hecht, and James Merrill—are essential figures in the study of blank verse in the middle and later twentieth century. The work of these poets alone would be sufficient to prove the continued vitality of the meter during those decades, and each of them merits a more detailed discussion than space permits. We may attempt at least to outline their achievements if not to explore them in depth.

Howard Nemerov is a notable figure for discussion both because of his commitment to blank verse over the whole span of his career and because of the multiplicity of poems that resulted from this. Looking for blank verse in Nemerov's work is as untaxing as looking for dandelions on the lawn in July. It is only a slight exaggeration to say, Turn a page, or two, and it will be there. It does not appear that Nemerov felt in any way defensive about his use of the form; he has little specific to say in his criticism about versification, although here and there we happen upon remarks that may pertain. Consider this acidulous view of the free-verse revolution, which Nemerov rates as decidedly old news from the standpoint of one trying to write poetry in the 1950s or '60s:

> Nowadays, if you want to write in free verse, or "cadenced verse," or no particular verse at all, you can do it and no one will object so long as you don't write a manifesto proclaiming your courage and wits to (or against) the world. In fact it is also probable that no one will even notice what you are doing unless you write a manifesto, for if the "revolution" won freedom for poetry it also won for large parts of the world freedom from poetry. And why poets should still be found, fifty years later, fighting for that "freedom to experiment" as though they did not have it, is a mystery, but maybe one of the sillier mysteries.[7]

This robust, unapologetic stance, in which traditional verse is as viable an option as any of the no-longer-new strategies of the modernists, seems to be one Nemerov shared with the other poets to be discussed in this section. In them we see a recommitment to formalism that was less consistently in evidence among many poets just a few years older. As the colossal rubble of World War II began to be swept aside, a mid-century formalism emerged in the United States. (In England, the postwar poets known collectively as the Movement— Philip Larkin and others—were in certain ways analogous.) Despite the successive waves of free-verse poets that were to challenge them (Black Mountain poets, Beats, Deep Image poets, and others), Nemerov and a number of his peers pursued extended careers without breaking faith with traditional forms.

Unflaggingly prolific for half a century, Nemerov applied blank verse to an expansive array of tasks. He wrote dramatic monologues: the somewhat unconvincing "Death and the Maiden" and the later, more satisfying "The

Beekeeper Speaks . . . and Is Silent." He wrote narratives such as "The Pond" and "A Day on the Big Branch." And he wrote quantities of shorter pieces: meditative, elegiac, or descriptive lyrics, and philosophical or satirical epigrams. Throughout his career he wrote both tighter and looser versions of the meter; the liberties he accords himself, however, are rarely as ostentatious as those in vogue in the thirties. Rather than docilely adhering to the modernist program with any great consistency, Nemerov's loosening of the pentameter usually seems designed to mesh with some demand of tone or momentary emphasis. His aberrations are typically localized, and the metrical norm is rarely difficult to recognize in a passage of more than a few lines.

His few dramatic forays aside, Nemerov used blank verse principally as a vehicle for his own voice responding to the visible world around him and speculating about realms beyond the range of even a keen observer's senses. Many of his pieces are nature poems, deriving from Wordsworth, no doubt, but like Frost's marked by the disillusionments of the twentieth century. The voice in his poems is level and controlled; emotion and idealism are held in bounds by irony and skepticism. The result in his blank-verse pieces is a highly identifiable conversational style, one of the most successful of many such to emerge in mid-twentieth-century poetry. Line after line, his poems offer examples of the almost limitless possibilities of accommodating natural speech rhythms within an iambic pattern. To illustrate, here are an earlier and a later passage:

> People are putting up storm windows now,
> Or were, this morning, until the heavy rain
> Drove them indoors. So, coming home at noon,
> I saw storm windows lying on the ground,
> Frame-full of rain; through the water and glass
> I saw the crushed grass, how it seemed to stream
> Away in lines like seaweed on the tide
> Or blades of wheat leaning under the wind.
>
> ("Storm Windows," 1–8)

> Landowska said, to end an argument,
> "Why don't you go on playing Bach your way
> And let me play Bach his way?" putting down

Whoever-it-was forever; music's not
All harmony, Landowska too is dead,
Spirit acerb, though her records remain
Hermetically kept where time not much corrupts
Nor quite so quick.

                        ("Playing the Inventions," 46–53)

By the standards of modernism, the liberties taken are modest indeed; yet they are audible, and are among the stylistic features that give this poet's voice its distinctive character. They enhance the verisimilitude of the poetry as speech. Often the variations Nemerov employs are more interesting than the heavy doses of anapests favored by other poets. For example, in

            x   /   x   /   /   x   /   x   x   /
            Or blades of wheat leaning under the wind

and

            / x x /   /   x / x   x /
            Spirit acerb, though her records remain

we find two trochees in a row substituted as the third and fourth feet. (In the second of these lines, there is also an initial trochee, which further accentuates the oddity.) The naturalness of Nemerov's phrasing and the generally regular movement of the passages in which such lines are contained may help their anomalies pass muster for many readers. What is interesting here is the economy of such gestures. Nemerov seems to have discovered early that, to avoid monotony, some very slight sidestepping of the paradigm may serve just as well and less distractingly than the wholesale bendings and stretchings of the later Stevens.

In speaking of a poet who has written so much, we are bound to admit the limits of generalization. At times Nemerov's conversational style indulges in a less agreeable slackness:

After a time we talked about the War,
about what we had done in the War, and how near
some of us had been to being drowned, and burned,

and shot, and how many people we knew
who had been drowned, or burned, or shot;
and would it have been better to have died
in the War, the peaceful old War, where we were young?

("A Day on the Big Branch," 83–89)

It is interesting that this sort of rhythmic lumpiness and line stretching often goes together with a deliberately hardheaded tone: it is as if the more ingenuous feelings (as well as the more regular meter) have to poke their way through a willfully assumed carapace of cynicism.

In his better poems Nemerov adjusts the movement of lines far more sensitively. Sometimes the verse is imitative in an obvious, even noisy way, as in the last lines of "Gyroscope." The passage begins with the instrument in full spin:

A silver nearly silence gleaning a still-
ness out of speed, composing unity
From spin, so that its hollow spaces seem
Solids of light, until it wobbles and
x / x / x / x x / /
Begins to whine, and then with an odd lunge
x / x x / x x / x /
Eccentric and reckless, it skids away
x / / / x x / / x x
And drops dead into its own skeleton.

(9–15)

The lines move brilliantly through the sustained, delicate balance of the object while spinning, suggested by the enjambments, to the contrasting wobble, lunge, skid, and final fall. From the spondee emphasizing the "odd lunge" in line 13 to the end, the stress displacements track the motion cunningly: the final line captures the clatter of the gyroscope's fall so exactly that the effect is as witty as the striking metaphor. When Pope recommended that in poetry the sound should seem an echo of the sense, this is one sort of thing he had in mind, and it is a rare skill in any era.

Less flamboyantly, but no less brilliantly, Nemerov plays off regular against irregular lines in a more solemn lyric, "Moment":

Now, starflake frozen on the windowpane
All of a winter night, the open hearth
Blazing beyond Andromeda, the sea-
Anemone and the downwind seed, O moment
Hastening, halting in a clockwise dust,
The time in all the hospitals is now,
Under the arc-lights where the sentry walks
His lonely wall it never moves from now,
The crying in the cell is also now,
And now is quiet in the tomb as now
Explodes inside the sun, and it is now
In the saddle of space, where argosies of dust
Sail outward blazing, and the mind of God,
The flash across the gap of being, thinks
In the instant absence of forever: now.

The poem's fifteen lines are written as a single sentence, albeit a run-on one. The small disruptions of meter are mostly located in the opening and closing of the poem, while the movement is more regular in the middle. This distinction corresponds to the imagery: the elemental images at the beginning and those which begin as elemental and become transcendental at the end are conveyed in lines that sweep beyond the meter's bounds. The various images of confinement that typify human experience at the center of the poem are themselves confined in a more regular metrical movement suggesting the sentry's pace or the tick of a clock. The way sound echoes sense is subtler here than in "Gyroscope," requiring much less displacement of stress to make its thematic point. Nemerov made himself a master of such small but telling adjustments over the course of his career.

Although the conversational mode was habitual for him, he sometimes allowed himself a richer sound, as in the beautiful "A Spell before Winter":

Now I can see certain simplicities
In the darkening rust and tarnish of the time,
And say over the certain simplicities,
The running water and the standing stone,
The yellow haze of the willow and the black
Smoke of the elm [. . .]

(8–13)

Or in the meditative sequence "Runes":

> Sunflowers, traders rounding the horn of time
> Into deep afternoons, sleepy with gain,
> The fall of silence has begun to storm
> Around you where you nod your heavy heads [. . .]
>
> (III, 1–4)

Nemerov's poems in the meter range in length from a few pages to a few lines; longer pieces yielded dominance to shorter ones over time. He tried the form successfully in stanzas of varying size: "The May Day Dancing" and "After Commencement" are likable examples. It would not be feasible to list all the worthwhile poems Nemerov wrote in the meter. Besides those already cited, a selective list would include "Lightning Storm on Fuji," "Deep Woods," "To Lu Chi," "The Icehouse in Summer," "Learning by Doing," "To D———, Dead by Her Own Hand," "The Western Approaches," "Boy with Book of Knowledge," "Larkin," "The End of the Opera," and "Trying Conclusions." The meter's versatility gave apparently inexhaustible scope to the poet's virtuosity.

Richard Wilbur's poems in blank verse are much less plentiful than Nemerov's, but they are indispensable to our study. They display the same high-spirited verve we find in Wilbur's more numerous rhyming poems, an ability not merely to satisfy the demands of a form but to unleash its full expressive potential in lines of peerless elegance and imaginative power. In Wilbur's handling the meter is normally close-woven; he is less likely than Nemerov or many other poets to bend the line in pursuit of speech mannerisms. The even movement of meter and the usually subtle shifts in rhythm keep the prosody of his poems in the background, directing attention instead to the energy and finesse of Wilbur's language. Even the lesser pieces—the childhood memory called "Digging for China," the acerbic epigram called "The Rule"—are graced with Wilbur's gift for finding the right word, which somehow he exercises without fussiness or pedantry.

Wilbur's major blank-verse poems are long for one who is primarily a lyric poet, but they are quite compact when viewed alongside precedents that the tradition offers. The longest, "The Mind-Reader," a dramatic monologue, runs a bit over four pages. Yet this piece and its slightly shorter counterparts—"Walking to Sleep," "Lying," "All That Is," and "This Pleasing, Anxious Being"—are so concentrated in style that they seem more imposing and consequential than their size would lead one to expect. These poems are not identical in theme, but in them a number of the poet's preoccupations recur and overlap. A baldly abstract summary would say that they explore, from various angles, the interactions of perception and memory with reality and speculate on the hows and whys of such negotiations. It is with something of a shock that the reader realizes that these are didactic poems, since they shun the abstraction of the previous sentence and make their points by amassing patterns of indelible imagery. They offer an argument of images, often of similes and metaphors. They exemplify what they are about, because the poet's keenness of perception and the substantial presence of what he describes are equally vivid in his lines.

In an essay of 1948, Wilbur wrote in defense of traditional verse forms; although some of his remarks were intended to discuss art in general, they have a particular relevance to these blank-verse poems that he was later to write: "Neither the mysterious world nor the formative mind can be denied. . . . In the best paintings of Cézanne you are aware of the tremendous mass, immediacy, and entity of the world, and at the same time of the mastery of the mind which got that into a frame."[8] What he says of Cézanne would serve equally well as an assessment of lines like these, from "The Mind-Reader":

> The mind is not a landscape, but if it were
> There would in such case be a tilted moon
> Wheeling beyond the wood through which you groped,
> Its fine spokes breaking through the tangled thickets.
> There would be obfuscations, paths which turned
> To dried-up stream-beds, hemlocks which invited
> Through shiny clearings to a groundless shade;
> And yet in a sure stupor you would come
> At once upon dilapidated cairns,
> Abraded moss, and half-healed blazes leading
> To where, around the turning of a fear,
> The lost thing shone.

> (32–43)

And what Wilbur says later about versification in his defense of formalism could be a description of his own combination of freedom with discipline:

There are not so many basic rhythms for American and English poets, but the possibilities of varying these rhythms are infinite. One thing modern poets do not write, thank heaven, is virtuoso poems of near perfect conformity to basic rhythms, as Byron, Swinburne, and Browning did in their worst moments. By good poets of any age, rhythm is generally varied cleverly and forcefully to abet the expressive purposes of the whole poem. Modern variations on basic rhythms are likely to suggest the speech patterns, phrasing, and familiar beats of contemporary life, and this is desirable. But the rhythmic variations cannot do this unless the whole expression of a poem reflects a contemporary sensibility: rhythm cannot be modern per se: it may, however, be modern in the ensemble of a poem, in the way it works with words.[9]

In fact the "whole expression" of "The Mind-Reader" or of Wilbur's other blank-verse poems seems not so much contemporary but timeless, attuned equally to modern and traditional properties of poetry. The photographic sharpness of Wilbur's imagery and his conciseness, for instance, are modern. But many other qualities of the above verse excerpt bespeak a consciously valued heritage. Certainly here, as in much of Wilbur's blank verse, the presiding genius is Milton. The exquisite patterns of assonance, the arrangements of images in sequences like the links of a chain, the gracefully sustained and extended syntax that leads a reader along the path followed by the description, the judicious placement of Latinate words ("obfuscation," "dilapidated," "abraded") among plainer ones—all this suggests Milton. It is Milton tactfully scaled back from epic proportions to those of lyric meditation, but Milton nonetheless. And Wilbur's mastery of these tactics has sufficiently made them his own so that we are not distracted by the influence. For Eliot and Pound, Milton and the iambic pentameter model he established were the enemies; for Wilbur and for fellow formalists of his generation, the feeling was different, and Milton was one of many available resources. Wilbur argues in his essay: "A basic rhythm is as timeless and noncommittal as the triangle. The horses of the nineteenth century did not run in iambs, any more than the Studebakers of the twentieth do."[10] If iambic pentameter is a wholly artificial construction, it follows in his view that it cannot be seen as the property of any particular era or of the poets who then made use of it: it is fully transposable to the time of any poet able to master its ins and outs.

"Lying" is perhaps the most complex of Wilbur's blank-verse poems, and is one of the most remarkable verse essays ever written. Beginning with the trivial example of a fib told to fill a silence at a party, the poem studies the human relation to reality, centering its vision on the unchecked abundance of God's creation to anchor its bold assertion: "We invent nothing, merely bearing witness / To what each morning brings again to light" (17–18). That is, the wonders of the world are already in existence, including ourselves, and we can only perceive them or mirror them; we cannot bring them into being out of nothing as the story of Genesis depicts God as doing. As for nothing itself, Wilbur argues that in this world of ours, nothing is in fact something:

> And so with that most rare conception, nothing.
> What is it, after all, but something missed?
> It is the water of a dried-up well
> Gone to assail the cliffs of Labrador.
>
> (33–36)

The poem alludes to Milton's Satan, as the would-be negator of divine plenitude, and even quotes a phrase from *Paradise Lost*. It fills out its theme of the human way of making as a seeing of what-has-been-made by cataloguing examples:

> Closer to making than the deftest fraud
> Is seeing how the catbird's tail was made
> To counterpoise, on the mock-orange spray,
> Its light, up-tilted spine; or, lighter still,
> How the shucked tunic of an onion, brushed
> To one side on a backlit chopping-board
> And rocked by trifling currents, prints and prints
> Its bright, ribbed shadow like a flapping sail.
>
> (47–54)

We might be reminded of Milton's masterly catalogues and expanded similes, but this is not stylistic antiquarianism in any simple sense. The catbird and the onion skin could have come out of early twentieth-century imagist lyrics, where they would not have been presented by means of iambic pentameter. Wilbur's eclectic grasp of multiple strands of tradition has resulted in something new, and moreover something whose novelty is not compromised by the historical and literary associations it calls to mind. About the verse in this poem, Wilbur comments interestingly:

> Did I choose blank verse because I glimpsed Milton in the offing? I suspect that I was more influenced by the fact that the pentameter is the most flexible of our meters, and the best in which to build large verse-masses; I must have sensed that, though the drift of the poem would finally be simple, I would wish to deal fluently and amply with the sensible richness of things, and with the world as a dense tissue of resemblances.[11]

It is characteristic of Wilbur in this and in the other more discursive poems to begin with a slight, even fanciful premise and "build large verse-masses" that are indeed imbued with "the sensible richness of things." What might be flimsy and spun-out in lesser hands acquires substance and luster in his. Although essayistic poems of this kind, listed above, are his grander works in the meter, there are some noteworthy pieces of other kinds. The eerie, elegiac lyric "The Mill," the disturbing night-piece "In Limbo," and the gentle tribute "The Reader" are striking in disparate ways. The one poem that seems not to work as well is "The Agent," in which the habitually punctilious imagery clogs the progress of a would-be narrative, which may in fact be more an improvisation based on old spy movies than a more customary sort of story-in-verse.

If narrative is one of the smaller facets of Wilbur's talent, it is paramount among Anthony Hecht's—at least in regard to his writing in blank verse. At times he overlaps genres by using a fictive narrator to tell the story, whether forthrightly or indirectly, and narrative and drama are thus intricately inter-meshed. The stories told in these poems are typically not happy ones. Hecht is one of the few recent poets whose work has the authentic note of the tragic—not in the devalued, journalistic sense of "a tragic three-car collision" but in the sense that Sophocles would have recognized. Like Wilbur, he finds the genres and techniques of the tradition fully equipped to deal with modern concerns—even, in his case, traumatic ones. His renderings of suffering, whether on an individual level or that of a global catastrophe such as World War II or the Holocaust, are made more memorable by virtue of his formal control.

Although there is a fine poem in his first (1954) volume about the sufferings of soldiers, "Christmas Is Coming," Hecht did not make use of blank verse with frequency until he was middle-aged. From his third collection, *Millions of Strange Shadows* (1977), through his seventh and last, *The Darkness and the Light* (2001), he employs it forcefully in poems large and small. Late in his life he contributed a six-page essay, "Blank Verse," to the anthology *An Exaltation of Forms*. In it he sketches the history of the form and provides examples of lines from a number of poets to illustrate "the pronounced rhythmic differences" the meter can accommodate.[12] The more provocative portion of his piece discusses the relation of blank verse to prose. He quotes from *Moby-Dick* to show how Melville puts into service the rhythms of Shakespearean drama in utterances of his characters. He then quotes a note that Wordsworth wrote to himself on the difficulties caused by the affinities of blank verse to prose. Here is Wordsworth's statement:

> Dr. Johnson observed, that in blank verse, the language suffered more distortion to keep it out of prose than any inconvenience to be apprehended from the shackles and circumspection of rhyme. This kind of distortion is the worst fault that poetry can have; for if once the natural order and connection of the words is broken, and the idiom of the language violated, the lines appear manufactured, and lose all that character of enthusiasm and inspiration, without which they become cold and insipid, how sublime soever the ideas and the images may be which they express.[13]

Hecht then summarizes Wordsworth as arguing that blank verse "should observe the directness and expediency of prose discourse, yet at the same time contrive to make itself manifestly distinguishable from prose," and concludes:

> A skill of enormous delicacy as well as strength is being proposed, and not least when we consider that "the natural order and connection of the words" and "the idiom of the language" are by no means constant and unvarying factors. Being, as he was, a poet of genius, he was able to write a blank verse of distinction, originality, and flexibility, and, most impressively, of both naturalness and grandeur. But the problem for any given poet remains, and a new idiom must be found by each new poet, allowing for the changes in prose as well as poetic conventions.[14]

Hecht may well have been personally focused on the issues surrounding the meter's links to prose because of his narrative bias. He is one of the twentieth-century poets who devoted exceptional energy to reclaiming for poetry some of the territory it had earlier appeared to cede to prose fiction.

His sizable narratives, such as "The Short End" and "See Naples and Die," required, besides poetic talent, the skills of a short story writer; even lengthier, "The Venetian Vespers" has the feel of a short novel in verse. These, briefer monologues like "The Grapes" and "The Transparent Man," and the memoiristic "Apprehensions" all seem to perform with great dexterity the tightrope walk between verse and prose that Hecht desiderates for blank verse. In his longer poems especially, Hecht unites the gifts of poet and storyteller in descriptive passages of eidetic power. Like Wilbur, he is a master of catalogues, and makes ample use of the meter's hospitality to them. Nearly half of the first section of "The Short End" is an account of the souvenir pillows collected by the protagonist, a woman plagued by alcoholism and depression. Here are just a few lines:

> Pillows from Kennebunkport, balsam-scented
> And stuffed with woodchips, pillows from Coney Island
> Blazoned with Ferris Wheels and Roller Coasters,
> Pillows that fart when sat on, tasselled pillows
> From old New Orleans, creole and redly carnal [. . .]

> (I, 12–16)

Here the verse line seems, as it were, overstuffed, and intimates an accumulation (and, by implication, a life) that has gone beyond control.

Hecht's catalogues have a different quality than Wilbur's: Rather than being an index of appealing abundance, they hint at distortions in his characters and in the often uncongenial world they inhabit. Rather than being emblems of divine plenitude, they frequently serve as portents of the narrative's dire progress and grim outcome. The effect, not only in catalogues but other elaborately detailed descriptions, is one of barely controlled dread, as images inscribed by trauma deep in a character's consciousness make their way to the surface. Brilliant as visual description, and also as a metaphor for the mind's attempt to recover the past, here is a salient passage from "The Venetian Vespers." The speaker imagines a silent film run backward "for the sake of the children in the house" (I, 132):

> Here, in pure satisfaction of our hunger,
> The Keystone Cops sprint from hysteria,

From brisk, slaphappy bludgeonings of crime,
Faultlessly backwards into calm patrol;
And gallons of spilled paint, meekly obedient
As a domestic pet, home in and settle
Securely into casually offered pails,
Leaving the Persian rug immaculate.
But best of all are the magically dry legs
Emerging from a sudden crater of water
That closes itself up like a healed wound
To plate-glass polish as the diver slides
Upwards, attaining with careless arrogance
His unsought footing on the highest board.

(I, 140–53)

The ironic wishfulness of this innocent return to the past, undoing the finality
of events, is underscored when the protagonist's own memories erupt in later
parts of the poem, as when detailing the fate of a soldier he knew:

He was killed by enemy machine-gun fire.
His helmet had fallen off. They had sheared away
The top of his cranium like a soft-boiled egg,
And there he crouched, huddled over his weapon,
His brains wet in the chalice of his skull.

(III, 144–48)

In his essay on blank verse, Hecht notes sensibly that the form's

nature and uses cannot be construed by examining any *single line* because
iambic pentameter (rhymed) is used in many stanzaic verse forms from
Chaucer to this day; and the way we evaluate any single line is inevitably determined by *context*: certain poetic voices insist on colloquial directness, others on
impersonal grandeur. The liberties permitted in a long poem might seem
conspicuous blemishes in a short one.[15]

It is obvious from these few quotations that Hecht is willing to allow himself
"liberties"; wider reading will show that while he is often direct he is not
markedly colloquial. In fact, some of the impact of his work issues from the

precarious balance struck between a lofty manner and painful or grotesque subject matter. As to versification, even if Hecht is less regular than Wilbur, he gives an overall impression of formal polish, perhaps because of his at times lapidary diction. While he frequently permits himself extra unstressed syllables, he is not as jagged as Nemerov in handling transitions from irregular to regular lines. His speech effects are somewhat more austere even when they verge on the demotic. In general, technical differences among these three mid-century formalists are less telling than their similarities as fashioners of fluent, civilized styles. Hecht's level of accomplishment in the form is high. "The Venetian Vespers" is one of the finest narrative poems of the late twentieth century, setting a story of war, family betrayal, and psychic malaise against the gorgeous and sinister backdrop of Venice. Similar in method, "See Naples and Die" charts the dissolution of a marriage parallel to another morbid travelogue. "The Transparent Man" is one of the finest dramatic monologues of the period: spoken by a woman dying of leukemia, it blends resignation, sorrow, and odd touches of humor to achieve a memorable pathos. And to these may be added mention of a wide assortment of other pieces: "Coming Home," adapted from the poet John Clare's journals of his insanity (discussed briefly in chapter 1); "The Feast of Stephen," a meditation on masculinity and violence; "The Deodand," a study of imperialism and the brutal backlash it inspires; and some late, more lyrical examples: "Memory," "Illumination," and "Lot's Wife."

James Merrill was enough younger than the three poets just discussed to have missed their formative experience of combat in World War II. His stylistic preferences were much in keeping with theirs, however, and he shares with these other formalists a wide range of cultural reference. The cosmopolitanism we see in Hecht (and to a lesser degree in Wilbur and Nemerov) is accentuated in Merrill's writing. The son and heir of a founder of the world's largest brokerage firm, Merrill traveled extensively and for decades resided half the year in Athens. As one realizes when contemplating the 869 pages of his *Collected Poems* (in which his 560-page *magnum opus*, *The Changing Light at Sandover*, is not included), it was not a life of leisure. Merrill's unremitting poetic labors accomplished an *oeuvre* as distinguished in exacting craftsmanship as it was formidable in quantity.

Like the other poets studied in this section, Merrill was unapologetic in his embrace of blank verse. The present writer recalls hearing him speak of his disesteem for the theories and practice of Ezra Pound: "All this talk about breaking the pentameter—it's always suited me just as it is." Merrill's attraction to the form did not deter him, however, from modifying it to match his sense of a particular poem's overall shape. It is not impossible to find short poems that eschew noteworthy variations (say, the early "Charles on Fire" or the late "Big Mirror Outdoors"), but Merrill's approach more often is eclectic. The longer the poem, the more likely he is to diversify its formal constituents. The opening lines of "Lost in Translation," an intricate, six-page narrative based on childhood memories, give a sample of the poet's assertive prosodic moves:

> A card table in the library stands ready
>   x x /   x / x   x   /   / x   / x
> To receive the puzzle which keeps never coming.
> Daylight shines in or lamplight down
> Upon the tense oasis of green felt.
> Full of unfulfillment, life goes on,
> Mirage arisen from time's trickling sands
> Or fallen piecemeal into place:
> German lesson, picnic, see-saw, walk
> With the collie who "did everything but talk"—
> Sour windfalls of the orchard back of us.
> A summer without parents is the puzzle,
> Or should be. But the boy, day after day,
> Writes in his Line-a-Day *No puzzle.*
>
>   (1–13)

We notice that when Merrill stretches line 2 beyond pentameter length, he does something more interesting than merely substituting anapests for iambs: while doing so with the first and the third foot, he also reverses stress to make the last two feet trochaic. This seems to tighten the line at the end, counteracting a burgeoning slackness. The sort of loose Stevensian approach favored by many poets might well have produced something like this:

>   x x /   x / x   x   /   x x / x x / x
> To receive the puzzle which keeps on not ever arriving.

Fortunately, Merrill wrote as he did, curbing the flow of the line to suggest the boy's impatient frustration. And other lines are docked of a foot or a syllable: lines 3, 5, 7, 8, and 13 are all shortened one way or the other. Without unduly stiffening the movement, this approach (compressing rather than stretching) suggests a more consciously composed utterance than we sense in conversational styles with looser prosody. Merrill's easy mastery of tone (typically gentle, rueful, reflective) may seduce readers into thinking that here is something casual and unassuming. Reading more closely, of course, reveals a highly artful intelligence at work in ways that are by no means spontaneous. The wordplay on "puzzle" highlights with the most delicate of touches the central matter of the boy's loneliness as he is left with his governess for the summer. The one rhyme in the passage ("walk" / "talk") also serves to point to the missing human companionship for which that of the collie is an inadequate substitute.

Rhyme is a subject worth dwelling on in regard to such poems by Merrill. "Lost in Translation" makes more extensive use of rhyme before it ends. Besides the fairly numerous rhymes that occur without a regular pattern, the poem features an inset passage in *Rubaiyat* (*aaxa*) quatrains. Merrill alternates blank verse with stanzaic passages in other poems as well ("Chimes for Yahya," "Verse for Urania," and others). This implies that Merrill is interested not only in expressive modifications of the pentameter line by line, but in balancing off masses of blank verse against other forms within the structure of a single poem. One might be reminded of musical structures, as when the movements of a symphony may contrast markedly with one another. By orchestrating his pieces as he does, Merrill diversifies his capacities as a narrator. Rhyme may be used to emphasize a central theme or signal a climax; or it may lead us into a digression—a different avenue of the narrative that nonetheless is parallel to its main course and contributes to the overall progression. While other poets before and after Merrill have engaged in similar variations of line length and rhythm in blank verse, none has yet equaled him in this penchant for mingling blank verse with rhyme. What is remarkable is that the disparate forms, in Merrill's hands, dovetail smoothly and coherently. It helps that Merrill, who published two novels, combined sophisticated narrative skills with his mastery of verse technique.

This many-faceted acumen is on full display in the blank-verse pieces thus far mentioned and in others, including "After the Fire," "Strato in Plaster,"

"The House Fly," and "Overdue Pilgrimage to Nova Scotia." The most expansive display of it, though, is in the trilogy *The Changing Light at Sandover* (1982), which has been called an epic. In its final form this work collects three lengthy poems—*The Book of Ephraim, Mirabell,* and *Scripts for the Pageant*—and adds to them a brief coda, "The Higher Keys." The finished poem is an unparalleled amalgam of oblique autobiography and occult speculation. Merrill tells the story of his consultations with the Ouija board over many years in the company of his longtime companion, David Jackson. In the course of reporting his conversations with the spirits of ancient and modern personages, he incidentally conveys a wealth of information about his life, loves, friendships, travels, and art, as well as puzzling through what his informants tell him about the fate of souls after death—an elaborate system of reincarnation—and the spiritual forces governing the destiny of the universe.

Blank verse is essential to Merrill's enterprise in *Sandover,* which features much the same jumping into and out of rhyme that we see in his shorter works in the form. Additionally, it daringly incorporates various voices in dialogue, if that is what exchanges with a Ouija board can be called. Here are some lines to illustrate; as he does throughout the poem, Merrill "transcribes" the spirit's words in block capitals:

> Correct but cautious, that first night we asked
> Our visitor's name, era, habitat.
> EPHRAIM came the answer. A Greek Jew
> Born AD 8 at XANTHOS Where was that?
> In Greece WHEN WOLVES & RAVENS WERE IN ROME
> (Next day the classical dictionary yielded
> A Xanthos on the Asia Minor Coast.)
> Now WHO ARE U We told him. ARE U XTIANS
> We guessed so. WHAT A COZY CATACOMB
> Christ had WROUGHT HAVOC in *his* family,
> ENTICED MY FATHER FROM MY MOTHERS BED
> (I too had issued from a broken home—
> The first of several facts to coincide.)
>
> (*The Book of Ephraim,* "C," 1–13)

Later on in the work, Ephraim's voice is joined or superseded by those of others, including the recently deceased W. H. Auden. Merrill's dexterity in alternating voices draws on the long tradition of blank verse as a dramatic medium. As with the transitions from rhymeless to rhyming lines, one admires the smooth meshing of different voices in a passage and often enough within a single line. The trilogy has been highly esteemed; in his two-volume history of modern poetry, for instance, David Perkins hails it as the greatest long poem in English after the Second World War (having awarded Eliot's *Four Quartets* the palm for the preceding period).[16] One may greatly admire it without suppressing all caveats. This long poem has its *longueurs,* especially in its later parts, as the finely gauged proportions of *The Book of Ephraim* shift into something less balanced. The second part of the trilogy is longer than the first; the third is longer than the second—an ominous progression. Story becomes more and more outweighed by oneiric revelations as the poem goes on, and not even Merrill's ready wit and impeccable style can keep this material from being fatiguing. Nevertheless, the work is a major achievement, and one that relies throughout on blank verse for its scaffolding, the standard background against which other forms are brilliantly and successively exhibited.

The blank verse written by this quartet of poets offers a generous gamut of examples to engage the attention of students of style and technique. While all four share a certain urbanity (backed, in each case, by prodigious literacy), each has an unmistakable voice, and to project it each exploits different elements of the meter. Reading them in any depth, we grow acquainted with Nemerov's acerbic toughness, Wilbur's contemplative composure, Hecht's distillation of sorrow, Merrill's seemingly effortless pyrotechnics. All of them—even the doom-conscious Hecht—may be said to have mastered various kinds of serious playfulness. In relation to traditional versification, Wilbur's blank verse is the purest. Yet Wilbur and (more conspicuously) the other three profit from the long trend toward accommodating speech effects of less formal, even demotic, sorts in the pentameter's hospitable span. The quick shifts in rhythm practiced by Nemerov, the more even (though audibly distinctive) movements of Wilbur and Hecht, the baroque juxtaposition of blank verse and rhyme in Merrill—all these are signs of the meter's adaptability. Then, too, the work of this group exhibits a notable range in scale: Nemerov writes his numerous pieces of about the size of a sonnet, Merrill his gargantuan trilogy, and all four their plentiful and estimable poems of middle length. The spread of subject matter pursued by the four is encyclopedic. This imposing corpus of blank verse fully justifies the faith that these poets shared in the continuing potency of the form; and in this they were joined by a growing contingent of poets their age or younger in the second half of the twentieth century.

IV

Because so many other poets born in the 1920s and 1930s—contemporaries or younger contemporaries of Nemerov, Wilbur, Hecht, and Merrill—wrote representative or memorable blank verse, the discussion of them in this section must be not only selective but ruthlessly compressed. In certain cases the poets, in advanced stages of their careers, continue to write, and assessments must remain tentative as long as the record is incomplete.

The record is regrettably complete in regard to Sidney Keyes, who left Oxford to serve in the British army and died in action, as a very young officer, in Tunisia in 1943. Keyes, who is little known in the United States, was already a highly adept writer of blank verse when he died at the age of twenty. The thought of what he might have accomplished during a normal life span prompts feelings of significant loss. He deserves notice not only for the quality of his work but for its unusual stylistic leanings. Keyes was a thoughtful student of romanticism—not only the English but the German variety—and in many of his poems he vaults back over many of the colloquial gestures favored by modernism to embrace the more richly textured idioms they supplanted. This obviously runs a risk of antiquarianism. Moreover, in his lesser work there is a mismatch between the opulent, assured style and the less mature tissue of attitudes it conveys. But his best poems manage to avoid dated poses while seeking their memorable resonance. If Keyes is attracted to the romantic sensibility and shares some of its fixations—most noticeably, a preoccupation with death—he complicates his themes by intruding traces of a more modern skepticism. The result is a sophisticated layering, both in the sound and the substance of his poems. The terse "Against Divination" is simultaneously sturdy and visionary as it argues against seeking wisdom (as, for instance, Yeats did) from the dead:

> Truth is not found in book or litten glass
> At midnight. Ghosts are liars. None may turn
> Winter's hard sentence but the silly man,
> The workless plowman or the unhoused poet
> Who walks without a thought and finds his peace
> In tall clouds mounting the unbroken wind,
> In dry leaves beating at the heavens' face.

(6–12)

The handling of assonance here is impressive, and Keyes brings the same finely developed ear to many poetic modes. In dramatic monologues such as "Gilles de Retz," "Schiller Dying," and "William Byrd" he creates a distinctive voice for each speaker and gracefully incorporates historical background. His control of the pentameter serves him equally well in brief symbolic lyrics ("The Kestrels," "Figure of a Bird and a Ring") and in more elaborate meditations ("Troll Kings," "The Expected Guest"). The poems he is known to have written in North Africa just before his death have not come to light, but there are some fine pieces derived from his military training in Northern Ireland, such as "Two Offices of a Sentry" and "Ulster Soldier," which recalls Edward Thomas's "Rain." It begins:

> Rain strikes the window. Miles of wire
> Are hung with small mad eyes. Night sets its mask
> Upon the fissured hill. The soldier waits
> For sleep's deception, praying thus: O land
> Of battle and the rough marauders lying
> Under this country, spare me from my mind.

> (1–6)

The startling symbolism of another war poem, "Timoshenko," lifts it above particular historical occasions. The famous Soviet marshal of World War II is depicted as consumed with pity for the soldiers he is soon to order into battle, and yet, simultaneously, as a robotlike iron man (in Keyes's grotesque image, "ten-sworded, every finger / A weighted blade" [1–2]). At the end of the piece, the marshal completes his battle plan:

> He turned, and his great shadow on the wall
> Swayed like a tree. His eyes grew cold as lead.
> Then, in a rage of love and grief and pity
> He made the pencilled map alive with war.

> (20–23)

In reading Keyes, as well as the other poets previously discussed who served in the war, we notice some differences between their military poems and those of World War I. There are not as many direct treatments of combat; battle is often alluded to, or anticipated, or recalled rather than simply being depicted in progress. Battle pieces exist, but they have to share the stage with treatments of other aspects of military life. Just because it is something of a rarity, this seems a good place to mention Louis Simpson's 1957 blank-verse narrative "The Runner." A bit over twenty-five pages, the poem recounts episodes from the Allied invasion of Europe in 1944 with a focus on one soldier's frontline experience. Simpson's verse is determinedly prosaic in phrasing, at the opposite end of the stylistic spectrum from Keyes' high lyric manner:

> From their lifted bows
> The gliders were disgorging jeeps and cannon.
> Riflemen formed their ranks and marched away.
> Dodd's section took its place in the company.
>
> (II, 15–18)

The poem is referred to as "fiction" and as "a story" by the author in a prefatory note which supplies the historical background. It is intelligent, readable writing, but it seems curiously situated as to its aim and method. Put simply, there appears to be no reason at all for it to have been written in verse. The unemphatic rhythms and the subdued documentary style lead one to imagine that this "story" might have been told just as well in prose. This may point to a perennial challenge facing poets of recent decades when they try to make poetry out of historical materials—even when the poet has taken part (as Simpson did) in the events described. Poetry in our times must contend not only with the novel but with the newspaper (and now, electronic media) if it proposes to tell stories. In attempting to reclaim certain types of material from these other modes of transmission, should poetry attempt to be a similar, less-nuanced sort of medium? That evidently is Simpson's strategy, and to many it will seem as self-defeating as it is self-denying. One is tempted to imagine how much more memorable the poem might have been if Simpson had availed himself of even a few of the many poetic resources he ascetically forswore. However much one might admire the pursuit of "truth" that most likely motivates such an approach, it appears that the restrictively documentary manner stints reality of some of its dimensions.

Edgar Bowers also served in the war and, afterward, in the occupation of Germany. Following this he studied with Yvor Winters at Stanford and wrote in the traditional verse forms that Winters championed. As we have noted,

Winters wrote very little blank verse. Bowers and a few other Stanford for-malists wrote a lot of it. For Bowers the commitment to the form deepened over time. In his first (1956) collection there is a dramatic monologue, "The Prince," which is a dignified but not altogether successful poem. It packs too many plot turns into too brief a length, and the movement of the pentameter lines is tense with rigidity:

> Giddy with lack of hope, my mind foresaw
> Itself, still barely human and by duress
> Bound in heroic trance, take glittering
> Impassive armor up and crowd the niche
> Of time with iron necessity; and, hard
> With loss and disbelief, approved its choice.
>
> (23–28)

The heavy stressing on the enjambed words seems to resist rather than facilitate the flow of one line into another. Bowers developed an easier manner and a more supple handling of rhythm for his meditative sequence "Autumn Shade," in ten brief sections, published in his second collection (1965). A few lines are enough to suggest his new level of mastery:

> My shadow moves, until, at noon, I stand
> Within its seal, as in the finished past.
> But in the place where effect and cause are joined,
> In the warmth or cold of my remembering,
> Of love, of partial freedom, the time to be
> Trembles and glitters again in windy light.
>
> (10, 1–6)

The language, which in the earlier poem seemed to be clanking about in armor, here trembles and glitters in consort with the "windy light" it evokes. "Autumn Shade" is one of the most eloquent poems written in the twentieth century on a poet's relation to his inspiration and other aspects of his expe-rience. Although deliberately modest in style and scale, it recalls Rilke, Stevens, and Eliot in its sensitive and suggestive probings of the mysteries of the poetic process. It belongs on any list of the century's best poems in blank verse.

Having assumed command of the meter, Bowers turned to it with increasing frequency in his later writing. A proliferation of themes and modes exhibits the versatility of the meter as the poet turns his hand to disquisitions on culture ("For Louis Pasteur," "In Defense of Poetry"), epigrammatic lyrics ("Living Together," "Insomnia"), personal reminiscence ("Elegy: Walking the Line"), narrative ("Clothes," "Clear-seeing"), and portraits of persons and places (the series "Thirteen Views of Santa Barbara" and several others). Bowers's late blank verse is relaxed without being slack, as we see from the opening lines of "Hang Gliding":

> When hang gliders wait for the wind, they wait
> Together in a row. The mountain light
> Recalls the young man from his solitude.
> Then, leaping out from off the farthest ridge,
> Will open to the wind's will, over his
> Lone shadow's long companionship, he rides
> His valor's widening circles toward the city—
> The roofs, white buildings, playgrounds, streets, and gardens.
>
> (1–8)

Compared with the stiff enjambments in "The Prince," these, like those of "Autumn Shade," have an airy grace. The student of blank verse will find much that is instructive in comparing earlier and later phases of this fine poet's technique.

Two other Stanford formalists, Helen Pinkerton and Charles Gullans, applied the meter to individualized purposes with memorable results. Pinkerton, a scholar of Melville and other nineteenth-century American writers, draws on her formidable knowledge of the period's history, personages, and culture in four substantial dramatic monologues. All of these poems refer to the Civil War, in progress or in retrospect, and delve deep into the moral and ethical dilemmas that were so explosively resolved by the conflict—to the extent that they were resolved. Pinkerton's refusal to oversimplify complex historical or emotional situations leads her to present her characters in the throes of mental struggles that yield to no easy answers. Perhaps as an inevitable consequence, the poems are not easy in the demands they make on the reader: the rigorous application of intellect that went into their writing assumes a correspondingly serious commitment on the part of the audience. Fortunately, notes are supplied to sketch the sometimes complicated historical backgrounds. Our focus on prosody forbids any detailed discussion of content; suffice it to say that the knottier passages submit to (and reward) a reasonable measure of attention.

The more accessible of the poems are "Lemuel Shaw's Meditation" and "Crossing the Pedregal." Both are portraits of the defeated. The eponymous speaker in the first, Herman Melville's father-in-law, contemplates the outbreak of the war that he had hoped to prevent by his rulings, as a Massachusetts Supreme Court chief justice, upholding the Fugitive Slave Act although abhorring slavery. Nearing death himself, Lemuel Shaw faces his bitter realization: "Now, argument, / Reason's persuasive eloquence, gives way / To grand unreason" (358–60). Before reaching this conclusion, the poem draws intricate parallels between Melville's novels—*Moby-Dick, The Confidence Man,* and *Billy Budd*—and the incendiary, mutually demonizing debates that led to secession. The poem's exposition of the moral conflicts between private conscience and public duty, both in life and as embodied in great fiction, is deep and finely articulated. "Crossing the Pedregal" is in the voice of Mary Custis Lee, imagined as writing to her husband, Robert E. Lee, on the fall of Richmond. A more emotionally volatile piece, this scouts the multiple temptations to despair faced by the losing side and sharply highlights the female perspective:

> You spend your wrath in battle while I cannot,
> And if you fall, you always have your men,
> Who will keep bright the flame of your repute,
> Whether we win or lose our independence.
> Why, what have I to do these long dull hours
> But knit and hear of you and the brave men
> You have infused with your strong stoic will,
> Aurelius's patience and Roman dignity,
> With more success than you have had with me
> Or my reluctant will.
>
>   (127–36)

Pinkerton sometimes permits herself more relaxed rhythms, but her general approach to prosody is traditional and disciplined. Her nineteenth-century settings and the epistolary framing of some of these poems calls for a more formal choice of diction than we find in many recent dramatic monologues. She wields this style with enough conviction that readers are more likely to find it impressively articulate than stilted or stuffy. She has also written several epigrammatic poems on works of art in the meter and a few more personal poems, among which the theological debate "The Return" stands out.

If Pinkerton's use of the meter for personal expression is rare, the opposite is true of Charles Gullans, an overlooked figure even among the often critically neglected formalists of his generation. There is no hint that we are to take the "I" in his poems as a persona; and if we consider simply the occasions he addresses—most often, love affairs gone wrong—we might think of the confessional poetry of Lowell and others. This would be a mistake. Gullans is engaged not in venting his painful feelings therapeutically but in analyzing them with riveting precision. The poems are sparse in circumstantial detail. Lovers are described in only the most general terms. The poems insistently probe the emotional havoc wrought by love (or sometimes merely lust): the patron of this poetry is that familiar deity Gullans calls "Eros the Terrible" ("Local Winds," 5.17). What we have, then, might seem a relapse into full-blown romanticism. But this judgment, too, would be a mistake. Gullans subjects the theme of passion in its most inflammatory form to an icy, unsparing examination by way of reminiscence and introspection. A most unusual poetry results, seeming almost as though it takes its emotional core from Shelley and its technique from Yvor Winters. Gullans uses contemporary, though not strenuously colloquial, diction, and his versification is nearly always regular—more punctilious than that of other Winters associates such as Bowers or Pinkerton. Here are some representative lines from the sequence "Many Houses," in which the speaker, knowing their relationship is winding down, hears his lover typing in the next room:

>   Your voice
> Is falling word by word upon a page
> In the next room, making a new event
> Inalterably dead. The intimate
> And personal are also true. And love,
> Love which was once the fluid and unfixed,
> Becomes a memoir or scenario,
> Another book upon another shelf;

Another piece of minor history,
This poem on this page. In a few days
You will get up and walk across the room
And turn the handle of the door and leave,
And leave behind unalterable loss.

(I, 5, 21–33)

Setting has more than incidental importance in many of Gullans's blank-verse poems. Los Angeles, with its insistent sunshine, luxuriant flora, and hedonistic youth culture, provides an ironic counterpoint to the regrets of an aging, unsuccessful lover. Place, in fact, is what anchors the poems so troublingly in reality, since Gullans is reticent in descriptions of persons. The poems are unhappy, and in no trivial sense, but with the disturbing resonance we find in poets like Hardy and Larkin. Especially memorable is the studied clash between subject and style, the harsh situations and settings rendered in smooth, unruffled lines:

Here, we are told, we find the city's best,
A bottomless, topless, go-go discotheque.
Where barmaids in their scandalous, baroque
Articulations of their surfaces
Move with a mannequin's austerity,
Remote and chill. Music is mindless here,
With the insistent mindlessness of sex,
As they grind out the motions of the brothel
With all a whore's indifference to her trade.
The neighborhood adonises cavort
Between the dart board and the pool room
With Roman noses, with their grecian asses
Stuffed into jeans like sailors in tight whites.

("Los Angeles Place Names: West Hollywood," 1–13)

For Gullans, the missing unstressed syllable in line 11 is a rare deviation. The general tautness of the lines reminds us, usefully, that traditional blank verse is capable of dealing with rough subjects without becoming blatantly rough in its rhythmic movement. For modern readers, iambic pentameter may be an unexpected medium for a description of the West Hollywood disco scene, but it serves the purpose more than adequately. Other absorbing poems in the meter by Gullans include the sequence "Local Winds," "The Chart House" (a haunting piece about a passing encounter with a hustler), and an austere meditation on death, "The House of Exile."

Modes of autobiography bulked large in later twentieth-century blank verse. Each of the many poets to use the meter in this way has given the egotistical an individual flavor. L. E. Sissman's pieces are often exercises in nostalgia, replete with circumstantial detail that sometimes atomizes a reader's attention rather than fixing it on the events presented. Sissman's reach for irony does not disguise his sentimental attachment to his past—especially to his time at Harvard in the late 1940s. Here he approaches his off-campus apartment to await an afternoon visit from a girlfriend:

> With gin, *prosciutto,* and Drake's Devil Dogs
> In a brown-paper bag, I climb the Hill
> On Saturday, the thirty-first of May,
> Struck by the sun approaching apogee,
> Green comments issued by the Common trees,
> Mauve decadence among magnolias,
> The moving charcoal shadows on the brown
> Stone of the moving brownstone where I live,
> And a spring breath of Lux across the Charles.
> My key mutters the password: I step in
> To the dense essence of an entire past:
> Rugs, chicken, toilets, Lysol, dust, cigars.
>
> ("In and Out: A Home Away from Home, 1947," 1–12)

Sissman wrote many poems on similar material in couplets and quatrains, and that may have been the better formal choice. The verse is handled well enough, but turns of wit such as line 5 and the further wordplay on "moving" and "brownstone" seem waiting for a snappy rhyme to pin them down. Writing like this has the charm of period and local color (in details like the once-prominent soap factory nodded to in line 9). But these trophies of a near-photographic memory are woven together in lightweight confections. The trouble is that Sissman's life experiences, the occasions for these diverting embellishments, are not especially interesting. Some writers succeed brilliantly in extracting significance from the mundane, but Sissman, though he commands respect for the artfulness of his descriptions, is more likely to be remembered for the poems in which he comes to terms with the Hodgkin's disease that killed him at the age of forty-eight. Some of his accounts of his diagnosis and treatment are unnerving—jaunty, but without the slickness that often compromises his other work. Something tougher and wiser emerges:

> Why must the young male nurse who preps the plain
> Of my knife-thrower's-target abdomen
> With his conversant razor, talking snicks
> Of scything into my sedated ears,
> Talk also in his flat and friendly voice,
> So far from showdowns, on a blasé note
> Of reassurance, learnt by classroom rote?
> It is that he must make his living, too.
>
> ("Homage to Clotho: Hospital Suite," 4, 1–8)

Some other intriguing poems featuring the meter in whole or in part are "The West Forties: Morning, Noon, and Night," "Dying: An Introduction," and "Three American Dreams: A Suite in Phillips House." (Sissman, who had a successful career in advertising, seems not to have learned the art of the headline. His titles tend to be straggling and appositional.)

For all the poets who in this period cultivated a traditional prosody, there were more who favored a more relaxed approach. The "anapestic stretching" that Donald Justice sees in the late Stevens became, as he asserts, a common tactic, and it was joined by other deliberate tweakings of the line. (In the background of some of these were such precedents as Eliot's Websterian lines and Frost's conversational effects.) Mona Van Duyn presents an example of this approach at its most attractive, although her practice might frequently make a stringent prosodist wince. She developed an effectively articulate style, and it is by no means clear that her formally conscious poems would be "better" if they took fewer liberties with versification. Her modifications usually seem choices rather than accidents. Still, one may wonder why she, like some other poets, should have found the pentameter insufficiently roomy. She is drawn

to a longer line—hexameter, or longer—and even in pentameter poems where
the stretching is not as frequent, it generally crops up at intervals.

In "Marriage, with Beasts," she recalls visiting the zoo with her husband.
This, for Van Duyn, is a relatively tight passage:

> As far distant as they can get from the hose
> that flushes away bones, flies and urine,
> snooting the praise of their dumpy audience,
> the cats stride with the strained hauteur of fashion
> models, back and forth, rippling their coats.
> We're tired of disguises, but what else can we look at?
> Wait. A mountain lion stops and gazes
> at me. He comes straight at me up to the bars
> and stays there, looking me in the eye. He neither
> implores nor threatens, he is only after some sight.

(84–93)

In lines 89 and 93, which both have thirteen syllables, the stress patterns are
not identical. It is within reason to propose five strong stresses for line 93:

```
     x   /   x   / x   x x / x / x   x    /
     implores nor threatens, he is only after some sight
```

is a possible rendering of the emphases; but many readers would demand a
stress on "he," which would make the line a stretched hexameter. Line 89 offers
even more points for debate because the monosyllabic phrase after the comma
is hard to scan convincingly.

```
       x   /   x  x  / x   x   / /   x   x  /   x
       We're tired of disguises, but what else can we look at?
```

is possible, but so also is the more interesting

```
       x   /   x  x  / x   x   x  \   /   x  /   x
       We're tired of disguises, but what else can we look at?
```

Cases could be made for other readings as well. This sort of line expansion is
Van Duyn's most usual modification, though occasionally she will move in

the opposite direction: "The Cities of the Plain," a provocative monologue for Lot's wife, intermittently draws back to tetrameter length. Other striking poems, which in various degrees exhibit her idiosyncratic prosodic maneuvers, are "The Challenger," "Photographs," "Evening Stroll in the Suburbs," "Last Words of Pig No. 6707," and "The Burning of Yellowstone." To say that in such pieces Van Duyn's versification "works for her," even if true, is not the same as recommending it as a model. Setting to one side matters of stress and syllable, what we remember from her poems are her attractive empathy, lively phrasing, and imaginative reach. But there are great numbers of poets who lack those assets and therefore risk providing more conspicuous distractions when wrenching or diluting their meters.

Satire has been less often a feature in recent blank verse than one might have expected, although, as we have seen, it formed one of the harsher strands of Nemerov's work in the form. For Turner Cassity it is the dominant mode, whether he is writing in neat, ruthless rhymes or equally astringent unrhymed pentameters. Cassity specializes in goring sacred cows. His triumphant flaunting of American iconoclasm reminds one of the funnier side of Mencken or the more serious side of Twain. Organized religion, government, family values, social and political icons ranging from high to low and from left to right, celebrities and nobodies, and simply any hopeful views of human nature are all equally likely to be cheerfully skewered by his deftly aimed lines. In "Stylization and Its Failures" he compares the American eagle to a vulture, beginning: "The vulture, at the least, has not the look / Of flying money, or a Seal of State / Become a Frisbee" (1–3), and, after enlarging on this, concluding:

> Ambitious Scout whose merit badges mass,
> Would you continue if you knew the end
> Is Court of Honor for a scavenger?
> Bald Eagle, Vulture of the Naked Neck,
> Are both of you one bird? One carrier
> To whose one message there is no reply?
> It was mere chance that a Samaritan
> Should happen by; mere chance that he was good.
> The body by the roadside nonetheless
> Would have received attention, in due time.

(17–26)

In "The Mount of the Holy Cross" he writes of the famous "Cross of Snow," using it as an occasion for discussing American disputes concerning church and state and noting that nature is not especially deferential to either side: "One arm has melted" (35). But, more recently,

> Snow that in the Great Salt Lake
> Has inundated dance pavilions has,
> Upon the peak at Leadville, nailed again
> The full crossarm and thousand-foot upright.
> A chair lift might exploit it. Postcards show,
> Already, colored helicopter views.
> It is the merest tic of time before
> Evel Knievel, say, decides to ski
> From wound to wound, or, every Saturday,
> Weekend stunt pilots write I. N. R. I.
>
> (42–51)

It seems evident that Cassity's prosody and his dry, deadpan manner are all of a piece in creating the amusing, outrageous, uncomfortable effect such passages have. The tightness of the line makes the utterance more lethal: no anapestic stretching here. In Cassity's longer pieces the satirist's targets split and recombine like globules of mercury. "The Mount of the Holy Cross," for instance, takes aim at traditional piety, religious kitsch, sport and tourism and the industries they support, and the American appetite for tackiness in general. Some of the greatest satire—parts of Swift's, for instance—extends its reach so much as to become a misanthropic nihilism. There are touches of this—more than a few—in Cassity. Yet his best work, often quite disturbing, has a traditional moral foundation: a sense that all human pretensions are mocked by mortality. We have already seen how this kind of chilly conclusion works in the eagle and vulture poem, and it is equally forceful in many another. Often the point is made with a twist: we are not merely mortal, but are drawn to death as murderers or victims, the Cain and Abel archetypes playing out through history. "Acid Rain on Sherwood Forest" mounts a sardonic defense of the arms manufacturer Baron Krupp, concluding:

> Had Cain
> No weapons but his hands he would be Cain,

And Abel dead of strangulation. Child
Of nature, little boy of five or six,
Why have you pulled the rubber suction cup
From off your arrow and begun to sharpen it?

(21–26)

Other provocative pieces in this vein include "Man of the Century," "Days of Labor," "Berlin-to-Baghdad," "Eniwetok Mon Amour," "Enola Gay Rights," and "Why Geriatrics Are Not Sacrificed." Some that seem lighter until one thinks twice about them include "The Glorified Go One by One to Glory," "Retouching Walker Evans," and memory pieces like "Mainstreaming" and "Hedy Lamarr and a Chocolate Bar." The daunting African landscape of "Oued Draa" shows Cassity on a rare occasion using blank verse for description with minimal commentary.

Like Cassity, Miller Williams mines rich veins of the Deep South and its folkways in his work. Also like Cassity, he has a robust talent for comedy. The tone of this is different, however. Williams can be sardonic, but he does not attempt anything like the ferocity of Cassity's black humor. His view of human nature and society is less likely to shock, but is often capable first of amusing, then of leaving an ache. Williams has written numerous pieces of blank verse, of which the shorter ones can be quite effective, sometimes in ways reminiscent of Nemerov. A few memorable examples are "The True Story of What Happened," "Form and Theory of Poetry," and "Going Deaf." Increasingly over the course of his career, he has developed his talent for the dramatic monologue. At the turn of the century he may be the most energetic and inventive poet to have followed Frost's lead, both in his preference for "ordinary" people as speakers and in his fine ear for the unobtrusive poetry of their speech. Frost's ruminations on "the sound of sense" find countless illustrations in Williams's hauntingly rendered voices.

Williams favors titles that outline for the reader the speaker, the occasion, and sometimes the audience within a monologue: "The Ghost of His Wife Comes to Tell Him How It Is," "The Art Photographer Puts His Model at Ease," and the like. (The tactic is a venerable one: Browning's "The Bishop Orders His Tomb at Saint Praxed's Church" is a well-known instance.) Unlike Frost, who in many pieces is leisurely and indirect at the outset, Williams is typically abrupt in his openings, suggesting the dominant emotion from the start. If his handling of characters is more indulgent than Turner Cassity's, his prosody, too, is more relaxed. "Relaxed" may be a misleading description, though, for only an alert sensitivity to speech inflections could produce his intelligent gravitations between regular and less-regular lines. Here is an excerpt from "She Talks to Her Sister, Briefly By on the Way to West Memphis." Lamenting her lack of closeness to her husband, now retired and "underfoot," the speaker recalls her suspicion of an infidelity on his part, then goes on to say:

> x   /   x   /   x   /   /   x /
> Well, that was back a long time ago.
>
> The time when people ought to be together
> /   x   /   x   /   /   x   /
> night and day like this, day and night
> are those first years, when nothing seems enough.
> x   /   x   x   /   x   /   x   / x x   /
> Not now, when a brushing touch can do for a day.
>
>   /   x   /   x   /   x   /   x /   x
> What this does, you know, it makes it harder
> x / x x   / x /   x   x / x   /
> for one to go on alone when the other dies.
> You get too used to being half of something.

(30–37)

Williams brings a welcome variety to his rendering of conversational rhythms. In lines 34 and 36 he uses the familiar anapests for markedly different effects: of wincing delicacy in the first instance, and of disruption capped by finality in the second. But his other slight modifications are just as telling. Line 30 has nine syllables and line 32 is even shorter, with eight. The poet has pared unstressed syllables from this or that iamb in aid of an unstudied manner of speaking. The calculation involved is evident; it would be easy to recast the lines to impose a regular iambic pattern:

> x   /   x   / x /   x   /   x /
> Well, that was back a long, long time ago.
>
> x   /   x   / x   /   x   /   x   /
> each night and day like this, each day and night

Line 35 is decasyllabic and at first presents a puzzling stress pattern. But minimally rewriting it—

<pre>
    x   /   x   /   x   /   x   /   x   / (x)
And what this does, you know, it makes it harder
</pre>

—reveals that it is a regular line with a feminine ending whose first foot has been docked of its first syllable. All this evidences a careful ear, and it should not be thought that Williams's handling of standard-patterned lines is any less sure. "You get too used to being half of something" has the fatalistic, proverbial ring of such sentences in Frost, a sense of language attempting to control pain by locking it in an adage.

A list of all Williams's dramatic poems in the meter is infeasible, but, besides those mentioned, some of the best are "Ruby Tells All," "Rituals," "Adjusting to the Light," "She Prays for Her Husband, the Good Pastor, on His Deathbed at Last," and the remarkable "Clutter of Silence: Invention for Two Voices," which in symmetrical sections sets forth the views first of a wife, then of a husband trapped in a failing marriage. The way the voices develop parallel themes as the speakers say what they can never say to each other is as memorable as it is sad.

It has often been noted that after the first few decades of the twentieth century the center of poetic activity shifted from England to the United States. One beneficial consequence of this for poetry in America has been the increased presence of poets drawn here from abroad to read or to teach. The West Indian Derek Walcott and the Irish Seamus Heaney are two of the most prominent poets to have lived here for prolonged periods in recent decades.

Walcott is sometimes spoken of as one who has written much blank verse. The description is problematic. He has written a great deal of iambic pentameter, but his habit, like James Merrill's, is to intersperse rhymed with unrhymed lines. There is in fact a noticeably higher incidence of rhyme in his work than in Merrill's, and the rhymes are not commonly set off in stanzaic sections but scattered throughout. Such an approach raises difficult questions of definition. When does "occasional rhyme" become more than occasional? One can certainly find poems in which it is less immediately apparent. "Europa" contains thirty-two lines. Six of these—three pairs—rhyme, which might not seem a large percentage. However, if one adds in what are obviously or arguably off rhymes, one can count eleven more "rhyming" pairs, albeit unobtrusive and sometimes very widely spaced. In a longer poem (forty-seven lines), "The Flock," the first seven lines end in full rhymes. The poem then avoids rhyming up through line 18, after which the next four lines rhyme in an *abba* pattern. From there to the end we find one pair of lines fully rhyming (lines 26 and 28), and a few possible off rhymes not conforming to any observable pattern. As sometimes with Merrill, we may wonder in which cases the blank-verse label is apt. Perhaps it is more accurate to docket this sort of thing as a hybrid form, especially when, as Walcott often does, the poet uses even more rhyme than in these examples.

Regardless of the formal questions raised by Walcott's writing, his colorful language and energetic rhythms are easy to appreciate. Like many of his generation he is less than punctilious about including a syllable more or less. The following is unusual, for Walcott, in maintaining iambic movement to the degree that it does, and unusual also in forgoing rhyme. Here the poet, watching a religious procession, blends images of colonialism and of the Holocaust:

> Now I have come to where the phantoms live,
> I have no fear of phantoms, but of the real.
> The Sabbath benedictions of the islands.
> Treble clef of the snail on the scored leaf,
> the Tantum Ergo of black choristers
> soars through the organ pipes of coconuts.
> Across the dirty beach surpliced with lace,
> they pass a brown lagoon behind the priest,
> pale and unshaven in his frayed soutane,
> into the concrete church at Canaries;
> as Albert Schweitzer moves to the harmonium
> of morning, and to the pluming chimneys,
> the groundswell lifts *Lebensraum, Lebensraum.*
>
> ("The Fortunate Traveler," II, 1–13)

Seamus Heaney's approach to the form is less complicated by outcroppings of rhyme. His blank verse shares with his other poetry the benefits of a densely textured idiom. Heaney draws on his farm background as a boy in Northern Ireland to invest his vocabulary with words of rural and agricultural heritage, and he melds these smoothly to others more urbanized and contemporary. This unique blend of the archaic and marginal with the more ordinary forms of diction gives his style strength and a sense of mythic timelessness.

In some of Heaney's early poems in the meter, the strength is evident in the vivid descriptions and is supported by an almost excessively muscular approach to verse movement. Here are the last lines of the well-known poem of childhood memory, "Death of a Naturalist":

> Right down the dam gross-bellied frogs were cocked
> On sods; their loose necks pulsed like sails. Some hopped:
> The slap and plop were obscene threats. Some sat
> Poised like mud grenades, their blunt heads farting.
> I sickened, turned, and ran. The great slime kings
> Were gathered there for vengeance and I knew
> That if I dipped my hand the spawn would clutch it.

> (26–32)

The plentiful assonances enrich the sound. The title poem of Heaney's first volume, this is commanding in its use of the meter but a bit ponderous in pace. Earlier in the poem there are some awkward enjambments. This earthbound handling of the meter is thematically suitable here, but it might not serve as well for airier subjects. In fact, Heaney over the years has developed a lighter rhythmic touch, and has grown capable of pentameters considerably more graceful. The opening of "Casting and Gathering," from his eighth collection, *Seeing Things,* displays a more diversified mastery of sound and movement:

> Years and years ago, these sounds took sides:

> On the left bank, a green silk tapered cast
> Went whistling through the air, saying *hush*
> And *lush,* entirely free, no matter whether
> It swished above the hayfield or the river.

> On the right bank, like a speeded-up corncrake,
> A sharp ratcheting went on and on
> Cutting across the stillness as another
> Fisherman gathered line-lengths off his reel.

> (1–9)

If at first Heaney's verbal inventiveness outpaced his prosodic sophistication, this was remedied in due course, and in his later work the two go hand in hand. A few more of his estimable pieces in the form are "The Wife's Tale," "Shore Woman," "Seeing Things," "Wheels within Wheels," and "The Sharping Stone."

Space constraints require even briefer discussion of work by poets of this age group who have used the form more sparingly. While some of the poems about to be mentioned are formally disparate from the bulk of their authors' work, they should interest anyone who values the meter, and some of them deserve to be better known. Lisel Mueller's gifts of elegance and economy are well displayed in her rare blank-verse poems. In "The Queen of Sheba Says Farewell," she brings a light touch to the contentious topic of gender differences and neatly makes the point that there are things about women that Solomon despite all his wisdom will never trouble to learn. Another piece, "The Power of Music to Disturb," casts the meter in nine-line stanzas to pursue its title theme. Mueller dexterously situates her speaker's apparently calm, lamplit, domestic scene between the sounds of animals hunting in the woods outdoors and the music pouring from the radio which, as she hears it, "drives / toward death by love, for love, because of love / like some black wave that cannot break itself" (7–9). Love as simultaneously seductive and destructive, and music's ability to express love's light and dark sides are points eloquently expounded in Mueller's meditation. The poem reflects its central paradox formally. With one exception, each stanza is written as a single sentence, and the smoothness of the verse movement, reinforced by extended syntax, suggests the beautiful flow of the music as it carries, like the poem, a disturbing message. The final stanza brings home a sense of inexorability:

> But O my love, I cannot beat it back,
> neither the sound nor what the sound lets loose;
> the opulence of agony drowns out
> the hard, dry smack of death against the glass
> and batters down the seawalls of my mind,
> and I am pulled to levels below light
> where easy ways of love are meaningless
> and creatures feel their way along the dark
> by shock of ecstasy and heat of pain.
>
> (37–45)

In a period in which blank verse has more commonly gravitated toward unornamented talk, an exuberant verbal device like Daniel Hoffman's "Mi-Carême" stands out. Hoffman summons festive sound effects, recalling the early Wallace Stevens somewhat, as he describes a French carnival procession of giant effigies heading for a ritual bonfire:

> A pair of osier giants, heads like eggs
> The last roc laid before the earth grew cool,
> In couthless courtship dipped and ducked and danced,
> Joy's colossi, rathe for ridicule,
> Tunes tattered the air festooned with flags then
> As instrumental joculators wove
> In sinuous undulations in between
> His lumbering ankles and the porte-cochère
> That a nest of pulleys held in her skirts aloft.

> (19–27)

Hoffman's other pieces in the meter, equally accomplished and widely varied in tone and topic, include "The Hermit of Cape Rosier," "The Great Horse Strode without a Rider," and "Asleep."

Donald Justice's forays with the form were sparse to the point of seeming surreptitious. These few poems, however, are made with his customary grace, an apparent casualness that deepens as we read to something other than casual. "The Telephone Number of the Muse" is a sly and clever piece of satire. "The Miami of Other Days" and "The Sunset Maker" are compact, pungent assemblages of nostalgia, autobiographical in the first case, fictional in the other, both infused with Chekhovian melancholy.

Richard Howard is best known as a writer of Browningesque monologues for literary and historical figures (he has in fact written one for Browning himself). Many of these are in open form or elaborately choreographed syllabics. Readers in search of blank verse will find some well-crafted pieces, though. While some of Howard's reanimations of the famous dead are little more than repositories of high-toned gossip, at his best he brings together a formidable historical knowledge, a psychoanalytic shrewdness, and a spirited style to achieve memorable feats of portraiture. The especially clever "Family Values" uses blank verse in its first two sections. Based on paintings of Milton dictating *Paradise Lost* to his daughters, these give voice to those much-put-upon women. "Venetian Interior, 1889" is not formally dramatic, but it contains effective inset dialogue as it presents the elderly Robert Browning visiting his son and daughter-in-law. Here are a few lines in which Browning gives his impressions of Disraeli:

> With that olive cast and those glowing-coal-black eyes
> and the mighty dome of his forehead (to be sure,
> no Christian temple), as unlike a living man
> as any waxwork at Madame Tussaud's:
> he had a face more mocking than a domino—
> I would as soon have thought of sitting down
>
> to tea with Hamlet or Ahasuerus . . .

                                                                    (79–85)

We notice the pun on "temple" and wonder if Browning was in fact as devoted to wordplay as Howard is. Such questions hardly matter when, as in this piece, the poet creates an altogether persuasive *mise-en-scène* for his equally persuasive speakers. Other notable pieces in blank verse by this poet include the fine ecphrastic poems "Thebais" and "*Les Travaux d'Alexandre*" and the compact, decadent monologue, "Further Triangulations." Howard's style is relentlessly self-conscious, and in its less inspired moments can be arch and chatty.

Another prolific and sophisticated poet of the time, though one more muted in style, is Howard Moss. His ambience and his manner are both urban and urbane, displaying an understated glossiness that fit the tone of the postwar *New Yorker,* where Moss was ensconced for decades as poetry editor. Once widely published (not least by his own magazine), Moss has faded in reputation since his death. His pentameters are thoughtfully made, at times crimped or stretched, at times admitting occasional rhyme. There is more polish than passion in this work, and when Moss reaches for either comic energy ("Ménage à Trois") or tragic profundity ("Buried City"), the results are strained. More modest and intimate pieces, often in a vein of urban pastoral, succeed better —"The Roofgarden," "The Dune Wig," "Someone," "Rules of Sleep," and "Rome: The Night Before," to name a few. The highly likable "The Pruned Tree" may be a witty and urbanized recasting of Karl Shapiro's "A Cut Flower." The tree's inhuman worldview is evoked in a naively self-centered voice:

> As a torn paper might seal up its side,
> Or a streak of water stitch itself to silk
> And disappear, my wound has been my healing,
> And I am made more beautiful by losses.
>
> (1–4)

Even more impressive is a later piece for an inanimate speaker, "Einstein's Bathrobe," which moves from homely details about the physicist at the breakfast table to a cosmic grandeur:

> From signs Phoenicians scratched into the sand
> With sticks he drew the contraries of space:
> Whirlwind Nothing and Volume in its rage
> Of matter racing to undermine itself,
> And when the planets sang, why, he sang back
> The lieder black holes secretly adore.
>
> (43–48)

Here is one case in which the poet's reach did not exceed his grasp.

For some poets of this age cohort, blank verse figured as part of a youthful formalist phase that was superseded by a preference for open form. It is not always remembered that Adrienne Rich was one who followed this pattern. The poems in dutiful blank verse that appeared in her first two volumes are something of a footnote to a career that shaped itself in less traditional ways. They are good reading, though, and in a few cases point intriguingly toward the poet's future. Even while they exemplify an esthetic Rich was to rebel against, they display her analytical sharpness and, in certain cases, the feminist concerns that were to be central to her later writing. "Mathilde in Normandy," for instance, comments mordantly on the lives of women left at home while men go off to war, drawing its example from the Norman invasion of England in ways that would strike a chord for any of the hosts of later women living through later wars. The monologue "Autumn Equinox" gives voice to an intelligent woman trapped in an unsatisfactory, conventional marriage. After stultifying decades in a small-town college with her clueless professor husband, she has reached the point at which frustration gives way to numb resignation. The poem moves briskly through her memories and discontents with touches of astringent humor, as when she recalls courtship:

So Lyman came to ask me of my father:
Stiff-collared, shy, not quite the man I'd dreamed—
(Byron and Matthew Arnold vaguely mingled
Without the disadvantages of either.)
And yet he seemed superb in his refusal
To read aloud from Bryant to the ladies
Assembled on the boarding-house piazza
Among the moth-wings of a summer evening.
His quick withdrawal won my heart. I smile
Sometimes to think what quirks of vanity
Propel us toward our choices in the end.

(58–68)

Whatever smile this prompts for the reader is fleeting, for the balked condition of the speaker and the subdued bitterness of the piece make it depressing. It is fascinating to compare this muted, fictionalized treatment of a theme with some of Rich's later work—first-person, overtly and radically politicized, and (of course) unmetered.

As it sometimes was in earlier generations, blank verse could be enlisted for decidedly odd purposes. The Scottish-born George Macbeth wrote a ten-page narrative, "Driving West," that attempts to describe the plight of survivors of a nuclear war. The imagery is like that of the disaster films that were to become popular in the sixties and seventies; here, fire reaches a wrecked subway train:

They smelt it coming. Acrid hint of smoke
Under carriage-cloth. Rake of hot-iron heat
Flaming on cheeks. And then that fast-back lick
Of its long tongue, flickering through each crack
In plastered skin and bone, liquid like knives
Cutting and salting. Wincing in its wounds
The whole train split like stitches.

(IV, 13–19)

Subtlety is not this poet's strong suit. It is difficult for a reader to remain committed to a piece that is climax from beginning to end; beneath such a barrage of obvious horrors and histrionic postures the mind grows restive. Such poetry tends to date itself through its excesses, and most of the interest this work can now hope to garner is as a Cold War document, a cultural artifact of the nuclear arms race of the sixties and the paranoia it engendered.

V

This allusion to the sixties and its tensions prompts further reflections on the relation of poetry to the broader culture during the period. For certain poets the formalist style they began with came to seem ill-suited for addressing urgent political or social concerns, or for projecting an authentic sense of self. The Vietnam War, the struggles for civil rights and women's rights, and, within poetry, the emergence of extreme self-revelations in the confessional mode all fed a tendency toward personal expression in antitraditional forms. The impersonal, paradigmatic qualities of meter no longer commanded the loyalty of traditionally schooled poets like Adrienne Rich, James Wright, W. S. Merwin, or (in certain phases) Robert Lowell. The assumption of such poets and the readers drawn to the jaggeder contours and tonal intensity of their new styles was that the turbulence of the times was being appropriately mirrored in free verse. From midcentury on, the most visible "movements"—Black Mountain, beat, confessional, deep image—all explicitly or tacitly favored free verse. As the previous section demonstrates, however, meter did not disappear, even when faced with opposition just as strenuous and even more widespread than that posed by Pound's and Eliot's earlier challenge. Poets like Wilbur and Hecht, refusing capitulation, continued to write the pentameters deemed extinct by trend-spotters. And eventually, in one of those swings of the stylistic pendulum that seem to accelerate progressively, new groups of young formalist poets appeared and reinvigorated the traditional poetics that had been beleaguered during years of unrest.

This outline of the history of blank verse concludes in this section with a look at the work of these poets, all of them born in 1940 or later, and many of them associated with what has come to be called the New Formalism. Many of these poets also work in rhyme and in syllabics; for some blank verse has been an occasional option, for others a more prominent one. By the end of the twentieth century, after all the passing tornadoes of modernism and postmodernism had subsided, poets were left with a pervasive mood of pragmatism, in which blank verse was seen as a readily available, highly adaptive resource, without presuming that it could or should be the primary one. If not indispensable, it was and continues to be an important tool in the contemporary poet's toolbox, and one for which fresh uses continue to be found.

One of the most prolific and versatile writers of blank verse today is Rachel Hadas. Her writing typifies the flexibility of structure and argument that contemporary poets tend to bring to their work in the form. Hadas writes what may be termed essays in verse; but these are rarely abstract, being grounded in personal experiences sensitively described. Autobiography and topical essay overlap, and the meter proves to be an efficient medium for bridging genres. Essayistic poems—especially extended ones like some of Hadas's—encounter all the risks of didacticism as well as of diffuseness. Blank verse may not be of much help in avoiding the latter; we recall Karl Shapiro's caution, quoted above, that it is perilously easy "to wander on and on" when writing it. Hadas's best work bypasses these pitfalls through a careful balance of personal and general concerns, a sure-footed progress from point to point, and, not least, a disciplined shaping of verse lines. "Performances, Assortments," conjures the spirit of Hart Crane, sixty years after his death, to respond to the sort of energetic New York street scene that captivated him:

> You saw beyond advertisements. Behind
> each paper face lurked splittings of the soul,
> its mask or its persona. "Janus-faced
> capture," or—grotesque arresting image
> suggesting mutilation and impalement
> x / x /   x / x / x
> but also somehow exhibition,
> a spit revolving in a restaurant window
> / x /   x / x / x /
> closely watched by hungry passersby—
> "I, turning, turning on smoked forking spires."

> (27–35)

This is trenchant literary criticism, at once brisk, sympathetic, and shrewd. The exacting pace of argument is complemented by the tightness of the verse. There is little stretching and in two cases notable snipping of lines. Line 32 discards its final stressed syllable while line 34 makes do without an initial un-stressed syllable. One hears the modification more obviously in the first case than in the second. Such shortened lines are frequently met with in Hadas's work, and in that of a number of other contemporary poets. This clipping seems to have grown in favor, perhaps as a counterweight to the Stevensian stretching that earlier enjoyed so great a vogue.[17] Although it may seem im-pressionistic to say so, the recurrent shortened lines contribute to a generally tighter feeling in such verse—a sense that the poem is less likely to ramble be-cause it is being kept on a shorter leash.

Some of Hadas's finest work in the meter is in sections of her long discur-sive poem "The Dream Machine," which meditates on such Wordsworthian subjects as memory and imagination in ways that confirm the persisting fas-cination of these matters. Other memorable pieces include "Peculiar Sanctity," on the effect of the AIDS epidemic, and "Genealogies," a tribute to the poet's father. The short poem "Props" grimly crystallizes a sense of tragedy through concentration on an unobtrusive image. The rose petals strewn by the Queen on Ophelia's grave in a performance of *Hamlet* remain lying on the stage while the final scenes are enacted, so that at last,

> Even when they lift the body
> high, while the livid King and Queen are sprawled
> half-in half-out of armchairs, some few white
> remembrances remain to be discerned
> by your sharp eyes.

(9–13)

Because the midcentury formalists remained active over the course of long careers, they were available as models and mentors for younger poets, and it is no surprise to see continuities between the generations. For example, J. D. McClatchy, who was to become one of James Merrill's literary executors, had his first book selected for publication by Richard Howard. Like that of both these elders, McClatchy's work is esthetically sophisticated, steeped in cultural awareness, polished in style. The work differentiates itself from such models through its voice, which is individualized and by no means belletristic, and, especially in recent years, through its willingness to engage subjects of an edgier kind. In "Sniper," the speaker recalls an incident from Vietnam: the shooting of a boy on a bicycle on his way to deliver guns and ammunition to the Viet Cong:

> You drop him.
> You'd do it again, even as you watch him kick
> In the dirt, the wheels still slowly turning.
> The spotter's bugged, but you explain they flop
> Around a lot when you shoot them in the head.
>
> (36–40)

The use of "you" sets up a tense ambiguity: either the speaker is recounting the sniper's own actions to him, using elements of the sniper's diction, or the poem is the sniper's own account, in which he distances himself from the act through avoidance of the first-person pronoun. A poem that operates in a more domestic sphere, "Cancer," is in its own way equally unsparing. The narrator tells of being brought as a child to celebrate his soon-to-die grandmother's birthday in her hospital room:

> Through the pleated, angled straw she took in
> A burning mouthful of champagne, and rebuked
> Her son-in-law for his expensive joke,
> Drawing, hairless, an imaginary comb
> Through memories of what pleasure anger gave,
> Then smiled, "I'd stop all this if only I could."
>
> (3, 6–11)

In some of the poet's earlier work the material is less wrenching. An especially memorable piece, "At a Reading," describes a poetry reading by Anthony Hecht during which a man in the audience repeats every word for the deaf woman accompanying him to lip-read. The poem raises startling points about the portability of poetry, challenging our conventional expectations of the ways it may reach its audience. There is in all these poems, as in most of McClatchy's work in the meter, an embrace of rougher movements in pursuit of natural turns of speech.

Description of place continues to find in blank verse a congenial medium. Emily Grosholz has written many poems of travel, usually sidestepping the clichés that dog the form. Many of her pieces are simultaneously love poems and poems of place: the scene is imbued by a consciousness of the lover's companionship or (in some instances) absence. Grosholz is a professor of philosophy, and her work, like Hadas's, is alert to the metaphysical suggestions offered by the ordinary. At the same time, she has an unabashed appreciation for natural beauty, and we find these intuitions finely balanced in a poem like "The Cliffs at Praiano," which after surveying a "lush obvious haven / for romantics" (2–3) concludes:

> We have been happy in a truckstop south
> of Roanoke, where shadows of semis loomed
> across the windows, browning the yellow neon.
> Love can do without the props of romance.
> And yet Praiano moves us with its wild
> theatrical display of elements:
> headlands, currents, breezes, strands of light.
> Look at the cliffs, I say, and mean instead
> that you are irrevocable. Reflected
> sea-light gleams on cliffs day has abandoned
> just as you stand before me, in my words.
>
> (23–33)

Grosholz's poems in the meter include briefer place descriptions in the form of unrhymed sonnets and several epistolary poems which include a good deal of intelligent response to scenery. The poem-as-letter is an underused form in our time, and Grosholz has an appealing way with it, sustaining tones that are intimate but not cloying. The same careful control of tone distinguishes poems centering on friendship ("Waiting for News of Jackie's Firstborn"), family lore ("Legacies"), and parenthood ("The Shape of Desire").

Mary Jo Salter is another observant traveler who distills the essence of far-flung settings in memorable glimpses. Blank verse is not her most frequent choice of form in which to do this, but the examples are distinguished. The early "Shisendō," set in Japan, is a triumph of unforced particularity recalling Salter's mentors Elizabeth Bishop and Amy Clampitt. A garden in Kyoto, its pavilion (The Hall of the Hermit Poets), and much of the history and cultural context of these all smoothly dovetail in this 127-line poem. One is struck by the compression and connotative force of the imagery: "Bamboo-leaf breaks its shadows on the rocks / like a spoon dropped in a glass of water" (5–6), she writes, and:

> Time is safely kept here.
> You can almost see it spinning in a wheel—
> yet slowly, like those two birds overhead
> swaying as if suspended in a mobile;
> hung by the very hand, it seems, that frees
> (even now, in autumn) two white butterflies
> to spiral up in tandem, lift like kites
> tethered to earth by strings too thin to see.
>
> (51–58)

Salter has written other alert and adept travel pieces ("June: The Gianicolo," "The Accordionist"), a dramatic monologue ("Armistice Day"), a biographical portrait ("Frost at Midnight"), and a narrative cast in dialogue ("Crystal Ball"). In all of these her handling of the verse line is conversationally easy without being notably loose. Feeling in her poems is understated but compelling. "Midsummer, Georgia Avenue" transmits a mild chill when its speaker, while reading a book on the porch, reflects on the cemetery across the road:

> Not far,
> the distance between you and them: a breath,
> a heartbeat dropped, a word in your two-faced
> book that invites you to its party only
> to sadden you when it's over. And so you stay
> on your teetering perch, you move and go nowhere,
> gazing past the heat-struck street that's split
>
> down the middle—not to put too fine
> a point on it—by a double yellow line.
>
> (18–26)

Salter, like many contemporary writers of blank verse, may use rhyme for emphasis (as here, in the concluding couplet) or more profusely (though still intermittently) in the manner of Merrill and Walcott.

The confessional poetry of Lowell and others appeared to open startling new avenues for poets writing personal narrative. Yet the autobiographical mode was by no means new in poetry, and pioneers like Wordsworth and Coleridge may have been more decisive in pointing the way for later poets than more immediate precursors like Lowell, Sexton, or Plath. Wordsworth and Coleridge, of course, wrote much of their most personal poetry in blank verse. In his long sequence "1992" Alfred Corn gives an unusual twist to the form by shuffling chronology and bringing in additional story lines. Each section begins with a passage of personal reminiscence, usually centered around events of a trip or a sojourn away from home. This is followed by a passage sketching the life of another (no doubt fictional) person who lives in the place the poet has experienced in passing. It is an intriguing method for transcending the sometimes solipsistic limitations of autobiography, a way of adding context, parallels, or contrasts to each glimpse of the self, sandwiching one's own slices of life together with those of others. Corn uses blank verse with some frequency, while allowing himself a longer line in many extended passages. Here are some representative pentameters from an episode dated 1978, in which the poet recalls working on revisions of a poem while on the road in California:

> What exactly do we do when we revise?
> Hopes of enjoying more than what's there move
> across unrhythmed first thoughts to send out
> the play of word against word, psychic antennae
> alert for enharmonic changes clearing vistas
> onto a penetration that we hadn't known
> or felt how much we meant, until the right note
> sends thrums of voltage up the spine (a home
> remedy for professional infirmities
> like scoliosis writers tend to have)
> or like the smart crack of bat against ball,
> along with heightened tone in mind and muscle—
> the product of recreation (also, of work)
> as if we played a sport whose goal was truth.

> (12, 15–28)

The sequence is conceptually fresh and, as these lines indicate, deftly written, though some may find its abrupt shifts in focus and character hard to square with their habitual wish as readers for narrative coherence.

Corn has also written shorter pieces in the meter that are less tricky in structure. "An Xmas Murder," set in Vermont, reads like a harsh updating of a Frost narrative, with its grim materials of small-town narrowness, violence, and homophobia. At just over a dozen pages, it is expertly paced. Corn also writes his own version of the New York City poetry produced by Howard Moss and others in the post–World War II period. There are blank-verse sections in his book-length sequence about New York, *A Call in the Midst of the Crowd,* and a pleasant late reprise in the memory piece "New York Three Decades On." Here and elsewhere Corn's lines sometimes spill over the pentameter's rim:

> On the night of the Great Blackout, I skipped town
> to Jersey with a (distant) marriage prospect
> who was bunking at a friend's in East Orange.

(68–70)

This elasticity alternates in the poem with passages composed in tighter lines:

> but nobody challenged me, no flat-broke
> brothers hustled this out-of-it honky,
> it just now dawning on him where he was.

(16–18)

Undoubtedly, this is a libertarian approach to the meter, but the pentameter is identifiable as the poem's basic line despite intermittent expansions or crimpings of it. One finds similar relaxed standards of line length indulged in by many of the poets of this period. Corn takes a moderate attitude toward metrical variation in his short prosody manual, *The Poem's Heartbeat:* "The general rule is that the substituted feet in a line will never outnumber feet of the reigning meter: in iambic pentameter you may make as many as two substitutions, but not three—because then there would be more substitutes than iambs in the line."[18] Most of the lines quoted from two poems by this poet pass muster by this standard, though this does not preclude some jagged sound effects. In

> ```
>     x   / x x   / x    / x  /   /
> ```
> but nobody challenged me, no flat-broke

the anapest in the second position would be a minor ruffle by itself, but in combination with the single accented syllable that replaces the final iamb, it becomes something less familiar. The line that follows this—

> ```
>        /  x    /   x   x   /   x /   /  x
> ```
> brothers hustled this out-of-it honky

—would appear to transgress Corn's suggested standard by substituting trochees for three of the line's iambs. The justification for such variations is most likely an expressive one: a bit of jostling to reinforce the fantasy (never actualized) of violence with which the speaker is flirting.

Andrew Hudgins takes a deceptively light approach to autobiographical writing in his book-length sequence *The Glass Hammer,* subtitled "A Southern Childhood." Most of the individual poems in this work are less than a page long; many of them are in blank verse. The poems are freestanding, separate vignettes; reading them in sequence, one thinks not of the continuous flow of a reel of film but of turning page by page through an album of snapshots. Hudgins shows considerable tact in arranging these poetic snapshots to provide a many-faceted view of his past without undue redundancy. In attitude, the pieces tend to imply an emotional distance from their materials, an unsentimental understanding of characters and events. The poet as a boy grows impatient with a minister's "tight circles of illogic":

> The preacher said, "We know God's word is true."
> *Amen,* somebody called. "How do we know?
> We know because the Bible says it's true."
>
> ("Sit Still," 1–3)

The boy's discovery of skepticism is succinctly but effectively sketched in the seventeen-line poem, which ends,

> Up front, the preacher waved his thick black book.
> He fanned the pages, smacked it with his palm,
> and I sincerely wished that I were stupid.
>
> (15–17)

If lines like these show Hudgins's talent for meshing meter and rhythm closely together, we find him in other places ready and willing to push the envelope, as at the end of a poem about reading and daydreaming over forbidden spy novels, "James Bond Considers Career Opportunities in Library Science":

> I brooded about packing
> a Colt or a Beretta, and of the girls,
> I'd choose not Pussy Galore but Domino.
> Poor Daddy didn't know what to do with me.
> I wanted to be stirred, not shaken—whatever that meant.
>
> (9–13)

Aside from these tart, amusing short poems, Hudgins has made use of the meter in a well-known series of dramatic monologues focusing on a revivalist preacher and his family, "Saints and Strangers," and in sections of his book-length poem based on the life of the poet and Confederate veteran Sidney Lanier, *After the Lost War*. The latter work, an impressive web of narrative, dramatic, and historical threads, is considered by many critics to be one of the best long poems of the last fifty years.

Less prolific and less widely known than Hudgins, John Burt deserves greater notice for his own sensitive explorations of history in verse. Burt is a scholar of American literature and history, and his extended, richly detailed poems on the American past, usually in blank verse, may remind readers of Helen Pinkerton's longer works. Burt sometimes focuses on famous personages, as in "Plains of Peace," about Woodrow Wilson and his failed campaign for the League of Nations, or "Elizabeth Keckley," about Mary Todd Lincoln's widowhood and descent into insanity, as witnessed by her black servant. Other poems deploy fictional characters against dense historical backgrounds, as in "Victory at Sea," about a World War II naval battle, or "Anna Peterson," an absorbing Robinsonian narrative centered on an itinerant portrait painter of the 1840s. This last has something of the sad sweetness of a Hawthorne story as it tells of an over-the-hill painter who has been losing the battle with emergent photography. He gains renewed inspiration through falling in love with the spirit of the dead woman whose portrait he is painting from the daguerreotype that her grieving father thinks unworthy of her. The ghostly love story is delicately handled, but the poem succeeds in large part because of

Burt's capacious grasp of period detail. These are some lines describing the painter's templates, waiting to have personalizing features added:

> Each burgher's wife wore black, had folded hands
> (He'd never mastered hands), sat in the shade.
> He had a dozen types to choose among,
> And always one of them would be as like
> As he'd have made it had he worked from life.
> Or liker, maybe, since from practicing
> He'd got the habit of their bodies down
> And worked a few improvements year by year
> He'd not have had the skill for, standing there
> Before a live impatient fidgeter.
>
> (I, 73–82)

Burt also has written provocative briefer poems in the meter, many of which touch on historical ironies and tragedies, categories which in analysis often prove to overlap.

The historically based poems of Hudgins and Burt represent but one of many directions taken in the last thirty years by poets with a resurgent interest in narrative. What has sometimes been called the New Narrative may be seen as an offshoot or an ally of the New Formalism, with many poets bearing both labels simultaneously. Naturally, blank verse is a common choice for poets of this ilk. We find it used by poets who share a fascination with history but approach it in a mediated fashion, by viewing a family's experience as a microcosm of the nation's. Two notable examples are "The Country I Remember," by David Mason, and "The Long Home," by Christian Wiman. Mason's work alternates passages in the voice of a long-lived Civil War veteran reflecting on his past with passages in the voice of his equally long-lived daughter. This strategy affords a capsulized view of the war and of the settlement of the West (where this family moved in 1880). It also presents dramatic contrasts in the perspective and experience of the two speakers. The onetime soldier is stoical and matter-of-fact; recounting a failed attempt to escape from Libby Prison, he says:

> The Rebs recaptured nearly half the men
> who crawled out through the tunnel. Some they kept

below in cages where they fed on rats.
The whole business was a bit discouraging.

("Eighty Acres," 40–43)

The daughter is readier to reveal sensitivity, as in her haunted memory of the family's westward journey:

I remember looking out of the train at night,
trying to count the dark shapes passing by
and seeing our faces pressed against the glass
like children looking back from another world.
I thought of bones in the embrace of weeds,
of Indians who vanished on the prairie,
of hills that swayed and rumbled like our train.

("How We Came This Far," 22–28)

In addition to the events it relates, the poem through its bifurcated portraiture deals with the variability of heroism, generational change and continuity, and gender differences and expectations. A curious stylistic feature is Mason's decision to arrange his fifty-three-page poem in seven-line stanzas.

Wiman's forty-page narrative follows the fortunes of a Texas farm family in the early and middle years of the twentieth century. In its use of a female narrator, its opening with a family's westward odyssey, and its intricate tracing of memory's webs, it recalls Mason's work, though the two poets' voices (or rather, their characters' voices) are distinct. "The Long Home" depicts its share of ordeals: privations, drought, tornadoes, bereavements. None of these troubles is given the disproportionate weight that might mire the poem in melodrama; the narrative moves fluently. Some of the best writing captures the huge emptiness of the West in the eyes of the narrator, brought to Texas from the Carolinas as a child:

In such space
You might one night wake falling into stars,
Or with a full moon shining from inside
Of you. Working alone, sowing a field
Of light in spring, you might begin to feel

Your shadow is the only shadow in the world;
Or hear in late October wind one day
The whispering hours and distances, soft callings
In a voice so like your own you leave your work
And wander off, wading a level cloud
Of cotton blooming in a blackland farm
As far as you can see.

(I, 46–57)

Both Mason and Wiman sustain an elegiac tone and include painful or melancholy episodes. Yet both tilt in the end toward optimism because of their stress on endurance, survival, and the restorative power of memory. Some contemporary poets follow narrative threads that lead deeper into the dark. Dana Gioia's "The Homecoming" is a monologue by a murderer who escapes from prison expressly to kill his hated foster mother. The pathological self-portrait is insistently fleshed out, and some readers may feel that this character understands himself as only his creator could—too well, in the end, to be convincing. "Counting the Children" is disturbing in a subtler and more persuasive way. The central morbid image—an enormous collection of dolls scavenged from the trash by a deranged woman—is riveting when conveyed in the level tones of the narrator, an accountant doing an inventory of the dead collector's possessions. In this poem Gioia arranges his lines in Stevensian tercets but keeps a tighter rein on his lines than Stevens often did:

Some battered, others missing arms and legs,
Shelf after shelf of the same dusty stare
As if despair could be assuaged by order.

They looked like sisters huddling in the dark,
Forgotten brides abandoned at the altar,
Their veils turned yellow, dresses stiff and soiled.

Rows of discarded little girls and babies—
Some naked, others dressed for play—they wore
Whatever lives their owners left them in.

(I, 28–36)

As the poem goes on, taking us deeper into the narrator's feelings for his own child and juxtaposing these with the gothic image of the abandoned "children" on their shelves, it achieves a genuine poignancy. Gioia has written extensively in the meter: other notable examples are the monologue "The Room Upstairs" and lyrics in a variety of moods: "Sunday Night in Santa Rosa," "Lives of the Great Composers," "Cleared Away," and "Metamorphosis."

A recent collection as vigorous as *The Determined Days* (2000), by Philip Stephens, indicates that the vogue for narrative in blank verse continues to have momentum. Except for a prologue and an epilogue in couplets, all the rest of the narrative vignettes in this book—twenty-six of them—are in blank verse. Each is a few pages in length. The distant model may be Frost, but the work's concentration on squalor comes out of a seamier realism. Some of the poems are gritty georgics, depicting the backbreaking work of railroad signalmen repairing lines buried or strung high on poles; a symbolic resonance of height and depth threads through the tissue of obscene conversation that the workers rely on to stay human. Other pieces provide dyspeptic glances at the American wasteland:

> The days grew warm, and we pushed up the windows,
> So when a meth house cropped up one block west,
> Each night we'd hear the cries of wacked-out tweakers,
> The crack of fistfights, blaring horns of addicts
> Craving their fix, and traffic speeding past
> Our corner, heedless of the signs and limits.
>
> ("In the Neighborhood," 11–16)

The book is daunting to read through all at once because its emphasis on the dismal and the sordid is as unremitting as the presentation is stark. A problem for this kind of realism is that it comes to seem unreal through overinsistence or absence of counterpoint. Frost and Miller Williams write their share of dark poems, but these are accompanied by milder ones, and not all their humor is black humor. Stephens's book as a whole may seem narrow and even obsessive in its dwelling on cheerless and tawdry situations. Technically, though, the writing is sure-handed, even brilliant, repeatedly startling us into awareness of how forceful a medium blank verse can be for unvarnished expression, as in this scrap of dialogue between two laborers on the job:

> Smith and Sandoval recalled
> This girl they'd spoken to at 7-Eleven:
>
> "Good God, she had big tits."
>
> > "Shit yeah, she did.
> I can't believe you asked if she knew where
> There was a Pic 'n' Save. You're one sad fuck."
>
> "Just making conversation."
>
> > "She doesn't shop
> At Pic 'n' Save."
>
> > "She bought a cup of coffee
> At 7-Eleven."
>
> > "It's a convenience store."
>
> "Well, I'd convenience her."
> > "You would."
> > > "I would."
> > > > ("True Story," 14–22)

As we see here, extremely colloquial material—even what some would consider a kind of antipoetry—can conform to the pentameter length and standard pattern with not much strain. There are numerous contemporary poets, of course, whose approach to the line is less tailored. Looking at some poems by Edward Hirsch, to cite one example, we find an updated version of Eliot's concept of "the ghost of meter." Poems that have the look of blank verse on the page prove recalcitrant, more often than not, to being scanned as such. Here is a stanza from "The Night Parade," a colorful, surrealistic account of sleep and dreaming:

> The greatest moments of the night parade
> Take place under the open tent where muscular

> Sleepwalkers tiptoe across tightropes, carefully
> Holding up umbrellas, and two married acrobats
> Float through miles and miles of empty space
> Just to hold hands on a wooden platform
> Hammered into the air. Everyone laughs
> When the clowns of sleep mimic the lions,
> Tower over the midgets, and pinch the backsides
> Of beautiful bareback riders. And everyone
> Drifts home slowly when the half-moon dims
> And confetti falls from the sky like applause.
>
> (2, 25–36)

The first line of the stanza is regular. The others engage in various kinds of stress shifting, and we find expansion (as in 26, 27, and elsewhere) and, less frequently, contraction (35). Some of these modified lines are not hard to imagine as part of a verse passage in which they would be surrounded by more regular ones, but here, where one line out of twelve scans conventionally, they are the rule rather than the exception. (This is not to say that the aberrant lines are necessarily bad poetry:

<pre>
  /   x   / x x x /   /   /
Drifts home slowly when the half-moon dims
</pre>

is a striking line; it is just not iambic pentameter.) Eliot's idea of meter haunting rather than inhabiting the lines is applicable to such verse, though the specter here seems to be retreating from regularity much more often than approaching it. The line

<pre>
  x   x / x /   x   x / x x   /
And confetti falls from the sky like applause,
</pre>

with its lone iamb stranded among anapests, drops into prose with an unconfetti-like clunk.

There is much of this problematic type of verse to be found in contemporary poetry; some poets who occasionally write in regular meter at other times venture into this rougher terrain, and for some the aim seems to be to treat blank verse not as a form to be embraced but as a point of departure, a theme barely to be discerned through layers of superimposed variations. And yet, this busy activity at the margins of prosody coexists in our time with work that places itself at the traditional center. In his first and so far only book, *The Optimist*, published in 2004, Joshua Mehigan writes some of the more imaginatively charged and gracefully governed blank verse seen in recent years. Here we have not the ghost of meter but meter embodied in language of potency and pith:

> The fire transformed the bedspread into fire.
> It climbed the curtain like a nervous cat,
> and at the top it rained onto the floor,
> where vapor reeked from cracks between the boards.
> They slept a moment more but didn't wake
> until the gas was on them like a tongue,
> and then they were asleep again.
>
> ("The Spectacle," 1–7)

Mehigan explores traditional flourishes that have been underused in contemporary blank verse. Notice the deftly buried rhymes in the opening of "A Bird at the Leather Mill":

> The crane stood in the center of the floor
> of the mill, lost and tentative. Its bill
> looked like a fancy awl with a down handle.
> It wore its wings as though they were a shawl
> thrown on an idiot.
>
> (1–5)

An even more striking device is the use of feminine endings on all twenty-three lines of "A Questionable Mother." The scene is a police station where an unwed mother is being questioned about the death of her infant:

> Within, the suspect cried they must believe her.
> The female officer behind a window
> of thick green glass typed slowly without stopping.
> Beneath the squat cap holding in her hairdo,
> her face suggested she withheld her judgment.
>
> (16–20)

The sustained, *deliberate* monotony of the falling rhythm suggests the moral numbness of the situation, and the poem suggests a possible bitter pun in the term "feminine ending." Other excellent pieces of Mehigan's in the form are "A Cellar in Pankow," "The House Swap," "The Umbrella Man," "Déjà Vu," and "Introduction to Poetry."

Some highly accomplished poets within the penumbra of the New Formalism have written only sparingly in the meter thus far. This small body of work includes some masterly poems. For example, Timothy Steele, an expert prosodist as well as a superior poet, has written a moving Robinsonian portrait, "Ethel Taylor," the wry Los Angeles street scenes "Past, Present, Future" and "Freudian Analysis," the sad contemporary nature poem *Didelphis Virginiana*," and a plangent lament for our culture's apparent downward trajectory, "Pacific Rim," in which the ocean embodies nature's detachment from humanity:

> A brutal century
> Draws to a close. Bewildering genetrix,
> As your miraculous experiment
> In consciousness hangs in the balance, do
> You pity those enacting it? The headlands'
> Blunt contours sloping to the oceanside,
> Do angels weep for our folly? Merciful,
> Do you accompany our mortality
> Just as, low to the water, the pelican
> Swiftly pursues his shadow down a swell?
>
> (19–28)

This poem offers a piquant comparison, stylistically and temperamentally, with Robinson Jeffers's World War II–era poem on the Pacific, "The Eye."

To mention two other occasional pentametrists, A. E. Stallings and Catherine Tufariello are younger poets who have composed memorable pieces. Tufariello's "The Feast of Tabernacles" applies a relaxed form of the line to a retelling of the biblical exodus, highlighting (as the Bible does not) the experience of women:

> They must have thought they saw the land of Canaan
> Lushly shimmering in the middle distance

Just beyond the column of white smoke—
Never that the high drama of departure
Would be followed by forty years of tedium,
More than fourteen thousand evening meals cooked
And eaten, pots scoured and clothing scrubbed
With never enough water, by stooping women,
While dust and sand got into everything.

(16–24)

Stallings writes amusing, sometimes devastating glosses on Greek myths, often with a feminist slant. "Hades Welcomes His Bride" presents the King of the Underworld giving Persephone a house tour; the voice is that of a smooth movie villain of the 1930s:

Come, come. This is the greatest room;
I had it specially made after great thought
So you would feel at home. I had the ceiling
Painted to recall some evening sky—
But without the garish stars and lurid moon.
What? That stark shape crouching in the corner?
Sweet, that is to be our bed. Our bed.
Ah! Your hand is trembling! I fear
There is, as yet, too much pulse in it.

(28–36)

Stallings has written also a fine, less humorous piece on mortality, "A Lament for the Dead Pets of Our Childhood."

This survey must come to a close, although here, as at previous junctures, examples could be multiplied. While it is not suitable to discuss here the present writer's poems in the meter, it can be noted that these are many in number and various in kind, including lyrics ("Selva Oscura," "A Geode"), narratives ("A Piece of Rope," "Hide-and-Seek"), place descriptions ("A Mica Mine," "The Devil's Garden"), monologues ("Living Past 19"), biographical sketches ("Last Days in Camden," "An Exhumation"), historical meditations ("The Post Office Murals Restored," "Drowned Towns"), and metaphysical causeries ("Solving for X").

In the account of twentieth-century and later blank verse offered in this and the preceding chapter, many readers will have noted two points worth highlighting in closing. The first point, unsurprising in the context of modernism, concerns the prominence of experimentation in poets' approaches to the form. Few poets were unaffected by the modernists' challenge, and many of those who continued to stay close to a traditional verse movement nonetheless carried out their own experiments in applying the meter to untraditional modes and structures. The extraordinary rise of the short lyric or epigrammatic poem in blank verse is one of the most significant poetic legacies of the century. As to the stylistic divergence between traditional blank verse and its many less-than-regular offshoots, it is still very much with us, as the last two sections of this chapter will have indicated. The esthetic consequences for poems in the meter and the practical consequences for poets attempting to write them are matters that will be touched on in the next and final chapter.

The second point about twentieth-century blank verse is even more obvious—that there is a voluminous quantity of it, which is now in the new century being steadily augmented. Furthermore, even a survey like this one, obliged to give most individual poems little more than a passing glance, should indicate that the level of artistry and imaginative vigor in much of this work is high. If we begin by listing enduring poems like Robinson's "Isaac and Archibald," Frost's "Home Burial, " Yeats's "The Second Coming," Stevens's "Sunday Morning," Wilbur's "The Mind-Reader," Hecht's "The Venetian Vespers," Merrill's "Lost in Translation," Bowers's "Autumn Shade," and Cunningham's "Montana Fifty Years Ago" we have only scratched the surface. There are a host of remarkable pieces that reward thoughtful reading as well as these: Muir's "The Transfiguration," Pratt's *Brébeuf and His Brethren,* Hayden's "Witch Doctor," Shapiro's "A Cut Flower," Keyes' "Against Divination," Pinkerton's "Crossing the Pedregal," Moss's "Einstein's Bathrobe," Mueller's "The Power of Music to Disturb," and a generous handful from each of Nemerov's, Williams's, and Cassity's bodies of work in the form. And this is leaving unmentioned not only many of the fine early and mid-twentieth-century poems previously discussed but also the energetic contributions of poets born from 1940 on, whose careers are in full stride. Reaching the end of this outline of the history of blank verse, the reader might bemusedly recall the claim, quoted in chapter 1, from the *Princeton Encyclopedia of Poetry and Poetics* that "the advent of free verse sounded the death knell of this meter which was once and for long a powerful, flexible, and subtle form, the most prestigious and successful modern rival to the greatest meter of antiquity."[19] In light of the record assembled here, this judgment appears not merely hasty but preposterous. No one would argue that blank verse has been the paramount form in poetry since the modernist era, but that it is a form whose many virtues continue to attract a numerous, diversified, and accomplished array of poets cannot be doubted.

One is reminded of the story of Mark Twain, with thirteen years to live, responding to a rumor that he had died with a cable to the Associated Press: "The reports of my death are greatly exaggerated." Blank verse, born sometime in the sixteenth century, is alive and well in the twenty-first, and it will be surprising if this assertion does not hold true for much longer than the next thirteen years. The meter has shown an uncanny ability to accommodate changes in idiom, not only those wrought by the passage of time but those inspired by difference in locale as well: after all, it jumped the Atlantic. Poets have repeatedly applied it successfully to uses that have been neglected or not previously thought of. Such qualities bode well for the meter's future as a poetic resource. Literary history suggests that its periods of decline alternate with those of renewal, as, phoenixlike, it rises reborn from its own fragrant ashes.

WRITING BLANK VERSE TODAY

I

THE CONTEMPORARY writer of blank verse has more stylistic and technical leeway than poets of any earlier period. This is the residual effect of modernism, persisting long after modernist pioneers like Pound and Eliot have receded as poetic models. In the pluralistic arena of contemporary poetry we find no consensus on prosody. Traditionally strict blank verse has enjoyed a resurgence in the hands of some New Formalists, but freer approaches to the meter are common and probably still are more numerous. In this environment the young poet looking for models may feel intimidated by the panoply of available styles and bewildered by the nebulousness of current standards and definitions. J. A. Symonds's comment on blank verse, quoted in chapter 3, is worth repeating here: "Indeed, so variable is its structure that it is by no means easy to define the minimum of metrical form below which a Blank Verse ceases to be a recognizable line."[1] This observation from the late nineteenth century seems only to increase in relevance as each generation wrestles with the meter's technical properties and stylistic heritage.

Appeals to purity of traditional standards are common to most cultural endeavors. In a recent article about "hyphenated" Chinese restaurants—Chinese-Cuban, Chinese-Peruvian, and others—the *New York Times* reported one expert's objections to such culinary fusions: "'Chinese food is defined by a flavor principle of soy sauce, ginger, garlic and green onions' and methods including stir-frying and steaming, he said. 'Once you get too far away from these rules, it is no longer Chinese.'"[2] One recognizes the attraction of clarity in such matters, but the fact that some of this suspect food tastes better than merely good might complicate one's attitudes. Then again, there is that worrisome phrase, "too far away from these rules." Can metrical feet be seen as ingredients in a recipe? An anapest or a trochee might introduce a different flavor into an iambic line. Is more than one or two of these too many? One line or a number of lines in a blank-verse poem might resist scansion even under lenient standards. What should that mean to us as we attempt to construct categories? At the least, it means we should be cautious.

Lack of agreement on standards has produced commentaries that compound confusion rather than dispelling it. In *A Poet's Guide to Poetry* (1999), by Mary Kinzie, we find the following entry in a chapter entitled "Poetic Terms":

> Free Blank Verse   Verse that still exhibits the length and alternation of weak with strong syllables prominent in BLANK VERSE, but with significant loosening of the IAMBIC PENTAMETER model, as in these lines by Mark Strand in *Dark Harbor,* VIII:
>
> > Tell me that I have not lived in vain, that the stars
> > Will not die, that things will stay as they are,
> > That what I have seen will last, that I was not born
> > Into change, that what I have said has not been said for me.
>
> See also VERSET.[3]

The entry on "Free Verse," which immediately follows the one just quoted, states in part, "Types [of free verse] are PODIC FREE VERSE (sprung rhythm), FREE BLANK VERSE, IMAGIST FREE VERSE, and VERSET (biblical or sublime free verse)."[4] Some of these subcategories might be useful in certain contexts, but they are not much help here. Judging from the Strand quotation, we are looking again at the stretched line of the later Stevens. The same sort of blurring that we find in Donald Justice's discussion of the Stevens line is even more starkly conspicuous here, with the coinage of a term like "free blank verse" and a description that asserts, essentially, that this entity is something like blank verse (which, remember, is unrhymed iambic pentameter), but is not *really* iambic pentameter (thanks to "significant loosening"). If Kinzie, whose compendious book offers much useful information in other respects, had been content to speak of "loose blank verse," there would be little to bicker with. But positing a form that is at once metrical and without a fixed meter can only add to the murkiness that afflicts current discussions of versification.

Resisting the notion of "free blank verse" does not relieve us of the need to ponder the various forms of loose blank verse which, as the preceding historical discussion has shown, figure significantly in English-language poetry. Good—even great—poems have been written thus. One may have no difficulty in acknowledging that and yet wonder how vigorous a means of expression this is for poets writing today. The more self-conscious a stylistic revolution is, the more prone it is to run out of steam, especially if it is as successful in establishing its hegemony as modernism has been. The sort of transgressive excitement that may once have attended "breaking the pentameter" can no longer be assumed, and in fact is not often generated by recent poems that stray markedly from the pattern as they halfheartedly flirt with it. The Stevensian stretched line, with its self-indulgent spread and often concomitant limpness, is one example. But not all questionable pentameters from the modern and postmodern periods sound alike; the last two chapters have offered plenty of specimens of anomalous lines with differing contours, sought out and allowed to stand by poets for varying reasons.

A few further examples may help focus the issue. A poem by Weldon Kees, "Dynamite for Operas," begins:

> After the red rugs of the palaces,
> Roofs of those great hotels, views of the sea,
> I seem to be back in this familiar room again.
> Brought here, perhaps. It was February when I left.

(1–4)

The meter "goes out" in line 3 and returns infrequently in the rest of this seventeen-line poem. Intriguingly, two of the few additional pentameters are the last two lines of the poem, which creates a symmetrical framing effect in conjunction with lines 1 and 2. In between, the verse wanders. A more scattershot sort of movement toward and away from regularity can be seen in one part of a sequence called "Sixty-fifth Street Poems," by Bruce Bawer. The first sentence reads:

> It's barely the middle of January,
> and already the black leather gloves
> you bought me for Christmas are ruined,
> still and water-lined, their proud shine gone.
>
>   ("2. Gloves," 1–4)

Line 4 is heavily stressed at the end but is regular except for the unstressed syllable docked from its first foot. The lines preceding it, though, oscillate outside the standard pattern. In the rest of the poem occasional regular or nearly regular lines appear at unpredictable intervals. A comparable now-you-see-it, now-you-don't approach to the meter may be found in the opening of "Al Badr Street," by John Canaday:

> Each night at eight my neighbor hacks and spits
> a lump of sputum from deep in his lungs,
> like an old, mad rooster greeting the moon.
> All day the air was a blunt instrument
> weighted with sunlight, but now colors rise
> slowly from hollows, from under the stones,
> with the gentleness of roses unfolding
> in the warm shadow of a concrete wall.
>
>   (1–8)

There is iambic pentameter to be found in these passages, as in Kees; sometimes it exhibits standard variations. But there is not much sense of it as a norm. Lines like Bawer's short and largely anapestic

>   x   /   x x   /   x   x / x
> you bought me for Christmas are ruined

and Canaday's largely dactylic

>   / x   x   / x   x   / x   x   /
> slowly from hollows, from under the stones

offer no hint of a basis in iambic pentameter. When there is a more regular line in such passages it almost seems an intrusion. The case is much the same as with Edward Hirsch's "The Night Parade," discussed in chapter 4. In these poets' dealings with the meter we do not observe much that reminds us of Eliot's calculated wrenching of the line in "Gerontion." The effect here is more one of absentmindedness than of intelligent deliberation. The poems are not without intelligence: it is simply directed toward features other than meter. A reader of verse like this may feel trapped in a sort of halfway house. This is blank verse—for a line or two, and then it is not. One is tempted to echo the put-upon housewife in Katherine Anne Porter's story "A Day's Work." Weary of darning his socks, she berates her layabout husband: "'You ought either go barefoot or wear your shoes over your socks as God intended,' she said. 'Sock feet. What's the good of it, I'd like to know. Neither one thing nor the other.'"[5]

The passages we have been looking at date from the 1940s to the present decade: as the last two chapters make clear, it is nothing new to take liberties with the blank-verse line. There is reason to wonder, in fact, if there might not be fresher possibilities at the opposite stylistic pole. As far back as 1962, in "The Problem of Form," J. V. Cunningham addressed the exhaustion of modernist approaches to poetry:

> And here in naked reduction is the problem of form in the poetry of our day. We have lost the repetitive harmony of the old tradition, and we have not established a new. We have written to vary or violate the old line, for regularity we feel is meaningless and irregularity meaningful. But a generation of poets, acting on the principles and practice of significant variation, have at last nothing to vary from. The last variation is regularity.[6]

Cunningham's argument is directed generally to traditional formalist poetry versus free verse, but it seems particularly applicable to the state of blank verse in recent decades. After reading verse that departs from meter not out of revolt against convention but in unconsidered subservience to a set of mannerisms once radical but now commonplace, we may indeed wish to go in search of "the last variation . . . regularity."

Any appeal to regularity, of course, must acknowledge what good poets demonstrate in practice: to write regular blank verse is not (and should not be) the same as writing something monotonous. Carried to an extreme, regularity can be as irritating a stylistic fault as any of the prosodic distortions of modernism in its less engaging phases. At this, as at the other extreme, the message to the apprentice poet scouting for models is, "Go, and do not likewise."

To be excessively "regular" in the sense intended here is to write lines in which the rhythm stays so close to the metrical pattern that there is no play or tension between the two; what results is verse that is often called "singsong."[7] Such verse today is harder to find (at least in published poetry) than it once was. The modernists were not wrong in drawing attention to the deficiencies of this sort of rhythmically unadventurous poetry, and they succeeded so well in stigmatizing it that one has to go back some decades to find plentiful examples. Just a few will be useful in demonstrating the drawbacks of lines that are too "penty," as Pound used to say. John Masefield, who was the English poet laureate for many years, was one of those whose style remained untouched by modernism. He wrote vigorous rhyming narrative poems and the likable sea ballads for which he is now best remembered. He was all at sea, however, in the unflattering sense, when attempting blank verse. Here are some lines from a travel reminiscence, "Australia":

> Always above these memories is the sense
> Of charming people, ever kind and thoughtful;
> Most generous in thought, in word, in deed,
> And faithful in their kindness to the end.
>
> (86–89)

There is an almost stupefying redundancy of expression, and this tendency operates in mischievous collusion with the meter, producing what is often called "padding" of the lines. The "in . . . in . . . in" sequence of line 88 is typical. We find much the same in a poem about Ovid in exile, "A Letter from Pontus":

> But always Ovid as a charming host
> Cheered and distracted and delighted me [. . .]
>
> (41–42)

> Just one week later, seven days from then.
>
> (89)

>   and never any hope
> Of mercy or forgiveness or release
> As someone killed and buried and forgotten.
>
> (103–5)

Masefield is evidently terrified of dropping a syllable, and pads his lines with conjunctions or prepositions when not tarrying over outright tautologies like that of line 89. Together with the lack of rhythmic modulation or notable metrical substitutions, this results in lines that are wooden or insipid. One final example may indicate the disadvantages of so abject an adherence to the metrical pattern. These lines are part of a description of a ship:

> Her gear is white manila, nearly new.
> All is in choicest order, the mast-shrouds
> Are set-up by a method new to me.
> The shrouds turn-in on double-purchase-blocks,
> The lanyards reeve through dead-eyes on the rail.
> The masts are raked, each little thing aloft
> Is cared for with unusual seamanship.
>
> ("The Spanish Main Schooner," 14–20)

Here a few timid modulations are not enough to dislodge the desperate correctitude of the iambic movement. The lines are often heavily end-stopped, discouraging fluency; even enjambed lines seem to run into a wall at their ends. However unpleasantly jolted we may feel by the disruptions of meter in modernist poetry, making headway in verse like this is like floundering through quicksand.

Although, as previously noted, it is less than common, it is not impossible to find fairly recent poetry that embraces meter in too fervent a grip. To illustrate, here are some lines from "To A and B, My Friends Who Are Not in Books," by Charles O. Hartman:

> Thinking my leisure here would help me learn
> More than your winter nights of talk in bars,
> Gestures among the leaves on autumn walks,
> My friends, I've tried to make you characters
> Flat as the leaves of books, like leaves between
> The stiff, preserving pages of my books.
>
> (11–16)

Certainly, this is a step up from Masefield. The more frequent use of inverted first feet gives these lines a bit more impetus than they otherwise would have, but the lines in other respects plod along the same path at the same pace, and overall there is a lack of rhythmic energy. This poem has more of a point than Masefield's piece on the schooner, and it is in that regard an attractive utterance. But it misses the opportunity a poet always has to make versification a vital expressive force. When formalists query the liberties now often taken with iambic pentameter, they are not espousing anything like a metronomic approach. Rather than breaking the pentameter, as Pound would urge, or following its pattern in a lockstep fashion, as in Masefield's padded lines, there is a third alternative. That is to explore the elasticity coiled within the line, to discover, as many poets have, that it can bend quite a lot—even drastically—without breaking. Along the way toward making that discovery, the more thoughtful stylist will discover something equally important: that sometimes an apparently slight modification will yield unexpectedly memorable results.

II

Think of a tightrope walker. The rope he is walking on is one whose properties he is intimately familiar with; he knows how tautly stretched it is and what slight degree of give in it can be tolerated. This sturdy rope (the metrical line, let us say) provides firm support to his motions in performance—to steady feats of passage, colorful jugglings, unexpected pauses, even stumbles which may appear spontaneous but are carefully rehearsed. These motions of his act can represent for us the effects of rhythm played out from the beginning to the end of the line. And what if one of those suspense-creating stumbles is not rehearsed but genuinely accidental? The seasoned professional may recover his balance, and the performance may be all the more gripping in consequence. But suppose the equilibrist loses his balance beyond recall. He may then fall into the net, which we will call prose.

One assumes that ropewalkers acquire their skills first from observing accomplished masters of the art and then from arduous practice, a matter of trial and error which in this case will include a number of bruising falls. A poet seeking to master the pentameter line is in for a prolonged period of study and experiment. Just how far the line will allow him to go—how much give it has beneath the pressure he exerts on it—is something each poet needs to find out for himself. Robert Frost once made an interesting comment on metaphor:

All metaphor breaks down somewhere. That is the beauty of it. It is touch and go with the metaphor, and until you have lived with it long enough you don't know when it is going. You don't know how much you can get out of it and when it will cease to yield. It is a very living thing. It is as life itself.[8]

By now it should be clear that the same state of things applies to blank verse. Such inherent unpredictability seems itself unpredictable: isn't meter a matter of counting, and are not syllables either stressed or unstressed? One could write blank verse according to an unvarying formula; but poems are not written that way. Precision is necessary in certain fields: the ingredients in pharmaceutical products need to be measured out and combined equally in every capsule. Precision in poetry is necessary as well, but it is not a matter simply of measuring amounts (or, more precisely, gauging alternate degrees of accent and setting them down unvaryingly in rows of ten). In the extraordinarily complex labor of composition, the poet must decide what modifications allowed by the system will create the sought-for effect. This is precision not in the mathematical but the artistic sense. It recognizes the importance of rules and the inevitability of exceptions, and balances the technical means against the expressive end. Writing in what may be technically described as blank verse is not the same as writing what deserves to be called a poem in the meter.

To do that—to write blank verse that coheres in a poem rather than subsisting as an exercise—one needs to become acquainted with the strange tensions operating between meter and rhythm, and sometimes between meter and grammar or syntax. Preceding chapters are rife with illustrations, but here are yet a few more. One thing that should be noted (or rather, reiterated) here is that after the nineteenth century the pursuit of euphony evident in the blank verse of Tennyson and others lost ground to the kinds of dramatic speech effects of which Browning was for so many later poets a source. It is less common now, and has been less common for many decades, to find the sort of consciously melodic quality of famous lines like these:

> sweet is every sound,
> Sweeter thy voice, but every sound is sweet;
> Myriads of rivulets hurrying through the lawn,
> The moan of doves in immemorial elms,
> And murmuring of innumerable bees.

> (*The Princess*, 7.203–7)

Tennyson masterfully combines rhythm and assonance to make each of the last three lines evocative of the sound it describes. In line 205 the additional unstressed (or elided) syllables seem to speed the line they lengthen, and of course the shorter vowels of the first three stressed syllables help in this. Line 206 slows considerably, not only because vowel sounds lengthen at key points, but because abutting syllables such as "in im-" and "-al elms" resist being raced over. The final line, with its echoic mimicry, suggests both the ongoing hum and darting movements of the bees through its balance of longer and shorter vowels, heavier and lighter syllables. This is a virtuoso performance, unquestionably. But no one would consider it unobtrusive. The taste of succeeding generations has favored rhythmic modulations and aural patterns that are, in the main, less conspicuous.

Since the earlier discussion of Robert Frost laid some emphasis on the more extreme manipulations in his blank-verse poems, it is appropriate here to note that his work offers plenty of examples as well of a more restrained approach. Although modernism has made us predisposed to value irregularities, and thus regard favorably Frost's comments on his pleasure in bringing meter and rhythm into "strained relation," he has intriguing lines in which the dramatic effect depends on the *absence* of strain, in which meter and dramatic emphasis coincide in ways that are anything but humdrum. Consider this proverblike line from "The Self-Seeker": "Pressed into service means pressed out of shape" (148). If asked to say aloud either of the opposed phrases, our tendency would be to stress the past participle and the noun:

> /   x x / x
> pressed into service
>
> /   x x /
> pressed out of shape.

For these phrases, as parts of this line of verse, that clearly would not do. The proper emphasis here is determined by the formal balance of the statement, and is best obtained by reading the line as regular iambic pentameter:

> x / x / x   /   x   / x /
> Pressed into service means pressed out of shape.

This reading alone brings out the point of the sentence, the relation of these types of pressure to one another, which is one of either complementarity or

contrast, depending on how one looks at it. It may be objected—sensibly
enough—that a reader heading into a line like this in the midst of a blank-
verse poem might not initially discern a regular iamb at the beginning of the
line. It is true that we need to arrive at the contrast of "out" in order to grasp
the need for stressing the first syllable of "into." But in this and similar lines it
appears that Frost wants to force his reader to go back, reread, and hear the accent shifting to where it really ought to be. For the reader, the line induces a
kind of double take. And in this particular case a small clandestine joke haunts
such a shift in the neighborhood of the word "pressed," for what we feel here
is a sort of *pressure* exerted by the sense of the words on the movement of the
line. While there is no strain on the metrical pattern, which in fact is eased toward greater regularity, there is this subtle pressure on comprehension, prompt-
ing it to double back to see that emphases are accurately assigned.

Something similar can be seen in the first line of "An Old Man's Winter
Night." We would ordinarily be inclined to render the opening phrase, as an
isolated set of words, this way:

> /   x x   /
> All out-of-doors.

But as it occurs in the line, that would make for a reading insufficiently sensitive both to sound and to sense. It should be:

> x / x /   x   / x / x /
> All out-of-doors looked darkly in at him

—here highlighting the antithesis poised between the two ends of the line,
and thus highlighting the tenuous separation of the old man *in* his isolated
dwelling from all that is *out* there in the dark. In both of these cases the drama
is heightened not by breaking with the meter but by letting it have its way.
Frost's comment, quoted earlier, in which he cites "the speaking tone of voice
somehow entangled in the words and fastened to the page for the ear of the
imagination" seems as apt for these exploitations of metrical regularity as for
some of his carefully judged deviations from it in other cases.[9]

When Frost does depart notably from the standard pattern, there is usually
a more regular line in the vicinity; in fact both the norm and the deviation are
more clearly defined through such juxtapositions. In "The Death of the Hired
Man," Warren the farmer speaks approvingly of Silas's skill with a hayfork:

```
    x  / x  / x   / x  / x  /
You never see him standing on the hay
```

```
    x   / x  x /   / x  x / x  /
He's trying to lift, | straining to lift himself.
```

(94–95)

Notice that, while in scanning many earlier quotations we have opted for a less emphatic stress on words like "on," we award a full stress here to the preposition, because that is what is indicated by the context. "You never see him standing *on* the hay," says Warren. We move, then, from this designedly regular line to the next, just as designedly distorted. The unhappy result of standing on the hay in question is enacted by the successive anapest, caesura, and trochee in the middle of the line. Even better, the initial iamb that leads up to this has almost a plaintive quality, as its brave attempt to carry on the purposeful stride of the previous line is suddenly balked by the noniambic "straining" inhering in these features. This is another of Frost's little dramas, played out within the confines of a sentence, with metrical feet and rhythmic fluctuations supplying the cast.

Frost's success here is evident, but its judicious nature, its tactfulness, deserves to be remarked. To focus more sharply on this, imagine how a conventional, less rhythmically adventurous poet might write what could be called a Masefieldian version of the lines:

```
    x  / x  / x   / x  / x  /
You never see him standing on the hay
```

```
    x  / x  /  x  / x  \  x  /
He tries to lift, | contending with his weight.
```

No strain in the prosody here; only a strain on the reader's attention. On the other hand, imagine a version by a more recent poet who, like some we have glanced at, has a somewhat distant acquaintance with iambic pentameter:

```
    x  /  x x  / x   / x  / x  /
You don't ever see him standing on the hay,
```

```
    /  x  x /  x x /  x   x  /  / x  x
Straining against it along with his own bodyweight.
```

This is blank verse on steroids, and none the better for it. While the physical strain is energetically insisted upon, the flouting of the iambic standard sacrifices

the opportunity for dramatic contrast, and the rocking rhythms are too boisterous for what is being described: the movement suggests something more
like a lumbering waltz than strength futilely expended while going nowhere.
Experiments like these would appear to show that while unthinking regularity
in blank verse is soporific, wholesale distortion of the meter may be disaffecting in other ways. Small shifts can by their more modest means often create
deeply satisfying rhythmic runs.

One way to summarize the effect of modernism on blank verse is to say
that it made metrical substitutions more various and plentiful. Older variations such as the initial trochee and the midline anapest were augmented, so
that more than one such substitution might occur in a single line. We have
seen examples of such strenuously modified lines throughout the earlier chapters on the twentieth century. The way such shifts alter the sound of iambic
pentameter is clearly audible and not too difficult to analyze, in each particular
case, because the noniambic feet stick out like sore . . . thumbs? What is harder
to grasp for those first attempting to write blank verse is the array of rhythmic
gradations that can be discerned within so-called regular lines. The use of numerical scansion to denote different levels of stress is the usual academic tool
for more precise analyses. But notational precision is not necessary: hearing
the differences and arranging phrasing in awareness of their potential effects
is what is needed. Moving a key word into different positions within specimen
lines of similar content will illustrate the point:

> 1. I've never been afraid like that before.
> 2. I've never in my life been so afraid.
> 3. Afraid? Like that? Not ever in my life.

In each of these lines, "afraid" is an iamb consorting with other iambs, but
the degree of accent on its second syllable varies slightly in each case. The
stress on "afraid" in line 1 is by no means weak, but it becomes heavier in line
2 (no doubt because of the intensifying "so" and the terminal position). And
it is heavier still, as an abrupt rhetorical question, at the beginning of line 3.
These are not blatant differences in emphasis, but they will be apparent, even if
subtly, in any sensitive reading. Growing familiarity in working with iambic
meter fine-tunes a poet's ear for such nuances and the overtones they add to
meaning as well as to sound. If we imagined a speaker for each of the lines above,

we would probably sense in each case a different persona: speaker 1 is matter-of-fact; speaker 2, a bit prim and prissy; speaker 3, expansive and dramatic.

Here, lest these assertions become too dramatic, we must enter a caveat. Poetic rhythms can suggest qualities of feeling or imitate movement, but they do this only in conjunction with the words they animate. In themselves, rhythms and meters are abstract patterns, which is what makes them available for any content the poet desires. It is easy to demonstrate this. If we take the line for which we just posited a prim and prissy speaker—"I've never in my life been so afraid"—we can set other words to it that will follow the same rhythmic contour while projecting a different tone. Here, for instance, is a line that could go into a dramatic monologue whose speaker is one of the divines or magistrates of Salem in 1692: "We're always ready here to hang a witch." The rhythm, which complemented the timorous tone and slightly fussy-sounding phrasing in the first case, serves just as well for the second line, with its declarative force and its cheerful, can-do attitude.

More than a few poets over the years must at times have wished there were a Bureau of Prosodic Weights and Measures. As it is, each poet must by experiment become alert to the permutations available in casting a pentameter line because of the inescapable fact of relative stress. All that is needed to make an iamb is a second syllable that is more accented than the first, but the *degree* of accent will vary within the line from one foot to another. And those so-called unstressed syllables are of course not entirely without stress (if they were, they would be inaudible). These unstressed syllables are another feature much experimented upon by poets in the twentieth century. There is, as mentioned earlier, a debate among prosodists about the frequency or even the existence of spondees in English-language poetry.[10] Whether one wishes to champion the spondee or, with the skeptics, to speak of the "heavy iamb," it is indisputable that modern blank verse exhibits countless examples of a supposedly unstressed syllable receiving a degree of stress that lessens the distinction between it and the stressed syllable that follows it in the foot. Here are some lines illustrating the use of such extra weighting in each of the five positions of a pentameter. In keeping with earlier practice, the feet in question are marked as spondees:

> /   /
> Earth spawns no gangrene half so luminous
>
> (Peter Viereck, "For an Assyrian Frieze," 27)

              /   /
And what rough beast, its hour come round at last

                            (Yeats, "The Second Coming," 21)

             /   /
And every tree up stood a rotting trunk

                          (Frost, "The Census-Taker," 22)

                 /   /
One average mind—with one thought less, each year

                       (Pound, "Portrait d'une Femme," 10)

                 /   /
She hears, upon that water without sound

                       (Stevens, "Sunday Morning," 106)

The samples here are restricted to lines that exhibit regular movement except for the modified foot. The extra emphasis given to one normally unstressed syllable affects the overall movement in markedly different ways, depending on its placement in the line. Of course, one could easily cite modern examples in which the spondee or heavy iamb would be only one of a number of modifications. The point urged by these particular examples is, again, that a very small change—the weighting of one syllable—may significantly contribute to the expressive power of the line. The apprentice poet wishing to develop mastery of iambic pentameter might wish to investigate these and other more modest variations of the paradigm before attempting Websterian (or simply weird) contortions.

We can examine in depth the ways in which a given line of blank verse observes or challenges the metrical standard. But any conclusion we may reach is of limited value if it fails to recognize that the lines we have been considering in isolation are not, in fact, isolated. As virtually all writers on the subject eventually acknowledge, the quality of a poet's blank verse can be judged adequately only by taking account of context: not the single line but its interactions with the lines surrounding it, and hence ultimately its relation to the poem's entirety. Many of the quotations in this book (in the sections on modernism, most of them) exhibit deliberate veerings toward and away from regularity. In cases where regularity is hardly ever sensed, or has so little prominence as to be overshadowed by noniambic gestures, we face the question of whether blank verse is an apt label for what we are reading. But we notice repeatedly how cannily some poets can balance the regular line off against others that are anything but.

Here is an instance. Howard Nemerov's unrhymed sonnet "TV" devotes its octave to a capsulized account of Bishop Berkeley's philosophy, which holds that physical objects exist only through being perceived—first by God, then by us. TV, Nemerov asserts, would have pleased the bishop by demonstrating that "whatever is made / The object of your vision is so made / Because another is looking at it too, / A fraction of a second earlier" (5–8). From this playful generality, the poem moves on to harsher particulars in its sestet:

>   x / x   / x / x / x /
> The straying lens across the battlefield,
>
>   x / x x   / x x   /   x / x x   /
> The cameraman's quivering hand considering death,
>
>   x / x / x   / x x   / /
> The instant replay—all of them shopworn,
>
>   /   /   x   / x   x   /   x x   /
> All soiled and secondhand goods of this world
>
>   / x x   /   / x x   x / x   /
> Shaken in God's wavering attention just
>
>   x / x   x /   x / / x   /   /
> An instant before we see it as out there.

(9–14)

If we met with any one of lines 10, 12, 13, or 14 in isolation, we would be struck by its departure from the regularity of line 9 (paradigmatic) and line 11 (divergent only in the shifting of stress at the end). Why doesn't the passage collapse in prosodic chaos? Nemerov's control of the syntax is a powerful force for coherence: we have to read all six lines to reach the full stop. But also there is a sense that anomalies of movement are not whimsically random but nicely calculated. The stress displacements and added unstressed syllables track the sense of "quivering," "Shaken," and "wavering" in their respective lines, and the disorder of line 12, while not directly mimetic, highlights the concept of the world as a welter of "soiled and secondhand goods"—a sort of terrestrial junk shop overseen by an absentminded proprietor. Line 14 is subtler yet, with the delayed stress provided by the anapestic second foot—a checking of the progressive movement to represent the infinitesimal gap between God's (or the cameraman's) perception and our own. The "instant" is here fleetingly embodied by a single additional unstressed syllable. And after this, the balanced, heavy stressing of "see it" and "out there" (cunningly separated by "as," which underlines the ambiguity surrounding the reality of what is being looked at) seems to point an uncomfortably accusatory finger at viewers like us—safe and sound on our side of the screen that distances us from the carnage it displays. Startlingly, the poem manages to skewer simultaneously the idealist philosophy and the modern mass media culture.

This is a cooler, less obtrusive set of effects than Tennyson's moaning doves and murmuring bees. But in its own less melodious way, it is equally demonstrative of how the rhythmic ebb and flow of a blank-verse passage aggregates meaning not simply by modifying this or that single line but by linking them in complex patterns of choreography. Nemerov's highly expressive modifications here are easier to appreciate because of the anchoring presence of his more regular lines and a disciplined limit applied to the liberties he does take. The changes of line length, for instance, are from the addition of unstressed syllables, not stressed ones, in all but the final line. The beat of the pentameter is skewed, but not to the point of losing a sense of the accentual count. The additional beats loaded into the final line are perhaps suitable there, as a conclusive emphasis, in a way that would be harder to rationalize if they occurred elsewhere. How conscious would all this be on Nemerov's part, or any poet's? Some of these details most likely take form through intuitive leaps rather than a systematic narrowing-down of options to the best available. This would be the case, understandably, for practiced poets who have absorbed rhythmic patterns thoroughly. A well-exercised verbal imagination will occasionally or even often be favored with shortcuts. But even the most practiced of poets may labor for days to get a line or a phrase right.

Finally, although a poet may expend untold amounts of lapidary craftsmanship on a line of verse, it is not destined to be a solitary gem. Its nearest companion lines and the setting they share require active attention as well. Exercises such as the one conducted some pages back—rephrasing a line in different ways so that the words are moved into different stress positions—are helpful in developing an ear for different levels of stress and for the pentameter's rhythmic possibilities. But the single line must be joined to others, and here the labor becomes perhaps more architectural than lapidary. Passages like the sestet of Nemerov's "TV" impress us not simply through intriguing maneuvers within the line but through the overall coherence and momentum of the lines taken together. About this there is still more to say.

III

Throughout this book, discussions of verse technique have focused primarily on the handling of iambic feet, which in any given pentameter may be strict in movement or subject to rhythmic sway. We have investigated with some thoroughness the various metrical substitutions which evolving practice has come to allow in the blank-verse line. This emphasis—what might be called a stress on stress—is historically warranted, having preoccupied both conservative and innovative stylists since the emergence of modernism. Yet, as this discussion has intermittently suggested, such analysis does not account for all the technical devices that have made blank verse so durable, versatile, and expressive a form. Especially if we turn our attention, as we have begun to do, from the single line to the passage, we should pay heed not only to stresses but to the framework containing them, and consequently to matters such as syntax, enjambment, and the pause or caesura.

One of the prime attractions of blank verse for poets in past times has been its compatibility with extended syntax—with sentences more like Conrad's or Faulkner's than Hemingway's or Carver's. No one would argue the desirability of long sentences apart from other considerations. Yet it is notable that many modern and postmodern poets have tied themselves down to a short-winded style that fails to take advantage of iambic pentameter's capacity for amplitude. Are there alternatives? The grand master of extended syntax in English blank verse is Milton, but like any great but idiosyncratic stylist, he is not amenable to simple copying. The third section of chapter 2, above, discussed with regrettable but necessary brevity certain of the tactics on display in *Paradise Lost*. Some of these were founded on classical models, including inversions of word order that would be hard to employ consistently or persuasively in contemporary writing. A style of today that was intentionally and closely derivative of Milton's would appear willfully antiquarian or mannered in the extreme. Yet some of Milton's skills in giving blank verse a longer reach and a longer breath may, allowing for large differences in the stylistic preferences of our later period,

still be instructive. As noted in chapter 4, Richard Wilbur occasionally brings
Milton to mind in his longer blank-verse poems. It is not that his sentences are
outstandingly long, but that they intimate a capacity to extend themselves to
address matters fully. Wilbur keeps the reader alert by varying the length and
structural complexity of his sentences, and the elegantly paced sequences that
result can be seen as streamlined descendants of Milton's. The closing lines
of "Walking to Sleep" are composed of three progressively longer sentences.
The speaker, apparently an expert on how to "walk" to sleep while evading
nightmares, concludes the advice he has been offering this way:

> As for what turn your travels then will take,
> I cannot guess. Long errantry perhaps
> Will arm you to be gentle, or the claws
> Of nightmare flap you pathless God knows where,
> As the crow flies, to meet your dearest horror.
> Still, if you are in luck, you may be granted,
> As, inland, one can sometimes smell the sea,
> A moment's perfect carelessness, in which
> To stumble a few steps and sink to sleep
> In the same clearing where, in the old story,
> A holy man discovered Vishnu sleeping,
> Wrapped in his maya, dreaming by a pool
> On whose calm face all images whatever
> Lay clear, unfathomed, taken as they came.

> (127–40)

Starting with the curt and functional first sentence and moving to the balanced
weighing of possibilities in the second, the poem then moves on to the still
longer and more densely figurative final sentence which, like some of Milton's,
unfolds overlapping layers of simile and allusion. Blank verse, especially in
longer poems, is particularly capable of facilitating this sort of measured expansion of scope in a wide range of contexts—descriptive, narrative, meditative.

Occasionally a modern or postmodern poet will construct a truly gargantuan sentence for a special purpose. The first sentence of Edwin Muir's
"The Labyrinth," mentioned earlier, sprawls across thirty-four and a half lines
in branching intricacy emblematic of the Cretan maze it depicts. The twenty-

four-line sentence opening Catherine Tufariello's "The Feast of Tabernacles" emphasizes the prolonged, even seemingly endless wanderings of the Israelites in the desert. One must grant that these are difficult feats to bring off, and it is not surprising that many notably extended sentences in blank verse are catalogues requiring little grammatical complexity to frame their compendia of listed items. A somewhat more complex catalogue is that which details not separate items but different aspects of an object, elaborating on a single image. The memory-obsessed speaker of Anthony Hecht's "The Venetian Vespers" is fixated on an image from his childhood, and discourses on it in a sentence the length of a sonnet:

> Yes, but also the sight, on a gray morning,
> Beneath the crossbar of an iron railing
> Painted a glossy black, of six waterdrops
> Slung in suspension, sucking into themselves,
> As if it were some morbid nourishment,
> The sagging blackness of the rail itself,
> But edged with brilliant fingernails of chrome
> In which the world was wonderfully disfigured
> Like faces seen in spoons, like mirrorings
> In the fine spawn, the roe of air bubbles,
> That tiny silver wampum along the stems,
> Yellowed and magnified, of aging flowers
> Caught in the lens of stale water and glass
> In the upstairs room when somebody had died.
>
> (I, 22–35)

Here the syntax is "slung in suspension" in order to disclose the intensifying morbidity of the image, which is at last climactically realized in line 35. But this is not all: this imposing, slow-moving sentence is immediately followed by one contrastingly short, which intensifies the imagery in a different way, through ironic incongruity. We have no sooner arrived at the terminus of the long sentence's death reference than we proceed to this: "Just like the beads they sprinkled over cookies / At Christmas" (36–37). As with Wilbur, Hecht's mastery is apparent not only in drawing out the length and complexity of a sentence but in balancing it against others of differing profiles and proportions.

And the meter is a supple instrument for the purpose. The apprentice poet seeking to vary the pace and structure of his sentences, which have definite consequences for the verse lines singly and *en masse*, would be well advised to study such models.

Enjambment is another of Milton's superior skills.[11] More variety in the length and structure of sentences will tend to make enjambment figure more prominently in a verse passage; but mastering it is imperative in any case in order to write confidently in the meter. Enjambment (if it is not used in some unduly repetitive pattern) is an obvious help in fending off monotony. The lines by Masefield that we viewed with dismay some pages back are monotonous not only because of scarcely varying rhythm but because of much heavy end-stopping. A few lines from Edwin Markham's old chestnut "The Man with the Hoe" are even more single-minded in this way:

> Through this dread shape the suffering ages look;
> Time's tragedy is in that aching stoop;
> Through this dread shape humanity betrayed,
> Plundered, profaned and disinherited,
> Cries protest to the Judges of the World,
> A protest that is also prophecy.
>
> (27–32)

By liberating phrasing from the bounds of a single line, a poet transcends the rigid symmetries, the almost mechanical parceling of sound that unvaried end-stopping imposes. We see such a less-constrained approach in the opening lines of "A Lament for the Dead Pets of Our Childhood," by A. E. Stallings. All of these lines are enjambed until the sentence they form reaches its end with line 6:

> Even now I dream of rabbits murdered
> By loose dogs in the dark, the saved-up voice
> Spilt on that last terror, or the springtime
> Of lost baby rabbits, grey and blind
> As moles, that slipped from birth and from the nest
> Into a grey, blind rain, became the mud.
>
> (1–6)

A comparison of this with the preceding passage shows how a series of closely associated ideas or images may produce diminishing or mounting interest in the reader. The greater part of that interest is sparked by the ideas or images themselves, no doubt, but the absence or presence of enjambment is by no means a negligible factor. Stallings's elegantly varied run-on lines are livelier to follow than Markham's locked-in ones.

Enjambment enhances motion in poetry, sometimes tracking it directly. Notice how the enjambments increase the animation in Timothy Steele's description of city boys playing a street game ("rollerblading hockey players"):

> Innocent ids, the boys regroup; one cuts
> A circle sharply, swings his stick, and rifles
> The plastic ball that serves as puck between
> The pair of soda cans that serve as goalposts.
>
> ("Freudian Analysis," 12–15)

But no matter what is being described or discussed, enjambment can be seen (if perhaps somewhat too simply) as a suspense mechanism. It tantalizes us, forces us to look beyond the line's end to follow what is ongoing (or going on) to some deferred and at times surprising conclusion. Howard Nemerov's three-stanza poem "Flower Arrangements" describes how the flowers given him "twice a week / Or even oftener accumulate / In plastic cups beside me on the table" (1–3). The middle stanza describes the fading and withering of these offerings in sequence, as the poet absentmindedly fails to discard the older ones:

> Shrinking into themselves, they keep their cool
> And colors many days, their drying and
> Diminishing would be imperceptible
> But for the instance of the followers
> Arranged beside them in the order of
> Their severance and exile from the earth;
> In death already though they know it not.
>
> (8–14)

Nemerov's enjambments are variously hard or soft, more or less urgent in catching the reader's attention. The end of line 8 might be seen as a clandestine enjambment, since it is unclear that "they keep their cool" is incomplete until its slang sense has been modified to objective description by the addition of "And colors many days." But the enjambment in line 9, on "and," and that in line 12, on "of," are drastic, at first seeming more like cuts than bridgings. (They may in fact hint at the "severance" of the flowers.) Yet the bridging is accomplished, for the radical incompleteness at the line break propels us onward. Certainly the steady progress of the sentence over these noticeable gaps until it arrives at the semicolon that end-stops line 13 intimates the "imperceptible," unhaltable progress of decay. Not truly unhaltable, though; the final line of the stanza, also end-stopped, reminds us of the ultimate end, and it brings this sequence of observations to an end as decisively as a semicolon or period precludes further enjambment. There is plenty of motion in this apparently static scene, but it is the motion of the poet's mind giving thought free play for a time.

The value for apprentice poets in mastering enjambment is, as these examples indicate, twofold. It is an essential tool for maintaining the balance between formal design and freedom of movement found in the best blank verse. And it can deepen meaning, operating somewhat like a masked metaphor. Probably there are not too many situations that would produce the wonderfully witty aptness of Richard Wilbur's enjambment in "All That Is":

> One passenger
> Already folds his paper to the left-
> Hand lower corner of the puzzles page [. . .]
>
> (14–16)

The reader of the poem, feeling his eyes move leftward and downward to complete the hyphenated word, is absorbed in an unusually immediate sense in what he is reading. This is of course delightful, but the same transitional suspension can produce something more complicatedly witty, as in these lines from Anthony Hecht's "Devotions of a Painter":

> I am enamored of the pale chalk dust
> Of the moth's wing, and the dark moldering gold
> Of rust, the corrupted treasures of the world.
>
> (30–32)

It is unlikely that without the enjambment of line 31 we would be as strongly impressed by the paradoxical "gold / Of rust" which the painter celebrates. And the deferment of identification until after the line break of what in fact we are reading about provides a sense of discovery, of delayed but satisfying clarification. Enjambment so used (and it is often thus that Milton uses it) has a way of forcing the reader to pause and reevaluate what he has read. Since the mechanism depends on the suppression (or at least the diminishment) of the pause at the line's end, the paradoxical nature of this device is intriguingly evident. It is often enough something that hurries us along, but it can be at times decisive in slowing us down, forcing us to look back before we go forward. The poet's calculated use of this kind of enjambment can be similar in its process and outcome to propounding a riddle: the audience is encouraged to look in the wrong direction for the answer, which, when it comes, forces a revised understanding of what came before. Enjambment thus is properly regarded as a device not merely of sound but of sense. It is highly worthwhile to explore not only its aural consequences but its thematically expressive possibilities in writing blank verse.

The pause or caesura is another device that affects the sound and sense of passages in manifold ways. Altering its position from line to line or, at times, suppressing it entirely are yet further means of avoiding the dullness of repeated identical movement. Sometimes the pause is used as added emphasis. In Joshua Mehigan's "The Spectacle," we find it applied like a brake to the onrush of enjambed lines:

> The fire
> waited behind the front door like a person
> of great importance just about to step
> onstage. | The town stood back and watched [. . .]
>
> (7–10)

The effect is stronger when, as here, the pause is suppressed in the lines preceding it: when it comes, it is a bit like the caboose at the end of the train. Pauses can be used more plentifully for particular dramatic effects. At the end of Frost's "'Out, Out—'" the farmboy wounded by a buzz saw is in his last moments (we will mark end-stopping as well as other pauses):

He lay and puffed his lips out with his breath.|
And then— | the watcher at his pulse took fright.|
No one believed. | They listened at his heart.|
Little— | less— | nothing!— | and that ended it.|
No more to build on there. | And they, | since they
Were not the one dead, | turned to their affairs.

(29–34)

The emotional context for these many pauses (scrupulously marked by punctuation that is almost like stage directions for a reciter) is the statement "No one believed." The experience is only capable of being registered in increments, haltingly, like the boy's own labored breathing and slowing pulse. Even after the pace of life comes back, in the enjambed phrase ending line 33, it is interrupted once more in the last line to emphasize the bitterly unavoidable difference between the living and the dead: the boy's work is over, but these people have work that has to be done.

As we have noted earlier, punctuation is not an infallible signal, by its presence or absence, of the presence or absence of a significant pause. Frost is a busy punctuator in the passage above, and his use of dashes would seem to specify major pauses, as do his periods within or at the ends of lines. Commas are more questionable. The pause in the final line, after "dead," seems natural. The one near the end of the preceding line ("And they, | since they") seems more dubious. It is certainly not as marked a pause as the comma-linked one in line 34, and although it is grammatically necessary, a performer might well rush right over it and through the long-deferred enjambment. This may be an arguable point; but, conversely, it is unquestionably true that many lines of poetry have pauses not signaled by commas. Many pentameters have an unpunctuated pause, albeit often quite a light one, after the second or third foot, as in these lines from Dana Gioia's "Metamorphosis":

Forever lost | within your inward gaze

(22)

Beyond the rapist's hand | or sudden blade

(9)

This sort of midline pause can fall in the middle of a foot as well:

The admonitions | of the nightingale

(8)

Such lines have a much more traditional sound than the agitated ones by Frost, with their proliferation of additional pauses. Even though the verse in Gioia's poem has a smoother flow, we notice that there is still frequent shifting of the pause's position from line to line. Some early blank verse in English was doctrinaire (and irritating) in placing the pause so frequently in the same position (after the second foot). But theatrical blank verse and Milton's epic meter set it free, and poets today are willing to move, suppress, or multiply it within their lines for expressive purposes.

A pause as close as possible to the beginning or the end of a line is of course especially striking. Although we may scarcely register some midline pauses as we read, these less conventionally placed ones are meant to be noticed. The old medium in Frost's "The Witch of Coös," wondering why the spirit she was consulting broke her trance, says:

> Don't that make you suspicious
> That there's something the dead are keeping back?
> Yes, | there's something the dead are keeping back.
>
> (16–18)

Lines 17 and 18 are identical except in a single word and, of course, punctuation, but notice what a decisive emphasis comes with the pause after "Yes," breaking the line's first foot. There is some difference in movement and tone because line 17 is part of a question and line 18 is declarative. But the pause is vital, marking the difference between suspicion and certainty. If one were to write the emphatic pause out of line 18 (for instance, by rephrasing the line slightly as the flat assertion "There's something that the dead are keeping back"), the dramatic contrast between the two lines would be much diminished. Breaking the final foot of a line also seizes attention. Randall Jarrell does this (as well as breaking an initial foot of the same line) in a description of a World War II pilot taking off from the deck of a carrier. His lines follow the pilot through his preparations, finally picturing him

> As he breasts the currents of the bellowing deck
> And, | locked at last into the bubble, | Hope, |
> Is borne along the foaming windy road
> To the air [. . .]
>
> ("Pilots, Man Your Planes," 33–36)

Notice how the pauses and end-stopping play against the surrounding en-jambments: "Hope" is encapsulated by pauses as the pilot is locked into the "bubble" (the cockpit, literally, but also the hope of surviving the mission).

The more one studies pauses in pentameter lines, the more one is struck by their capacity for gradation. Just as the stress on an iamb's stressed syllable can be more or less heavy, pauses interact with their surroundings to cover a wide range of emphases. Howard Nemerov's "Moment," quoted in full in chapter 4, ends this way:

> and the mind of God,|
> The flash across the gap of being, | thinks
> In the instant absence of forever: | now.

> (12–14)

Both of the last two lines interpose a pause between the two syllables of a final iamb. But the enjambment of "thinks" with the following phrase keeps that pause from being as pronounced as the one before "now"—a word not only end-stopped but literally the end of the poem. In fact, if we go back to the be-ginning of the grammatical clause in line 12, we find that the pauses increase in force line by line: that in line 13 is more noticeable than the end-stopping of line 12, and that in line 14, as we have seen, is more noticeable still. Pauses can be arranged in a sequence that builds to a climax.

It makes sense to think of pauses and enjambments together, for both are welcome complications to the meter, and both owe their existence not to meter but to syntax. The verse that overruns the expected pause at the end of a line will sooner or later reach the barrier of a caesura. Attention to these fea-tures is a natural aspect of writing language that is simultaneously metrical and grammatical. While these features are predominantly structural, they are capable of taking on a figurative quality as well in special instances like this cunning nine-line poem by Miller Williams, "Form and Theory of Poetry":

> Think of how in a hurricane the winds
> build up from nothing at all and suddenly stop
> then start the opposite way and die down,|
> the way the traffic around a stadium
> builds to the game, | stops, | starts again
> going the other direction, | dies down.|

Think in the eye of a hurricane, | then, | of halftime.|
At a football game, | think of the Gulf Coast,|
Biloxi, | Mississippi, | blown away.

Here the pauses are so intricately in league with the developing metaphor that they almost steal the show from it. The ominously fitful movement that they impose on the words is itself an emblem of what is being described. It is an eerie effect (the more so given the prescience of the piece, which was published a number of years before Biloxi, Mississippi, was indeed blown away by a hurricane). It is a more complex and teasing device than it at first appears to be: we wonder, for instance, if line 2 is meant to be read as end-stopped or enjambed. The absence of a comma after "stop" in an otherwise heavily punctuated poem suggests one of two things. Either "stop" is enough of a stop so as not to need a comma, or this particular stop is so brief that it lacks the emphasis denoting the others, and we skim with it through the enjambment: stop then start. Readers will differ, but the general point to be drawn from this, as from the whole poem, is that pauses and enjambments can affect meaning as they affect movement, and thus can assist the poet in pursuit of a theme. Interestingly, the theme in this case is broached only in the title, not in the poem itself. We may take this to suggest that the form and theory of poetry are things so elusive that they are best approached by analogy or metaphor rather than head-on. This is a truth infrequently acknowledged by prosodists and literary critics.

IV

A good poem in blank verse, as in any other form, is dependent on inspiration. If that sounds alarming, let us say it is dependent on having an idea that is startling, or clever, or amusing, or touching, or terrifying. This initial conception, though, can only be realized through attention to each particular formal detail and to the patterns these create when set in place. It is exacting work to weigh degrees of stress against one another; and, as we have just seen, this is not all, for the gaps between those metrical units require measured adjustment as well. Absence of rhyme and of the confines of stanza form signals an apparent ease that quickly complicates itself as lines accumulate on paper.

Such a thought echoes Shapiro's and Beum's calmly paradoxical judgment that blank verse, "undoubtedly the easiest kind of verse to write," is nonetheless "one of the hardest to *master*."[12] This view was expressed more sardonically by Ambrose Bierce in *The Devil's Dictionary:*

> Blank-verse, *n.* Unrhymed iambic pentameter—the most difficult kind of English verse to write acceptably; a kind, therefore, much affected by those who cannot acceptably write any kind.[13]

By attending to technical concerns like those treated in this chapter, a poet will, without a doubt, be courting difficulty. But for a poet—for any artist— difficulty is beside the point, or it is of the essence: in any case, it is not something to be shunned. The difficulties peculiar to blank verse are not ineluctably mysterious, and can be overcome and even turned to advantage by poets who are prepared to explore the protean capacities of iambic pentameter. Such effort has kept legions of poets joyfully (if not gainfully) employed across the centuries, writing this resilient, limber, charismatic line. And many still are drawn to it today.

NOTES

Preface

1. John Hollander, *Vision and Resonance: Two Senses of Poetic Form* (New York: Oxford University Press, 1975), viii.

Chapter 1: The Sounds of Blank Verse

1. Julian Symons, *Mortal Consequences: A History—from the Detective Story to the Crime Novel* (New York: Harper, 1972), vii–viii.

2. Samuel Johnson, "Somervile," in *Lives of the English Poets,* ed. George Birkbeck Hill (Oxford: Oxford University Press, 1905), 2:230. The comment was provoked by William Somervile's poem *Rural Sports.*

3. John Addington Symonds, *Blank Verse* (New York: Scribner, 1895), 51.

4. John Milton, *The Reason of Church Government Urged against Prelatry,* in *Complete Poems and Major Prose,* ed. Merrit Y. Hughes (New York: Odyssey Press, 1957), 667.

5. "Journey Out of Essex," in *John Clare's Autobiographical Writings,* ed. Eric Robinson (Oxford: Oxford University Press, 1983), 154.

6. A helpful discussion of this distinction is in Timothy Steele, *All the Fun's in How You Say a Thing: An Explanation of Meter and Versification* (Athens: Ohio University Press, 1999). See especially chapter 1, "Metrical Norm and Rhythmical Modulation," 27–51.

7. For skepticism as to spondees, see Steele, *All the Fun's in How You Say a Thing,* 46–49, and W. K. Wimsatt and Monroe C. Beardsley, "The Concept of Meter: An Exercise in Abstraction," in Wimsatt's *Hateful Contraries: Studies in Literature and Criticism* ([Lexington]: University of Kentucky Press, 1965), 133–36.

8. A widely used system of this kind is that of G. L. Trager and H. L. Smith Jr., *An Outline of English Structure,* Studies in Linguistics Occasional Papers no. 9 (Norman, OK: Battenburg Press, 1951). In positing four levels of stress, Trager and Smith were preceded by the eminent philologist Otto Jespersen; see his "Notes on Metre," most easily accessible in *The Structure of Verse: Modern Essays on Prosody,* ed. Harvey Gross (New York: Fawcett, 1966), 111–29. For examples of passages scanned according to the four levels of stress, see Steele, *All the Fun's in How You Say a Thing,* 31–38, and Philip Hobsbaum, *Metre, Rhythm and Verse Form* (London: Routledge, 1996), 7–9. Jespersen casts some doubt on the efficacy of his own system of scansion by declaring that "in reality there are infinite gradations of

stress, from the most penetrating scream to the faintest whisper" ("Notes on Metre," 115). In "The Concept of Meter: An Exercise in Abstraction," Wimsatt and Beardsley emphasize this point to defend traditional foot scansion: "For all we know, there may be, not four, but five degrees of English stress, or eight. How can one be sure? What one can always be sure of is that a given syllable in a sequence is more or less stressed than the preceding or the following. Or, suppose that there are, as Jespersen and Trager-Smith seem to agree, just *four* degrees of English stress. The discriminations are not needed for discerning the meter—but only the degrees of more and less. How *much* more is always irrelevant" (*Hateful Contraries*, 131).

9. David Mason and John Frederick Nims, *Western Wind: An Introduction to Poetry*, 5th ed. (Boston: McGraw-Hill, 2006), 209.

10. For Symonds, see note 3, above. In addition to the works of Symonds and others discussed in this chapter, it is worthwhile to note one that is more narrowly focused: Edward Payson Morton, *The Technique of English Non-Dramatic Blank Verse* (Chicago: R. R. Donnelley, 1910). This University of Chicago PhD dissertation compiles statistics on the use of various prosodic devices by a number of canonical writers of blank verse. It has been reprinted (Folcroft Press, 1970).

11. George Saintsbury, *A History of English Prosody*, 3 vols. (London: Macmillan, 1906–10).

12. Robert Bridges, *Milton's Prosody*, rev. ed. (Oxford: Oxford University Press, 1921).

13. Edward Weismiller and T. V. F. Brogan, "Blank Verse," in *The New Princeton Encyclopedia of Poetry and Poetics*, ed. Alex Preminger and T. V. F. Brogan (Princeton: Princeton University Press, 1993), 140.

Chapter 2: Before the Twentieth Century

1. Saintsbury speaks of the prosodic situation at this time in England as being in a "state of chaos" (1:298). A useful study of the gradual development of metrical regularity in the sixteenth century is John Thompson's *The Founding of English Metre* (New York: Columbia University Press, 1961).

2. C. S. Lewis, *English Literature in the Sixteenth Century* (Oxford: Oxford University Press, 1954), 121.

3. Edward R. Weismiller, in his entry "Blank Verse" in *A Milton Encyclopedia*, ed. William B. Hunter et al. (Lewisburg, PA: Bucknell University Press, 1978), comments on this "extraordinary" use of "a *metrical* caesura (as distinguished from a simple pause, a sense break) for possibly the first and probably the last time in the history of English accentual-syllabic verse" (1:180).

4. "To the Memory of My Beloved, the Author Mr. William Shakespeare: and What He Hath Left Us."

5. Cited in O. B. Hardison Jr., *Prosody and Purpose in the English Renaissance* (Baltimore: Johns Hopkins University Press: 1989), 237.

6. Saintsbury, *History of English Prosody*, 2:6.

7. Ibid., 2:8

8. Symonds, *Blank Verse,* 30.

9. Saintsbury, *History of English Prosody,* 2:6.

10. Ibid., 1:349.

11. There is a chart of the percentages in *The Complete Signet Classic Shakespeare,* ed. Sylvan Barnet (New York: Harcourt Brace Jovanovich, 1972), 20.

12. George T. Wright, *Shakespeare's Metrical Art* (Berkeley: University of California Press, 1988), 6.

13. Some have conjectured that one reason blank verse became a mainstay in the theater of this period was its capacity as an aid to memory. As O. B. Hardison notes: "Renaissance actors had to commit a staggering number of lines to memory. Not only did they frequently play double or triple roles in a single play, they had to perform in more than one play in the course of a single week. . . . Blank verse survived at least in part because it is easy to memorize and provides a ready basis for faking when memory falters" (*Prosody and Purpose,* 256–57).

14. Wright, *Shakespeare's Metrical Art,* 17.

15. Symonds, *Blank Verse,* 46–47.

16. John Milton, *Paradise Lost,* in *Complete Poems and Major Prose,* 210.

17. For reasons of space, all examples of Miltonic blank verse are drawn from *Paradise Lost;* parenthetical references are to book and line. Milton's other uses of the meter—in parts of *Comus* and of *Samson Agonistes,* and in *Paradise Regained*—exhibit some interesting stylistic differences; but it was the verse of *Paradise Lost* that exerted the most influence on later poets.

18. For some fine analyses, see Weismiller's "Blank Verse" entry in *A Milton Encyclopedia,* 1:179–92.

19. Raymond Dexter Havens, *The Influence of Milton on English Poetry* (Cambridge, MA: Harvard University Press, 1922), 136.

20. The full title of the work, which no one uses, is *The Complaint: or, Night-Thoughts on Life, Death, & Immortality.*

21. Havens, *Influence of Milton,* 149.

22. Wrestling with the specter of Milton took numerous forms in the later eighteenth century. William Blake is scarcely known as a writer of blank verse, and yet in his first collection, *Poetical Sketches,* he included a quartet of lyric apostrophes addressed to the four seasons and a similar piece, "To the Evening Star," in all of which iambic pentameter is put strenuously to the test. John Hollander explains some of their more unexpected turns as being responses to Miltonic enjambment. Blake must be said to outdo Milton in this respect, in such lines as these from "To the Evening Star":

> Smile on our loves, and, while thou drawest the
> Blue curtains of the sky, scatter thy silver dew
> On every flower that shuts its sweet eyes
> In timely sleep. Let thy west wind sleep on
> The lake; speak silence with thy glimmering eyes,
> And wash the dusk with silver.

(5–10)

Blake's sporadically applied pressures on the meter foreshadow effects that were to become commonplace in the twentieth century. Hollander describes these poems as "flagrantly experimental" ("'Sense Variously Drawn Out': On English Enjambment," *Vision and Resonance*, 114).

23. William Wordsworth, "Preface to the Second Edition of *Lyrical Ballads*," in *Selected Poems and Prefaces*, ed. Jack Stillinger (Boston: Houghton Mifflin, 1965), 453.

24. Ibid., 451.

25. The late Victorian belletrist Edmund Gosse praises Milton for avoiding this sort of understressed third foot, which he sees as otherwise all too common: "A persistent weakness in the third foot has ever been the snare of English blank verse, and it is this element of monotony and dulness which Milton is ceaselessly endeavoring to obviate by his wonderful inversions, elisions and breaks" ("Blank Verse," in *The Encyclopaedia Britannica*, 11th ed., 4:42). This kind of complaint became less frequent in later periods, once the modernist assault on traditional versification had upended so many assumptions about standards of prosodic judgment.

26. Saintsbury, *History of English Prosody*, 3:71.

27. "Note by Mrs. Shelley," in *Shelley: Poetical Works*, ed. Thomas Hutchinson; new ed., corrected by G. B. Matthews (Oxford: Oxford University Press, 1970), 31.

28. Or is it, rather, to be scanned as follows?

/ x / / x x /   x x   /
Yielding one only response, at each pause

The line in either case may not be melodious, but it certainly is peculiar.

29. Saintsbury, in the midst of an almost idolatrous account of Shelley's blank verse, acknowledges as one of its traits "a certain breathlessness" (3:105).

30. Whether Keats *intended* to leave *The Fall of Hyperion* unfinished is disputed by scholars; the fragment of it that we have is about half as long as the earlier *Hyperion* fragment. A little over a year after his last work on it, Keats was dead. See Douglas Bush's note in his edition of John Keats, *Selected Poems and Letters* (Boston: Houghton Mifflin, 1959), 355.

31. This piece is one section of a travel diary Rossetti wrote during his tour. Accompanied by his fellow Pre-Raphaelite Holman Hunt, he viewed artworks in France and Belgium while chronicling impressions of the trip in verse—mostly sections of blank verse and sonnets. The other blank-verse passages have many fine lines but more stylistic and prosodic rough edges than "Antwerp to Ghent." John Hollander comments interestingly on this poem in his *Vision and Resonance*, 283–84.

Chapter 3: Blank Verse and Modernism

1. Robert Frost, "Introduction to E. A. Robinson's 'King Jasper,'" in *Collected Poems, Prose, & Plays* (New York: Library of America, 1995), 741. All quotations from Frost are from this edition.

2. Yvor Winters, *Edwin Arlington Robinson* (Norfolk, CT: New Directions, 1946), 108.

3. Ibid., 124.

4. David Perkins, *A History of Modern Poetry: From the 1890s to the High Modernist Mode* (Cambridge, MA: Harvard University Press, 1976), 130.

5. Winters, *Edwin Arlington Robinson*, 101.

6. Some prosodists use the term "Ionic" to refer to this combination (a pyrrhic followed by a spondee). Like some other terms drawn from classical prosody, this seems an unnecessary embellishment of a technical vocabulary that most readers find more than sufficiently complicated. While this particular modification is more common in twentieth-century poetry, earlier examples are not hard to find. The Shakespeare line discussed in chapter 1, "The quality of mercy is not strained," is a case in point.

7. For a much more fully detailed discussion of Frost's theory and practice of versification than can be provided here, see Timothy Steele, "'Across Spaces of the Footed Line': The Meter and Versification of Robert Frost," in *The Cambridge Companion to Robert Frost*, ed. Robert Faggen (Cambridge: Cambridge University Press, 2001), 123–53.

8. Frost, "Preface to an Expanded 'North of Boston,'" 849.

9. Frost to John T. Bartlett, July 4, 1913, 664.

10. Frost to Walter Pritchard Eaton, September 18, 1915, 690–91.

11. Frost to Bartlett, 665.

12. Frost to John Cournos, July 8, 1914, 680.

13. Frost, "The Figure a Poem Makes," 776.

14. Ibid.

15. Robert Francis, *Frost: A Time to Talk* (Amherst: University of Massachusetts Press, 1972), 96–97.

16. Frost, "Conversations on the Craft of Poetry," 854.

17. Frost, "Preface to 'A Way Out,'" 713.

18. Ibid.

19. Frost, "Preface to 'The Death of the Hired Man,'" 785.

20. It is true that there is a large quantity of blank verse in the three volumes of Hardy's historical drama *The Dynasts*. But this is a work that has yet to find an audience. Hardy was sensible in declaring it, in his preface, to be "a play intended simply for mental performance, and not for the stage." Even mental performances, one suspects, have been infrequent. Readers are bound to be intimidated by the pitiless exactitude of the subtitle: "An Epic-Drama of the War with Napoleon, in Three Parts, Nineteen Acts, and One Hundred and Thirty Scenes, the Time Covered by the Action being about Ten Years." There are good things, deeply interred, in *The Dynasts;* but these are principally some of the rhymed choruses. And of course, Hardy's major influence on subsequent poetry came through his rhymed lyrics.

21. Thomas reviewed *North of Boston* admiringly three times for various publications. Comments in all three pieces show his interest in Frost's way with blank verse. In one he imagines Frost's lines in "the unresisting medium of blank verse" printed as prose: "If his work were so printed, it would have little in common with the kind of prose that

runs to blank verse: in fact, it would turn out to be closer knit and more intimate than the finest prose is except in its finest passages. It is poetry because it is better than prose" (*A Language Not to Be Betrayed: Selected Prose of Edward Thomas*, ed. Edna Longley [Manchester: Carcanet, 1981], 127). Another remark signals his sensitivity to Frost's thinking about tonal qualities: "There are moments when the plain language and lack of violence make the unaffected verses look like prose, except that the sentences, if spoken aloud, are most felicitously true in rhythm to the emotion" (130–31).

22. Edmund Blunden's "Third Ypres," also in blank verse, provides an interesting comparison in its unvarnished description of a battle in progress.

23. For an extensive survey of attempts at verse drama in the first half of the twentieth century, see Moody E. Prior, *The Language of Tragedy* (Bloomington: Indiana University Press, 1966), chapter 5.

24. George Bernard Shaw, *The Perfect Wagnerite*, 1923 (New York: Dover, 1967), 113.

25. George Bernard Shaw, *Cashel Byron's Profession, by Bernard Shaw, being No. 4 of the Novels of his Nonage. Also The Admirable Bashville, and an Essay on Modern Prizefighting* (London: Constable, 1925), 287. When his early novel *Cashel Byron's Profession* was dramatized and staged in New York without his authorization, Shaw was compelled to write and stage his own version within a very short time to protect his rights to the work. *The Admirable Bashville* was the result.

26. *The Poems of Lascelles Abercrombie* (London: Oxford University Press, 1930), vi.

27. See, for instance, the admiring comments on Yeats's *Four Plays for Dancers* in Bottomley's "Note" to his own *Scenes and Plays* (New York: Macmillan, 1929), 121.

28. Perkins, *A History of Modern Poetry: From the 1890s to the High Modernist Mode*, 369.

29. Maxwell Anderson, "Poetry in the Theater," in *Off Broadway* (New York: William Sloane, 1947), 47.

30. Ibid., 50.

31. Prior, *Language of Tragedy*, 319.

32. Leaping even further ahead in chronology, we may note the verse plays of Glyn Maxwell, an English poet now resident in the United States. These enterprising works are based in fantasy or legend and are done in loose pentameters. Three of them were published in one volume, *Gnyss the Magnificent* (London: Chatto and Windus, 1993).

33. For extensive discussion of the emergence of free verse and its challenge to traditional meter, see Timothy Steele, *Missing Measures: Modern Poetry and the Revolt against Meter* (Fayetteville: University of Arkansas Press, 1990).

34. Ezra Pound, "A Few Don'ts for an Imagist," *Poetry* (March 1913).

35. T. S. Eliot, "Reflections on *Vers Libre*," in *Selected Prose*, ed. Frank Kermode (New York: Harcourt Brace Jovanovich and Farrar, Straus and Giroux, 1975), 33.

36. Ibid.

37. Ibid.

38. Ibid., 34–35.

39. Ibid., 35–36.

40. J. V. Cunningham, "How Shall the Poem Be Written," in *Collected Essays* (Chicago: Swallow, 1976), 268–69.

41. T. S. Eliot, "Tradition and the Individual Talent," in *Selected Essays* (New York: Harcourt, Brace, 1950), 5.

42. By the time of his death, Eliot's work was so widely accepted as canonical that even some erstwhile antagonists were moved to recant their earlier criticisms. John Crowe Ransom, for instance, who had questioned Eliot's prosody in "The Waste Land," made handsome amends in an essay analyzing the versification of "Gerontion." He describes Eliot's practice as energizing: "He favored a profusion of new rhythms replacing the steady old rhythms, which seemed worn to death; or keeping more or less the iambic pentameters of the blank verse he needed by 'counterpointing' them with smaller cross-rhythms" ("Gerontion," in *T. S. Eliot: The Man and His Work*, ed. Allen Tate [New York: Dell, 1966], 134). In comments on specific passages, this benign view is maintained; for example: "[R]arely does the old iambic rhythm hold up; that rule has been discarded, in the interest of fresher and more spontaneous rhythms for the modern ear" (140).

43. For evidence, see W. H. Auden, *Juvenilia: Poems, 1922–1928*, ed. Katherine Bucknell (Princeton: Princeton University Press, 1994). "The Watershed," early but in a mature style, is one rare exception to Auden's avoidance of blank verse that may be found in his collected editions.

44. Cunningham, "How Shall the Poem Be Written," 269.

45. Conrad Aiken, *Preludes* (New York: Oxford, 1966), v.

46. Ibid.

47. Edwin Muir, *An Autobiography* (London: Hogarth, 1964), 205.

48. For more extensive comment, see Harvey Gross, *Sound and Form in Modern Poetry* (Ann Arbor: University of Michigan Press, 1964), 68–70.

49. Both poems appear in the annotated E. J. Pratt, *Selected Poems*, ed. Sandra Djwa, W. J. Keith, and Zallig Pollock (Toronto: University of Toronto Press, 2000).

50. These two poems are most easily found in Louise Bogan's posthumous collection of prose and poetry, *Journey around My Room*, ed. Ruth Limmer (New York: Viking, 1980).

51. Raine has two poems thus titled. The reference is to the one beginning, "Never, never again."

52. Gross, *Sound and Form*, 237.

53. Line 1 may not be as odd (or odd in the same way), depending on Stevens's chosen pronunciation of "peignoir." English-language dictionaries allow stress either on the first syllable or the second. The latter is often preferred and is thought by some English speakers to be more French-sounding. (French is not an accentual language, so for a French speaker the syllables would not be noticeably differentiated by stress.) Either reversing the accent's position or attempting to be more accurate by giving both syllables equal stress would still leave the middle of the line disrupted.

54. This is not an easy line to scan persuasively. We may justify the stress on "is" in terms of not merely prosody but rhetoric, if we assume that when the poem begins the debate is already in progress. The speaker emphasizes his claim: "Poetry *is* the supreme

fiction." Of course, by this reasoning, one can frame readings of the line that would throw a stronger stress onto "the" or "supreme," depending on what particular objection offered by the old woman is being answered. No matter how the line is scanned, it is not close to being iambic.

55. Wallace Stevens to Morton Dauwen Zabel, March 13, 1933, in *Letters of Wallace Stevens,* ed. Holly Stevens (New York: Knopf, 1966), 265.

56. Gross, *Sound and Form,* 245.

57. Ibid., 243.

58. Donald Justice, "The Free-Verse Line in Stevens," in *Oblivion: On Writers and Writing* (Ashland, OR: Story Line Press, 1998), 29.

59. Gross, *Sound and Form,* 244.

60. Ibid., 246.

61. Justice, "Free-Verse Line in Stevens," 27.

62. Wallace Stevens, "A Note on Poetry," in *Collected Poetry and Prose* (New York: Library of America, 1997), 801.

63. Symonds, *Blank Verse,* 11–12.

64. See Justice, "Free-Verse Line in Stevens," 37–38. While he does not argue for the influence of Stevens exclusively on all the later poets he cites at the end of his essay, where he quotes passages from Spender, Schwartz, Jarrell, Bishop, and Strand, he concludes: "Stevens's version of this line is only his own very special adaptation of a line coming into general currency even as he developed it. Its development in his work, however, follows a straightforward and progressive course, and he uses it more systematically and persistently than other poets seem to have done. The Stevens line may therefore be seen as exemplary, both historically and practically. It remains one of the most important verse lines of the modern period, and Stevens is its most systematic master" (38).

Chapter 4: After Modernism

1. Delmore Schwartz, *Shenandoah,* in *Poetic Drama,* ed. Alfred Kreymborg (New York: Modern Age Books,1941). The alternation of prose with verse passages makes citation by line numbers impractical in this case.

2. Delmore Schwartz, *Genesis: Book I* (New York: New Directions, 1943), ix.

3. Here, again, alternation of verse with extended prose passages precludes line references.

4. Schwartz's essay of 1949, "The Literary Dictatorship of T. S. Eliot," is included in his *Selected Essays* (Chicago: University of Chicago Press, 1970).

5. Karl Shapiro and Robert Beum, *A Prosody Handbook* (New York: Harper, 1965), 141–142.

6. For nineteenth-century examples, see William H. Robinson Jr., ed., *Early Black American Poetry* (Dubuque, IA: Wm. C. Brown Company, 1969). This anthology includes even earlier examples, such as Phyllis Wheatley's "To the University of Cambridge, in New England," published in her collection of 1773 but written as early as 1767. Wheatley

exhorts the students at Harvard to steer clear of sin while enlarging their intellects: "Suppress the deadly serpent in its egg" (26).

7. "Attentiveness and Obedience," in *A Howard Nemerov Reader* (Columbia: University of Missouri Press, 1991), 260–61.

8. Richard Wilbur, "The Bottles Become New, Too," in *Responses: Prose Pieces: 1953–1976* (New York: Harcourt, 1976), 216.

9. Ibid., 221.

10. Ibid.

11. Richard Wilbur, "Some Notes on 'Lying,'" in *The Catbird's Song: Prose Pieces 1963–1995* (New York: Harcourt, 1997), 140.

12. Anthony Hecht, "Blank Verse," in *An Exaltation of Forms: Contemporary Poets Celebrate the Diversity of Their Art*, ed. Annie Finch and Kathrine Varnes (Ann Arbor: University of Michigan Press, 2002), 46.

13. Ibid., 48. Hecht does not identify the source of this quotation from Wordsworth.

14. Ibid., 49.

15. Ibid., 47.

16. David Perkins, *A History of Modern Poetry: Modernism and After* (Cambridge, MA: Harvard University Press, 1987), 659.

17. As noted in the previous chapter, the clipped line is a frequent device in the blank verse of Robert Graves.

18. Alfred Corn, *The Poem's Heartbeat* (Brownsville, OR: Story Line Press, 1997), 36.

19. See above, chapter 1, note 13.

Chapter 5: Writing Blank Verse Today

1. See above, chapter 3, note 52.

2. Julia Moskin, "Craving Hyphenated Chinese," *New York Times,* September 21, 2005, D8.

3. Mary Kinzie, *A Poet's Guide to Poetry* (Chicago: University of Chicago Press, 1999), 415.

4. Ibid.

5. Katherine Anne Porter, "A Day's Work," in *The Collected Stories of Katherine Anne Porter* (New York: New American Library, 1970), 388.

6. Cunningham, "How Shall the Poem Be Written," 250.

7. W. K. Wimsatt and Monroe C. Beardsley comment on this point in their magisterial essay "The Concept of Meter: An Exercise in Abstraction" (see above, chapter 1, note 7). See especially the following: "There is no line so regular (so *evenly* alternating weak and strong) that it does not show some tension. It is practically impossible to write an English line that will not in some way buck against the meter. Insofar as the line does approximate the condition of complete submission, it is most likely a tame line, a weak line" (140).

8. Frost, "Education by Poetry," 723.

9. See above, chapter 3, note 16.

10. See above, chapter 1, note 7.

11. One of the finest studies of Milton's enjambments, extending to a more general discussion of how enjambment affects the reading experience by assuming thematic weight, is John Hollander's "'Sense Variously Drawn Out': On English Enjambment," in his *Vision and Resonance*, 91–116.

12. See above, chapter 4, note 5.

13. Ambrose Bierce, *The Unabridged Devil's Dictionary,* ed. David E. Schultz and S. T. Joshi (Athens: University of Georgia Press, 2000), 27.

SOURCE LIST FOR VERSE REFERENCES

This list provides sources for all poems and verse plays quoted, discussed, or mentioned by title in the text and notes. (A few exceptions have been made for works fully cited in the notes.) Titles of individual poems are given only for ease of reference, as in many cases when more than one volume by a poet is listed. Many poems are of course available in editions other than those cited here, or in anthologies.

Abercrombie, Lascelles. *The Poems of Lascelles Abercrombie.* London: Oxford University Press, 1930.

Aiken, Conrad. *Preludes.* New York: Oxford University Press, 1966. (*Preludes for Memnon, Time in the Rock*)

———. *Selected Poems.* New York: Oxford University Press, 1961. ("The Wedding")

Akenside, Mark. *The Poetical Works of Mark Akenside.* Edited by Robin Dix. Madison, NJ: Fairleigh Dickinson University Press, 1996.

Alfred, William. *Hogan's Goat.* New York: Farrar, Straus and Giroux, 1966.

Anderson, Maxwell. *Eleven Verse Plays.* New York: Harcourt, 1940.

Arnold, Matthew. *The Poems of Matthew Arnold.* Edited by Kenneth Allott. London: Longmans, 1965.

Auden, W. H. *Collected Shorter Poems 1927–1957.* New York: Random House, 1966.

Bawer, Bruce. *Coast to Coast.* Brownsville, OR: Story Line Press, 1993.

Berryman, John. *Collected Poems 1937–1971.* New York: Farrar, Straus & Giroux, 1989.

Betjeman, John. *Collected Poems.* Enlarged ed. Boston: Houghton Mifflin, 1971.

———. *Summoned by Bells.* Boston: Houghton Mifflin, 1960

Blake, William. *Complete Writings.* Edited by Geoffrey Keynes. London: Oxford University Press, 1966.

Blunden, Edmund. *Overtones of War: Poems of the First World War.* Edited by Martin Taylor. London: Duckworth, 1996.

Bogan, Louise. *Journey around My Room.* Edited by Ruth Limmer. New York: Viking, 1980.

Bottomley, Gordon. *Gruach and Britain's Daughter.* London: Constable, 1921.

———. *Poems of Thirty Years.* London: Constable, 1925. ("The End of the World")

Bowers, Edgar. *Collected Poems.* New York: Knopf, 1997.

Browning, Elizabeth Barrett. *Aurora Leigh: A Poem in Nine Books.* New York: Thomas Y. Crowell, 1883.

Browning, Robert. *Poetical Works, 1833–1864.* Edited by Ian Jack. London: Oxford University. Press, 1970.

Bryant, William Cullen. *Poetical Works.* New York: D. Appleton, 1891.

Burt, John. *Victory at Sea.* Edgewood, KY: Robert L. Barth, 2001.

———. *The Way Down.* Princeton: Princeton University Press, 1988. ("Plains of Peace")

———. *Work without Hope.* Baltimore: Johns Hopkins University Press, 1996. ("Anna Peterson," "Elizabeth Keckley")

Byron (George Gordon, Lord Byron). *Selected Poems and Letters.* Edited by Edward E. Bostetter. New York: Holt, Rinehart, 1951.

Canaday, John. *The Invisible World.* Baton Rouge: Louisiana University Press, 2002.

Cassity, Turner. *The Destructive Element: New and Selected Poems.* Athens: Ohio University Press, 1998. ("The Mount of the Holy Cross," "Enola Gay Rights," "Man of the Century," "Days of Labor," "Berlin-to-Baghdad," "Eniwetok Mon Amour," "The Glorified Go One by One to Glory," "Retouching Walker Evans," "Mainstreaming," "Hedy Lamarr and a Chocolate Bar," "Oued Draa")

———. *No Second Eden.* Athens: Ohio University Press, Swallow Press, 2002. ("Stylization and Its Failures," "Acid Rain on Sherwood Forest," "Why Geriatrics Are Not Sacrificed")

Ciardi, John. *Lives of X.* New Brunswick, NJ: Rutgers University Press, 1971.

Coleridge, Samuel Taylor. *Selected Poems.* Edited by Richard Holmes. New York: HarperCollins, 1996.

Corn, Alfred. *A Call in the Midst of the Crowd.* New York: Viking, 1978.

———. *Autobiographies.* New York: Penguin, 1992. ("1992")

———. *Contradictions.* Port Townsend, WA: Copper Canyon Press, 2002. ("New York Three Decades On")

———. *The West Door.* New York: Viking, 1988. ("An Xmas Murder")

Cowper, William. *The Poems of William Cowper.* Vol. 2: 1782–1785. Edited by John D. Baird and Charles Ryskamp. Oxford: Oxford University Press, 1995.

Crane, Hart. *The Complete Poems of Hart Crane.* New York: Doubleday Anchor, 1958.

Crapsey, Adelaide. *Verse.* New York: Knopf, 1934.

Cunningham, J. V. *The Poems of J. V. Cunningham.* Edited by Timothy Steele. Athens: Ohio University Press, Swallow Press, 1997.

Davidson, John. *The Theatrocrat: A Tragic Play of Church and State.* London: E. Grant Richards, 1905.

Deutsch, Babette. *The Collected Poems of Babette Deutsch.* Garden City, NY: Doubleday, 1969.

Donne, John. *The Satires, Epigrams and Verse Letters.* Edited by W. Milgate. Oxford: Oxford University Press, 1967.

Eliot, T. S. *Collected Poems 1909–1962.* New York: Harcourt, 1963.

———. *The Waste Land: A Facsimile and Transcript of the Original Drafts Including the Annotations of Ezra Pound.* Edited by Valerie Eliot. New York: Harcourt, 1971.

Emerson, Ralph Waldo. *Poems.* Boston: Houghton Mifflin, 1904.

Evans, Sebastian. *Brother Fabian's Manuscript and Other Poems*. London: Macmillan, 1865.

Fitzgerald, Robert. *Spring Shade: Poems 1931–1970*. New York: New Directions, 1971.

Francis, Robert. *Collected Poems 1936–1976*. Amherst: University of Massachusetts Press, 1976.

Frost, Robert. *Collected Poems, Prose, & Plays*. New York: Library of America, 1995.

Fuller, Roy. *Collected Poems, 1936–1961*. Philadelphia: Dufour, 1962.

Gascoigne, George. *The Complete Works of George Gascoigne*. Edited by John W. Cunliffe. Vol. 2. Cambridge: Cambridge University Press, 1910.

Gibson, Wilfrid. *Collected Poems 1905–1925*. London: Macmillan, 1929.

Gilbert, W. S. *The Savoy Operas; Being the Complete Text of the Gilbert and Sullivan Operas as Originally Produced in the Years 1875–1896*. London: Macmillan, 1930.

Gioia, Dana. *Daily Horoscope*. Saint Paul, MN: Graywolf Press, 1986. ("The Room Upstairs," "Sunday Night in Santa Rosa," "Lives of the Great Composers")

———. *The Gods of Winter*. Saint Paul, MN: Graywolf Press, 1991. ("Counting the Children," "The Homecoming," "Cleared Away")

———. *Interrogations at Noon*. Saint Paul, MN: Graywolf Press, 2001. ("Metamorphosis")

Graves, Robert. *Collected Poems*. Garden City, NY: Doubleday Anchor, 1966.

———. "Recalling War." In *The Penguin Book of First World War Poetry*. 2nd ed. Edited by Jon Silkin. New York: Viking Penguin, 1981.

Grosholz, Emily. *Eden*. Baltimore: Johns Hopkins University Press, 1992. ("Waiting for News of Jackie's Firstborn," "Legacies," "The Shape of Desire")

———. *Shores and Headlands*. Princeton: Princeton University Press, 1988. ("The Cliffs at Praiano")

Gullans, Charles. *Letter from Los Angeles*. Santa Barbara, CA: John Daniel, 1990.

Hadas, Rachel. *Halfway Down the Hall: New and Selected Poems*. Hanover, NH: Wesleyan University Press, 1998. ("Performances, Assortments," "Genealogies," "Peculiar Sanctity")

———. *Indelible*. Middletown, CT: Wesleyan University Press, 2001. ("Props")

———. *Living in Time*. New Brunswick, NJ: Rutgers University Press, 1990. ("The Dream Machine")

Hardy, Thomas. *The Dynasts*. London: Macmillan, 1921.

Hartman, Charles O. *The Pigfoot Rebellion*. Boston: Godine, 1982.

Hayden, Robert. *Angle of Ascent: New and Selected Poems*. New York: Liveright, 1975.

Heaney, Seamus. *Death of a Naturalist*. London: Faber, 1966. ("Death of a Naturalist")

———. *Door into the Dark*. New York: Oxford University Press, 1969. ("The Wife's Tale")

———. *Seeing Things*. New York: Farrar, Straus and Giroux, 1991. ("Casting and Gathering," "Seeing Things," "Wheels within Wheels")

———. *The Spirit Level*. New York: Farrar, Straus and Giroux, 1996. ("The Sharping Stone")

———. *Wintering Out*. New York: Oxford University Press, 1972. ("Shore Woman")

Hecht, Anthony. *The Darkness and the Light*. New York: Knopf, 2001. ("Memory," "Illumination," "Lot's Wife")

———. *The Hard Hours*. New York: Atheneum, 1967. ("Christmas Is Coming")

————. *Millions of Strange Shadows*. New York: Atheneum, 1977. ("Coming Home," "The Feast of Stephen," "Apprehensions")

————. *The Transparent Man*. New York: Knopf, 1990. ("Devotions of a Painter," "The Transparent Man," "See Naples and Die")

————. *The Venetian Vespers*. New York: Atheneum, 1979. ("The Venetian Vespers," "The Short End," "The Grapes," "The Deodand")

Hirsch, Edward. *Wild Gratitude*. New York: Knopf, 1986.

Hoffman, Daniel. *Hang-Gliding from Helicon: New and Selected Poems 1948–1988*. Baton Rouge: Louisiana State University Press, 1988.

Howard, Richard. *Fellow Feelings*. New York: Atheneum, 1976. ("Venetian Interior")

————. *Misgivings*. New York: Atheneum, 1979. ("Thebais")

————. *Trappings*. New York: Turtle Point Press, 1999. ("Family Values I-V," "*Les Travaux d'Alexandre*," "Further Triangulations")

Hudgins, Andrew. *After the Lost War: A Narrative*. Boston: Houghton Mifflin, 1988.

————. *The Glass Hammer: A Southern Childhood*. Boston: Houghton Mifflin, 1994. ("Oh Say, Can You See," "Sit Still," "James Bond Considers Career Opportunities in Library Science")

————. *Saints and Strangers*. Boston: Houghton Mifflin, 1985. ("Saints and Strangers")

Jarrell, Randall. *The Complete Poems*. New York: Farrar, Straus and Giroux, 1969.

Jonson, Ben. *The Alchemist*. Edited by Alvin B. Kernan. New Haven: Yale University Press, 1974.

————. *The Complete Poetry of Ben Jonson*. Edited by William B. Hunter Jr. New York: Norton, 1968.

————. *Volpone*. Edited by Alvin B. Kernan. New Haven: Yale University Press, 1962.

Justice, Donald. *New and Selected Poems*. New York: Knopf, 1997.

Keats, John. *Selected Poems and Letters*. Edited by Douglas Bush. Boston: Houghton Mifflin, 1959.

Kees, Weldon. *The Collected Poems of Weldon Kees*. Edited by Donald Justice. Lincoln: University of Nebraska Press, 1962.

Keyes, Sidney. *The Collected Poems of Sidney Keyes*. Edited by Michael Meyer. London: Routledge, 1988.

Kunitz, Stanley. *The Poems of Stanley Kunitz, 1928–1978*. Boston: Atlantic–Little, Brown, 1979.

Landor, Walter Savage. *Poems*. Edited by Geoffrey Grigson. Carbondale: Southern Illinois University Press, n.d.

Lowell, Robert. *Collected Poems*. Edited by Frank Bidart and David Gewanter. New York: Farrar, Straus and Giroux, 2003.

Macbeth, George. *Collected Poems, 1958–1970*. New York: Atheneum, 1972.

Mackaye, Percy. *Jeanne d'Arc*. New York: Macmillan, 1906.

————. *The Mystery of Hamlet, King of Denmark; or What We Will, a Tetralogy, in Prologue to The Tragicall Historie of Hamlet, Prince of Denmark, by William Shakespeare*. New York: B. Wheelwright, 1950.

————. *A Thousand Years Ago.* Garden City, NY: Doubleday, 1914.

MacLeish, Archibald. *Collected Poems 1917–1982.* Boston: Houghton Mifflin, 1985.

Markham, Edwin. *The Man with the Hoe and Other Poems.* New York: Doubleday and McClure, 1899.

Marlowe, Christopher. *The Complete Plays.* Edited by J. B. Steane. Baltimore: Penguin, 1969.

Masefield, John. *Collected Poems.* London: Heinemann, 1932.

Mason, David. *The Country I Remember.* Brownsville, OR: Story Line Press, 1996.

McClatchy, J. D. *Hazmat.* New York: Knopf, 2002. ("Cancer")

————. *Ten Commandments.* New York: Knopf, 1998. ("Sniper")

Mehigan, Joshua. *The Optimist.* Athens: Ohio University Press, 2004.

Meredith, William. *Effort at Speech: New and Selected Poems.* Evanston, IL: Northwestern University Press, 1997.

Merrill, James. *Collected Poems.* Edited by J. D. McClatchy and Stephen Yenser. New York: Knopf, 2001.

————. *The Changing Light at Sandover.* New York: Knopf, 1993.

Milton, John. *Complete Poems and Major Prose.* Edited by Merritt Y. Hughes. New York: Odyssey Press, 1957.

Moss, Howard. *New Selected Poems.* New York: Atheneum, 1985.

Mueller, Lisel. *Alive Together: New and Selected Poems.* Baton Rouge: Louisiana State University Press, 1996.

Muir, Edwin. *Collected Poems.* New York: Oxford University Press, 1965.

Nemerov, Howard. *The Collected Poems of Howard Nemerov.* Chicago: University of Chicago Press, 1977.

————. *Inside the Onion.* Chicago: University of Chicago Press, 1984. ("She")

Norton, Thomas, and Thomas Sackville. *Gorboduc.* In *Early English Classical Tragedies*, edited by John W. Cunliffe. Oxford: Oxford University Press, 1912.

Philips, John. *The Poems of John Philips.* Edited by M. G. Lloyd Thomas. Oxford: Blackwell, 1927.

Pinkerton, Helen. *Taken in Faith.* Athens: Ohio University Press, Swallow Press, 2002.

Pitter, Ruth. *Collected Poems.* New York: Macmillan, 1969.

Pound, Ezra. *The Cantos of Ezra Pound.* New York: New Directions, 1948.

————. *Personae: The Collected Shorter Poems of Ezra Pound.* New York: New Directions, 1971. ("Erat Hora," "The Tomb at Akr Çaar," "Portrait d'une Femme," "Near Perigord")

Pratt, E. J. *Selected Poems.* Edited by Sandra Djwa, W. J. Keith, and Zallig Pollock. Toronto: University of Toronto Press, 2000.

Raine, Kathleen. *The Collected Poems of Kathleen Raine.* London: Hamish Hamilton, 1956.

Randall, Dudley and Margaret Danner. *Poem Counterpoem.* Detroit: Broadside Press, 1964.

Rich, Adrienne. *Poems: Selected and New, 1950–1974.* New York: Norton, 1975.

Robinson, Edwin Arlington. *Collected Poems.* New York: Macmillan, 1937.

Rossetti, Dante Gabriel. *Collected Poetry and Prose.* Edited by Jerome McGann. New Haven: Yale University Press, 2003.

Salter, Mary Jo. *Henry Purcell in Japan.* New York: Knopf, 1985. ("Shisendō")

———. *Open Shutters.* New York: Knopf, 2003. ("Midsummer, Georgia Avenue," "The Accordionist," "Crystal Ball")

———. *Sunday Skaters.* New York: Knopf, 1994. ("June: The Gianicolo," "Frost at Midnight")

———. *Unfinished Painting.* New York: Knopf, 1989. ("Armistice Day")

Sassoon, Siegfried. *Counter-Attack.* New York: Dutton, 1918. ("Repression of War Experience")

———. *Selected Poems.* London: Faber, 1968. ("Counter-Attack," "Prelude: The Troops," "Villa d'Este Gardens")

Schwartz, Delmore. *Genesis: Book I.* New York: New Directions, 1943.

———. *Selected Poems (1938–1958): Summer Knowledge.* New York: New Directions, 1967.

———. *Shenandoah.* In *Poetic Drama,* edited by Alfred Kreymborg. New York: Modern Age Books, 1941.

Scott, Winfield Townley. *Collected Poems: 1937–1962.* New York: Macmillan, 1962.

Shakespeare, William. *The Complete Signet Classic Shakespeare.* Edited by Sylvan Barnet. New York: Harcourt, 1972.

Shapiro, Karl. *Collected Poems: 1940–1978.* New York: Random House, 1978.

———. *Essay on Rime.* New York: Reynal and Hitchcock, 1945.

Shaw, Robert B. *Below the Surface.* Providence, RI: Copper Beech Press, 1999. ("A Mica Mine," "An Exhumation," "A Geode," "Hide-and-Seek")

———. *The Post Office Murals Restored.* Providence, RI: Copper Beech Press, 1994. ("Selva Oscura," "A Piece of Rope," "Last Days in Camden," "The Post Office Murals Restored")

———. *Solving for X.* Athens: Ohio University Press, 2002. ("The Devil's Garden," "Drowned Towns," "Solving for X," "Living Past 19")

Shelley, Percy Bysshe. *Poetical Works.* Edited by Thomas Hutchinson. New ed., corrected by G. B. Matthews. Oxford: Oxford University Press, 1970.

Simpson, Louis. *Selected Poems.* New York: Harcourt / Harvest, 1965.

Sissman, L. E. *Night Music.* Boston: Houghton Mifflin / Mariner, 1999.

Stallings, A. E. *Archaic Smile.* Evansville, IN: University of Evansville Press, 1999.

Steele, Timothy. *The Color Wheel.* Baltimore: Johns Hopkins University Press, 1994. ("Pacific Rim," "Past, Present, Future")

———. *Toward the Winter Solstice.* Athens: Ohio University Press, Swallow Press, 2006. ("Freudian Analysis," "Ethel Taylor," *"Didelphis Virginiana"*)

Stephens, Philip. *The Determined Days.* Woodstock, NY: Overlook Press, 2000.

Stevens, Wallace. *Collected Poems.* New York: Knopf, 1954.

Stickney, Trumbull. *The Poems of Trumbull Stickney.* Boston: Houghton Mifflin, 1905.

Surrey (Henry Howard, Earl of Surrey). *The Aeneid.* Edited by Florence H. Ridley. Berkeley: University of California Press, 1963.

Tate, Allen. *Collected Poems 1919–1976.* New York: Farrar, Straus and Giroux, 1977.

Tennyson, Alfred. *The Poems of Tennyson.* Edited by Christopher Ricks. London: Longmans, 1969.

Thomas, Dylan. *Collected Poems*. New York: New Directions, 1957.

Thomas, Edward. *Collected Poems*. London: Faber, 1949.

Thomson, James. *The Seasons and The Castle of Indolence*. Edited by James Sambrook. Oxford: Oxford University Press, 1972.

Thoreau, Henry David. *Collected Poems of Henry Thoreau*. Enlarged ed. Edited by Carl Bode. Baltimore: Johns Hopkins University Press, 1964.

Tufariello, Catherine. *Keeping My Name*. Lubbock: Texas Tech University Press, 2003.

Tuckerman, Frederick Goddard. *The Complete Poems of Frederick Goddard Tuckerman*. Edited by N. Scott Momaday. New York: Oxford University Press, 1965.

Van Duyn, Mona. *If It Be Not I: Collected Poems 1959–1982*. New York: Knopf, 1993. ("Marriage, with Beasts," "The Cities of the Plain," "Photographs," "Evening Stroll in the Suburbs," "The Challenger")

———. *Near Changes*. New York: Knopf, 1990. ("The Burning of Yellowstone," "Last Words of Pig No. 6707")

Viereck, Peter. *Terror and Decorum: Poems 1940–1948*. New York: Scribner's, 1950.

Walcott, Derek. *Collected Poems 1948–1984*. New York: Farrar, Straus and Giroux, 1986.

Warren, Robert Penn. *Brother to Dragons*. New York: Random House, 1953.

Warton, Thomas, Jr. "The Pleasures of Melancholy." In *A Collection of English Poems, 1660–1800*, edited by Ronald S. Crane. New York: Harper, 1932.

Webster, John, and Cyril Tourneur. *Four Plays*. Edited by J. A. Symonds. New York: Hill and Wang, 1956.

Whittier, John Greenleaf. *The Complete Poetical Works of John Greenleaf Whittier*. Boston: Houghton Mifflin, 1994.

Wilbur, Richard. *Collected Poems, 1943–2004*. Orlando, FL: Harcourt, 2004.

Williams, Miller. *Some Jazz a While: Collected Poems*. Urbana: University of Illinois Press, 1999. ("Form and Theory of Poetry," revised version)

Wiman, Christian. *The Long Home*. Ashland, OR: Story Line Press, 1998.

Winters, Yvor. *The Poetry of Yvor Winters*. Chicago: Swallow, 1978.

Wordsworth, William. *Selected Poems and Prefaces*. Edited by Jack Stillinger. Boston: Houghton Mifflin, 1965.

Yeats, W. B. *The Poems* (Revised). Edited by Richard J. Finneran. New York: Macmillan, 1989.

———. *The Collected Plays of W. B. Yeats*. London: Macmillan, 1952.

Young, Edward. *Night Thoughts*. Edited by Stephen Cornford. Cambridge: Cambridge University Press, 1989.

Zaturenska, Marya. *Collected Poems*. New York: Viking, 1965.

CREDITS

Bawer, Bruce. Excerpt from "Sixty-fifth Street Poems, 2. Gloves" from *Coast to Coast* (Story Line Press, 1993) reprinted by permission of Story Line Press.

Canaday, John. Excerpt from "Al Badr Street" from *The Invisible World* reprinted with permission of Louisiana State University Press.

Grosholz, Emily. Excerpt from "The Cliffs at Praiano": Grosholz, Emily; *Shores and Headlands*. © 1988 Princeton University Press. Reprinted by permission of Princeton University Press.

Hartman, Charles O. Excerpt from "To A and B, My Friends Who Are Not in Books" from *The Pigfoot Rebellion* by Charles O. Hartman reprinted by permission of David R. Godine, Publisher. Copyright © 1982 by Charles O. Hartman.

Heaney, Seamus. ©Reprinted by permission of Farrar, Straus and Giroux, LLC: Excerpt from "Casting and Gathering" from *Seeing Things* by Seamus Heaney. Copyright © 1991 by Seamus Heaney.

Heaney, Seamus. Excerpt from "Casting and Gathering" from *Seeing Things* by Seamus Heaney. Copyright © 1991 by Seamus Heaney. Reprinted by permission of Faber and Faber Ltd, London.

Hudgins, Andrew. Excerpts from "James Bond Considers Career Opportunities in Library Science" and "Oh, Say, Can You See?" from *The Glass Hammer: A Southern Childhood* by Andrew Hudgins. Copyright © 1994 by Andrew Hudgins. Reprinted by permission of Houghton Mifflin Company. All rights reserved.

Lowell, Robert. ©Reprinted by permission of Farrar, Straus and Giroux, LLC: Excerpts from "Death and the Maiden" and "Goethe" from *Collected Poems* by Robert Lowell. Copyright © 2003 by Harriet Lowell and Sheridan Lowell.

Nemerov, Howard. "Moment" and "What Kind of Guy Was He?" and excerpts from "Flower Arrangements," "Gyroscope," "A Spell before Winter," "Storm Windows," and "TV" from *Collected Poems* by Howard Nemerov (University of Chicago Press, 1977) reprinted by permission of Margaret Nemerov.

Nemerov, Howard. Excerpt from "She" from *Inside the Onion* by Howard Nemerov (University of Chicago Press, 1984) reprinted by permission of Margaret Nemerov.

Randall, Dudley. Excerpt from "Old Witherington" from *Poem Counterpoem* by Dudley Randall with Margaret Danner (Broadside Press, 1964) reprinted by permission of the Dudley Randall Estate, Melba J. Boyd, Literary Executor.

INDEX

The letter *n* following a page number refers to a note on that page.